The Farm Animal Movement

T0015187

THE FARM ANIMAL MOVEMENT

EFFECTIVE ALTRUISM, VENTURE PHILANTHROPY, AND THE FIGHT TO END FACTORY FARMING IN AMERICA

JEFF THOMAS

Lantern Publishing & Media ● Woodstock and Brooklyn, NY

2023
Lantern Publishing & Media
PO Box 1350
Woodstock, NY 12498
www.lanternpm.org

Cover design by Pauline Lafosse

Printed in the United States of America

Library of Congress Cataloging-in-Publication information is available upon request.

I miss you
continuously
and love you
infinitely

The question is not, Can they reason? nor, Can they talk? but, Can they suffer?
—Jeremy Bentham

CONTENTS

INTRODUCTION

Ending the World's Worst Suffering

If you are reading this book, you have freedom rare in human history and face the moral question of what to do with it. Given the numbers involved, the most significant action you can take to mitigate suffering in the world is to work in and donate to improving farm animal welfare. This book is a survey for people outside of the animal movement who want to learn about the opportunities for careers and activism, including financial support, inside the movement.

In less than a decade, farm animal compassion has moved from the realm of niche causes into the pantheon of established social movements. America is undergoing an unheralded ethical revolution regarding the industrial treatment of farm animals. A constellation of activists, capitalists, farmers, lawyers, philanthropists, politicians, scientists, teachers, and writers are using different tactics with the same motives and goals to address what they see as the world's most pressing and tractable problem. Collective actions previously impossible have become self-reinforcing as millions of Americans are making loud and clear statements about their priorities with their careers, investments, purchases, and votes. This book tells the stories of this revolution, from midwestern slaughterhouses to the halls of Capitol Hill to Ivy League universities and Silicon Valley laboratories.

Until recently, working to help farm animals was an isolating task for most Americans. It was nearly impossible to find people in your community who shared your values and could act on them. In the early 2000s, Dr. Michael Greger had a distinguished academic pedigree but lived out of his car as he drove around the country lecturing on the benefits of plant-based eating. After his 2015 book, *How Not to Die*, spent months as a *New York Times* bestseller, he used the proceeds to become one of the movement's leading philanthropists.[1] Dr. Greger's path is a microcosm.

Capital begets capital, and the charitable dollars going toward farm animal welfare increased geometrically in six years from $20 million in 2015 to $150 million in 2021 as the number of employees working in the farm animal welfare movement quintupled. The last several years have seen the emergence of an unprecedented, large-scale movement to recognize and address the causes of farm animal suffering. For the first time in history, many Americans are answering the moral question of what to do with their limited time on Earth by dedicating their lives to helping farm animals. What was once the province of itinerant vegan physicians has opened so it is now possible for you—yes, you—to dedicate your life's work to helping end the world's largest source of suffering.

NUMBERS DON'T LIE

Behind you stand the ghosts of the three hundred farm animals killed for every year you have lived.

Reading U.S. Department of Agriculture (USDA) slaughter reports shows the faces behind the billions: a lamb shot four times in the head with a .22 rimfire magnum before dying at Elkton Locker & Grocery in Elkton, South Dakota; a chicken drowned upside-down in a vat at the Tyson plant in Carthage, Texas; a turkey wandering a parking lot and crushed by a truck at Whitewater Processing in Harrison, Ohio; a pig shot with a captive bolt who jumped, with a bleeding head, out of the slaughter box only to be corralled by reassuring hands that delivered the *coup de grâce* at E.L. Blood and Son in West Groton, Massachusetts.

There is profound suffering within our own species, but the manpower and money required to prevent disease, poverty, and war mean it is difficult for any one person to mitigate those problems. What of the more-than-human world? Every year in America, three million dogs and cats are killed in shelters, seven million animals are killed for clothing, a few hundred million in laboratories, and ten billion in slaughterhouses. Though farm animals represent over 99 percent of the nonhuman animals killed by humans, they draw comparatively few advocates and resources—by one estimate, less than 1 percent of the dollars donated to animal charities, or 0.03 percent of all charity in the United States.[2] There are about twenty thousand lions on Earth and twenty thousand chickens killed in America each minute.[3]

Witnesses to farm animal suffering can't "unknow."[4] The pain of each baby animal they encounter on farms, in videos, or in books is too much for any person to feel. Yet it is not just one individual who is suffering, any more than it is just one person witnessing their pain. With ten billion animal deaths per year in America alone—times ten worldwide, times ten again if we include fish—compared to just seven billion people on the planet, animal agriculture is easily the greatest source of misery and death on the planet, one for which humanity bears responsibility.

But this book is not about death and suffering. I assume you already know the answer to Bentham's question. This book is about life and hope.

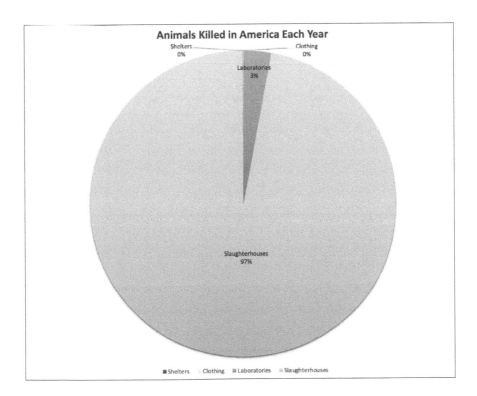

FAITH—AND A PLAN

"Books are a form of political action," said Toni Morrison. "Books are knowledge. Books are reflection. Books change your mind."[5] I wrote this book because I know what it feels like to be alone in this work. There are so many of us who are scattered to the wind, querulous and searching but isolated. John Ruskin wrote in *Sesame and Lilies*:

> Of all he has in his life, he feels like this is the one thing he knows and has. This is the one bit of real knowledge, or lucid truth that his experience and understanding has allowed him to own, and he feels compelled to write it down for posterity, or engrave it in stone, as if to say, "This is the best part of me. Everything else in my life was mundane—I ate, I drank, I slept and loved like everyone else. My life was as fleeting as vapor before I died, but I saw and knew this one thing. If anything in my life is worth remembering, this is it." And that is what he writes down. In his own small way, and with whatever inspiration or gift he might have had, that is what he leaves behind. And that is a real Book.[6]

I tried to write a real Book.

The most important farm animal book or film people read or see is the first one. Jane Goodall read *Animal Liberation*.[7]

> When I'm talking to people about eating animal products, I tell them that I read Peter Singer's book back in the 1970s. I didn't know about factory farms. I was shocked. The next time I saw a piece of meat on my plate, I thought, Goodness, this symbolizes fear, pain, death. Who wants to eat fear, pain and death? So I just tell them my story. I don't ever want to appear holier than thou. You've got to be reasonable. If you tell people, "You've got to stop doing that," they immediately don't want to talk to you. The main thing is to keep a channel open. Young activists, sometimes they're inexperienced and demand something. They ask my advice, and I say: Talk about how the issue is affecting you. How you feel about it. I think that's the way forward.

I wish that I had known about the farm animal movement my entire life. I was born in a city and knew nothing of those worlds. If I had given it any thought, I would have assumed the only thing to be done was to be a veterinarian. I met an evolutionarily optimized serotonin wolf (a dog) in college who changed me. I wanted to see what factory farms were all about and watched *Meet Your Meat*, PETA's twelve-minute exposé. The book for me was *The Food Revolution* by John Robbins.[8] I became a vegetarian, then a vegan a month later. Afterwards I began seeing beautiful pigs, radiant cows, and lovable chickens. I began feeling safety, love, and joy when I looked into animals' eyes. I came to the movement later in life, having finished graduate school before I realized that people can devote their lives to helping farm animals.

Writing is an act of faith in and hope for the future.

Faith is the pierless bridge
Supporting what we see
Unto the scene that we do not

reads Emily Dickinson's poem.

The good news is that nobody has to be brilliant to make an extraordinary difference for animals. Ordinary people can change millions of animals' lives. I know there will be readers who have yet to come across the worlds in these chapters. You can be a part of a community of altruistic, caring, creative animal lovers. There are now myriad paths carved out by dreamers who saw suffering and insisted they would do whatever it took to stop it. What was radical is now mainstream. If you care about animals and know the answer to Bentham's question, all that remains is to act on it. In these pages, I hope to give you a framework for doing so.

The nation's social and charitable impulses are changing, as evidenced most clearly by the spread of effective altruism. The epiphany of effective altruism is discussed in the next chapter. The same reasoning that finds farm animal suffering to be one of the world's most neglected and tractable problems can be focused on the issue itself: what is the worst suffering that farm animals face, and how can it be changed?

Following exposés of the horrors of animal agriculture in the 1990s and early 2000s, Americans have seen that, if the law is followed, most cattle can live lives of relative peace followed by a quick and hopefully painless death.[9] Furthermore, cattle cannot be raised or killed like chickens can, they cannot be stuffed head to tail by the hundreds of thousands. For this reason and for reasons of scale—98 percent of land animals killed in the United States are chickens—animal advocates have decided to focus their efforts primarily, though not entirely, on the painful slaughter of conscious animals; mutilations such as face branding and tail docking; and the lives of laying hens in battery cages, broiler chickens in barren barns, mother pigs in gestation crates, and calves in veal crates. Animal lovers do the most good by attacking and reforming the worst abuses; effective altruism provides a schema for doing this.

Harvard's random roommate assignment of Dustin Moskovitz with Mark Zuckerberg may have been the most fortuitous event in the history of animal welfare.[10] In Chapter 2, I discuss how the entry of Facebook co-founder Moskovitz's Open Philanthropy Project into the arena of farm animal philanthropy in 2015 has changed the movement.[11] Over the last six years, the movement's global budget has doubled to perhaps $200 million, with one quarter coming from Open Phil. This commitment was all the more remarkable for the fact that Moskovitz and his wife, Cari Tuna, do not have a particular interest in farm animals outside of effective altruism. Their foundation's staff merely applied the lens of effective altruism, a data-driven utilitarian ethic to end the most suffering, and found farm animal welfare was important, neglected, and tractable.[12]

Family farmers have been on the front lines, resisting the intensifying monopolization and corporatization of American agriculture responsible for driving animals onto factory farms. Farmers and vegan advocates form a natural rural–urban alliance that can find common cause with political power in state capitals and Washington, D.C., where secret— and not-so-secret—networks of politicians, lobbyists, and congressional staffers work to realize the humane visions of their constituents. Californians have twice given landslide victories to ballot initiatives so that consumers in one of the world's largest economies can purchase cage-free eggs and crate-free pork only from farmers adhering to more humane standards. The political tactics and victories of family farmers and vegan activists are revealed in Chapters 3 and 4, respectively. Learning from the movement's recent successes and failures will be critical for smart activists anticipating the next federal Farm Bill as well as those in subsequent years.

A number of successful nonprofits have been founded this century to address the problems of farm animal cruelty. One of the most successful is Mercy For Animals. The perspicacious leaders of that organization have fostered a culture of altruism and emotional intelligence that is a blueprint for the movement and other social activists. The stories, strategies, and visions of founder Nathan Milo Runkle and president Leah Garcés are profiled in Chapter 5.

No movement is without flaws and abuses of power, and no book on the modern animal movement in the U.S. would be complete without acknowledging the painful reality of discrimination and sexual misconduct at the Humane Society of the United States. Although I have a sense of the culture of many organizations, I had first-hand knowledge of this case as I worked twenty feet from the office of Humane Society CEO Wayne Pacelle and reported his mistreatment of women up the chain of command long before he was fired. This is the most personal chapter in the book, which tells stories that few know about and many would rather cover up. Readers will learn the inside story of the #MeToo movement at HSUS in Chapter 6. Neither the animal rights movement nor HSUS can heal without addressing this collective trauma and betrayal of trust.

Structural racism negatively affects the largely white animal rights movement in the United States by narrowing the pool of candidates for employment, volunteerism, philanthropy, and political support; restricting the audience receptive to messaging about the humane treatment of animals; and inhibiting alliances with other social movements. Mitigating racism in the animal movement is necessary for advocates to achieve their policy goals. However, there is a dearth of academic literature on racism in the animal movement in the United States. In Chapter 7, I review that literature and discuss potential reasons for the scarcity of quality research.

Changing the legal system has long been a chicken-and-egg problem, whose solution takes leadership, lawyers, and tacticians. For the legal education system, farm animal law is no longer in its infancy. The pathways for animal lawyers were planted by Bob Barker's endowments twenty years ago and have grown exponentially just over the past five years, especially at Harvard Law School under Professor Kristen Stilt and Executive Director Chris Green and at Yale Law School under Deputy Dean Doug Kysar. Their graduates are beginning to fill the ranks of future corporate and nonprofit leadership. The burgeoning field of farm animal law and policy is reported on in Chapter 8.

While agribusinesses are responding to increased consumer concern over animal welfare, they will soon have to answer for how they will compete in the brave new world of animal-less agriculture. Beyond Meat's 2019 initial public offering (IPO) was the most successful on Wall Street in nearly two decades, drawing billions of dollars of capital that will hire scientists, capitalists, and marketers looking to change the world and get rich doing it.[13] Biochemists have also made rapid progress toward fulfilling the promise of clean meat grown safely in food labs, without slaughter. What cost $330,000 for a prototype eight years ago now costs $600.[14] Clean meat is the most exciting technology for the future, but it might surprise activists on both sides to see that American agribusiness has been doing a great deal to advance the cause of the humane treatment of animals. When humans hang birds in shackles or shoot lambs in their heads, errors are inevitable. If clean meat promises to remove all animals from agriculture in the long term, today's humane tech promises to remove just some animals—us—to the benefit of all. Farm animal welfare has emerged from the province of family farmers and activists and entered into the boardrooms of the world's largest agricultural conglomerates. With efforts from all sides, from prominent academics like Temple Grandin to Wall Street, the near future shows the potential for pro-industry, pro-animal scientific advances that could save many millions of dollars and billions of lives. Forestalling competition will not work, if for no other reason than that there is too much money to be made by selling clean meat. If we can raise animals free from pain—and that is a big "if"—then agribusiness will be able to answer this question in a way that consumers can stomach. Chapter 9 discusses entrepreneurs who are developing clean meat and more humane technology.

Readers who are new to the movement or contemplating getting involved will benefit from this book. You can learn about the cutting edge, see where the possibilities and problems lie, and consider where your talents can be most effective. There is no book I know of that brings together these disparate threads for you. This is not a dry academic tome, but it is well grounded in research and social science methods. Those who want to explore more can look to the "Further Reading" section and the footnotes, or reach out to the people in this book who are accessible and always willing to help others find their niche. For those already working in the movement whose expertise on effective altruism, animal law, or clean meat far exceeds mine—indeed, some of whom I interviewed for this book—my unique contributions can be found in Chapters 2 and 5. Though the chapters are arranged for the best rhythm, it is not necessary to read them sequentially. Readers are welcome to begin with the chapter of their choice.

1

NUMBERS DON'T LIE

Effective Altruism and Venture Philanthropy

Peter Singer faced a moral quandary when he was a young academic who had already written two seminal works: *Animal Liberation* and "Famine, Affluence and Morality." "These were not the only issues around at the time," he recalls.

> The Vietnam War was still being fought, and the threat of nuclear war between the United States and the Soviet Union could not be ignored. I was already a vegetarian, had marched against the Vietnam War, and was donating to Oxfam. Where should I direct my time, energy, and whatever ability I might have to argue in favor of one of these causes? I didn't try to answer that question by thinking about which issue is the most urgent in the sense of Which issue is most in need of immediate action? or even Which issue is it most important to resolve?, but by thinking about where I could make the most difference. And that, I decided, was the issue of animal suffering because whereas there were many highly able people already campaigning and writing about global poverty, the Vietnam War, and nuclear disarmament, very few thoughtful people were advocating a radical change in the moral status of animals. There was an animal welfare movement, but it was mostly concerned with cruelty to dogs and cats and horses; only a

minuscule amount of attention was going to farm animals, where the overwhelming majority of the suffering humans inflict on animals was, and still is, occurring.[1]

"'What is the most urgent issue?' is not the right question to ask," concludes Singer. "Because [we] should be asking, 'Where can I do the most good?'"[2]

The philosophy leading many people to the farm animal movement is effective altruism, which is both simple to understand and radical in its implications. It strikes me as being as intuitive as the theory of natural selection: when one hears of it, it makes so much sense that it is surprising one had not thought of it before. Effective altruism is the ethic that we should end the most suffering we can. Importantly, we should be driven by numbers in determining where and how to apply our talents and resources. The numbers lead us to the large, neglected, solvable (or tractable) problems of extreme poverty, existential risks to civilization such as meteor strikes, and factory farming.[3]

"Every year, hundreds of millions of animals—*many times more* than the total number killed for fur, housed in shelters, and locked in laboratories combined—don't even make it to slaughter," write Matt Ball and Bruce Friedrich in *The Animal Activist's Handbook*. "They actually *suffer to death*."[4] The website Counting Animals estimates this suffering to death at 139 million chickens per year in the United States alone. "Given that an animal is suffering as much as a human, does the suffering of the animal matter as much as the suffering of the human?" Singer asks. "The answer to the ethical question should be yes."[5] Given the numbers of lives and relative timeframes, it is fair to rank factory farming as the highest priority.

Excellent books and articles have been written on effective altruism. There are complicated questions about the ethics toward one's children versus strangers, earning to give, organ donations, wild animal suffering, insect sentience, and other thorny issues. Singer's logic seems right, but I do not know for certain. I am not a dialectician, nor do I feel it is helpful to recount philosophical debates here. I am interested in helping people and animals by conveying to readers the practical importance of effective altruism as it relates to farm animal suffering.

WHAT IS THE WORST FARM ANIMAL SUFFERING?

The best comparative evaluation of American farm animal suffering I am aware of is in the magisterial *Compassion, by the Pound: The Economics of Farm Animal Welfare* by F. Bailey Norwood and Jayson Lusk, agricultural economists at Oklahoma State and Purdue, respectively.[6] Their work is sympathetic to animal farmers as well as to activists. "We have no formal affiliation with the animal production industries or with animal advocacy groups," they write. "Strangely, for authors of a book on farm animal welfare, we did not choose to write on this topic out of an intense concern about farmers or farm animals. We are passionate about science, economics, and the truth, and we were drawn to this topic because we felt the controversy needed a heavy dose of honest, objective, and dispassionate information."

Theirs is precisely the type of analysis effective altruists ordinarily embrace. The reader will see in later chapters that, despite the tremendous good it has accomplished, the vegan activist wing of the farm animal movement can be prone to epistemic closure and groupthink. Farmers and animal welfare scientists must be part of any political solution to factory farming. Nonvegans' views should be seriously considered when it comes to offering solutions to farm animal suffering.

Number of Animals Used and Killed vs. Money Donated to Animal Charities
Source: Animal Charity Evaluators

When we talk about animal suffering in the United States, we really are talking about chicken suffering, statistically speaking. Since 98 percent of all land animals killed by humans are killed for food, and 98 percent of those are chickens, others pale in comparison—strictly statistically, of course.[7]

The story of chicken's rise to the center of the American dinner plate is recounted in Christopher Leonard's *The Meat Racket*.[8] Several factors conflated to produce this transformation. First was the Industrial Revolution's inevitable encroachment onto American family-farm life. As labor moved into cities and suburbs, refrigeration, long-distance rail, and interstate truck transport permitted the shipment of chilled chicken meat to supermarkets hundreds of miles from the abattoir. Americans' economic hegemony, rising productivity, and increasing standard of living, including mass adoption of automobiles and ubiquitous fast food franchising, led to increasing consumption of meat and other luxury goods. Secondly, during World War II, the federal government rationed red meat but not chicken. Americans' chicken consumption tripled from 1940 to 1945.

Another key factor was the economy of scale created by the business savvy of Arkansan Don Tyson and his political patron on the make, the then governor of Arkansas, Bill Clinton. Tyson Foods was so central to Arkansas's economy that gadfly candidate Ross Perot derided Clinton as "the chicken man" during the 1992 presidential campaign.[9] Indeed, Clinton's first secretary of agriculture, Mike Espy, was indicted for bribery for accepting a slew of cushy gifts from Tyson; Espy was found innocent at trial but the company pleaded guilty to the felony in 1997. Tyson and his successors avoided the antitrust regulations facing Iowa pig farms, for example, and vertically integrated the poultry industry, maximizing or minimizing—depending on industry-crushing imperatives—every penny of profit traditionally given to farmers, truckers, slaughterhouses, packers, shippers, wholesalers, and retailers until competitors were forced to imitate, sell out, or go bankrupt. Independent cattle ranchers cannot be squeezed like contract poultry farmers can.

Fourth was appetite: over the last fifty years, health and environmental concerns have caused beef and pork consumption to be supplanted and then dominated by chicken consumption. Americans ate more

McNuggets and became fatter, as did their children, an epidemiological transition replicated as other countries became wealthier.

Finally, the unique biology of chickens facilitated their rapid genetic alteration and more efficient factory farming. Before they are shipped to slaughter at less than two months of age, a million broiler (meat) chickens can be raised in a single football field–sized industrial barn with a construction loan floated with a guarantee from the federal Farm Service Agency.[10] Selective breeding that causes rapid weight gain so debilitates these infant birds that they frequently die of heart attacks or cannot walk.

Picture of 9 chickens over time in years 1957, 1978, 2005
Source: Zuidhof, M., et al. (2014). "Growth, efficiency, and yield of commercial broilers from 1957, 1978, and 2005," Poultry Science, 93(12), 2970-2982.

The research has been conducted by poultry scientists at the world's leading agricultural facilities, America's public land-grant universities. Broiler chickens cannot maintain homeostasis in inclement weather and are vulnerable to a range of predators; they are in some measure dependent upon climate-controlled, enclosed systems. Hens laying eggs have longer lifespans and incur even cheaper costs. Raising chickens is astonishingly efficient: it takes about 8 pounds of food to produce one pound of beef; 3.9 pounds of food to produce one pound of pork; and just 1.9 pounds to produce one pound of chicken meat.[11] Any grocery shopper knows that chicken and eggs are so highly efficient and subsidized, they are not just cheaper than other meats but cheaper than most produce.

By comparison, American beef cattle are still grazed for the first six months of life largely in marginal, midwestern ranchland subsidized by taxpayers through artificially low federal grazing fees, followed by a few months at a feedlot, whose upper limit is 100,000 heads.[12] Calves' rumens restrict their food intake to grass and their mothers' milk, and cows only have one offspring per year, as opposed to ten for pigs or dozens for hens. American cattle ranching is inefficient on factory farms and has proven too competitive to be fully vertically integrated, though a handful of companies now have oligopolistic control over beef meatpacking. Meat pigs are born to mother pigs restrained in farrowing or gestation crates and are raised in concrete group pens that allow freedom of movement, but the animals' size and waste limit economies of scale. Furthermore, pork production is predominantly oligopolistic rather than monopolistic.

What farming practices cause farm animals the most suffering? Norwood and Lusk provide a detailed review of academic literature regarding farmed land animal consciousness, emotions, physiology, and behavior, as well as comparative stress, pain, and mortality indicators among different species and husbandry systems. (The authors did not consider aquatic animals.) It is well worth reading for those who are interested. The bottom line is as follows and illustrates why farm animal activists have chosen the tactics and targets you will read about in the following chapters.

All farm animals suffer and die premature deaths. For those who see no reason to differentiate between nonhuman and human consciousness, this is heartbreaking enough; we do not raise humans for meat. The conditions in which some farm animals are raised should not be considered as better than the conditions of others, only less horrible. Nevertheless, there are gradations of suffering among different species of farm animals and types of food. production

Beef cattle suffer least. If they were left to their own devices, surely a life spent grazing and chewing cud would be a top priority. Compared to the other farm animal species in America, beef cattle live the happiest lives. Their movements and autonomy are not highly restricted. They face problems with inadequate veterinary care, bad weather, aggression from other cattle in feedlots, and not infrequent inhumane slaughter.

Next come dairy cows and pasture-raised pigs, who see natural light and the outdoors, are able to move, and can have independent and to some degree, emotional lives. Dairy cows suffer additionally from mastitis, continual pregnancy and theft of offspring, and reproductive exhaustion.

Broiler chickens and hens in cage-free systems come next. They live unnatural lives in their indoor football fields. Aggression, genetic health, handling, transport, and slaughter are all significant problems and causes of mortality.

The worst suffering is endured by veal calves, breeder pigs in gestation crates, and laying hens in battery cages. They each suffer a similar fate: lives of darkness, being restrained so as to be unable to move or take a step, unloved and hardly cared for before the inevitable death by slaughter, reproductive exhaustion, or cannibalism. Veal calves are kept anemic and immobile and then killed. Pigs in gestation crates often demonstrate repetitive self-harm behavior tantamount to insanity as they are artificially inseminated and litter after litter of their babies are taken from them. Laying hens die after one or two years in the wire cages they share with six or seven others. Their bodies are removed when they begin to rot. In humans, such an existence would be called a living nightmare. Baby calves and mother pigs and hens in crates or cages "are individually the most miserable animals that have ever existed," concludes Yuval Noah Harari.[13]

Farm Animal	Welfare of one breeding animal	Welfare of one market (meat) animal
Beef	8	6
Shelter-pasture pork	4	4
Milk	n/a	4
Egg from cage-free system	3	2
Chicken meat	-4	3
Crate-free pork	-5	-2
Pork	-7	-2
Veal	n/a	-8
Egg from cage system	3	-8

Source: *Compassion, by the Pound*, Table 8.2.

Norwood and Lusk quantify the harrowing suffering faced by farmed land animals. They rank 10 as the best care, −10 as the worst, with a positive score indicating a life worth living despite the suffering and a negative score indicating that the animal's suffering is so unbearable that she or he would be better off dead.

It is important to consider the ways in which humans consume these animals' muscles and secretions. The average American dairy cow produced 23,391 pounds of milk in 2019.[14] Drinking 16 ounces of cow's milk per day one would require 23,391 days, or more than 64 years, to consume one dairy cow's annual output. One beef cattle produces the same amount of edible meat as roughly 250 broiler chickens, while chickens have six times shorter lives in worse conditions. Humanity's global shift from beef to chicken was the worst thing that could have happened to farm animals. Those animals who suffer the most are the most numerous in the factory farm economy.

What can we do about it?

THE OPEN PHILANTHROPY PROJECT AND LEWIS BOLLARD

The Open Philanthropy Project (Open Phil), the foundation of Facebook co-founder Dustin Moskovitz, did what any good foundation would do and looked to hire the best talent available in its grant areas. Lewis Bollard applied.

For a man now charged with ending more suffering than anyone in human history, Bollard is fairly grounded. Bollard's family has a legacy of meritocratic public service. The son of New Zealand's finance minister, who was himself the son of a distinguished botanist who led New Zealand's academy of science, Bollard had traveled with his family and witnessed the live animal markets of Vietnam.[15] He read *Dominion: The Power of Man, the Suffering of Animals, and the Call to Mercy* and was driven to visit a slaughterhouse at the age of fifteen.

> Huge chutes drove a pig every three seconds toward her death. As I stood on the kill floor, I watched the moment when each pig, emerging from the chute, sensed [her] fate; the sudden piercing squeal followed by the too-late attempt to turn and run—some pigs literally attempting to scramble up vertical walls—as metal shackles were clamped around their ankles. And I watched as the shackles hoisted each pig into the air and as the slaughterer's knife sent blood splattering across my overalls.[16]

His articles in *The Harvard Crimson* show a well-formed worldview, a gift for composition, and the remarkable ability to focus all of his columns on animals while remaining original. "I've never fully accepted any abstract theory of animal rights," he writes. "Nor do I think one needs to in order to sense that something has gone horribly wrong. For me, the horrors of the slaughterhouse and the suffering of the factory farm attest to that."[17] His empiricism is a useful outlook in the nonprofit world, where employees and organizations can become mired in indecision instead of moving forward. At Yale Law School, the only major law school without an animal law program at the time, he led a reading group on animal law and won a national competition with his review of the unconstitutionality of ag-gag laws.[18] Not only is he gifted, perhaps brilliant, but also he has exceptional emotional intelligence. It was no surprise when he was hired. He left a prestigious job at the Humane Society of the United States to help give away Moskovitz's fortune.

In a nod to transparency many of us would not relish if we were the subject, Open Phil made public its evaluation of Bollard's strengths and weaknesses as an applicant. They felt the twenty-eight-year-old possessed an impressive intellect and communication skills and was "a very strong generalist." However, they were wary that his few years of work experience and relative dearth of connections in the field would be problematic. They would be, but not for the reasons that his employers anticipated.[19]

The problem was not the cognitive nature of the work. It was the interpersonal. Bollard had to give away about $30 million to $60 million per year to charities, and there are only so many doing good work on farm animal welfare. He could easily increase all of their budgets by however much they needed and let them sink or swim. But from the moment he was hired, how could he ever fully trust anyone in the movement again? Every person he spoke to would be aware of his role as a funder, and all or nearly all would want to accentuate the positives about their organizations or causes and downplay the negatives. This is not to say there would be any nefarious intent: it is just human nature for animal advocates. After his three years as an employee in the movement, all at HSUS, he would never be able to work within it again to see how it functioned, to know the personalities, or to understand the cultures of the various charities. As meticulous and impartial as his own effective altruist calculations could be, the information brought to him by others might never be purely objective. He was the only person in the world engaged in this type of work at this scale. There were one or two dozen other major donors in the field, but at most they were volunteer board members. Bollard's knowledge of the movement already surpassed theirs.

The job was not without other pitfalls. Even for someone equipped as Bollard was, the work he was doing had never been done before. Whether or not he was the most qualified person for the job—and he likely was— to a large degree, the farm animal movement would follow his strategies. The decision on one grant could make or break an organization, a common-enough reality in the foundation world, but the opportunity cost of a wrong decision would be harm to millions of innocent creatures or more. Another risk for someone who fully understood the consequences was the burnout of inventing the field of farm animal philanthropy and working day in, day out on a cause with such uncertainties. It was a mental tightrope walk; it required not only single-minded passion, or even a degree of zealotry, to work on this or any other social justice issue, but also the discipline to turn one's mind off at night in order to recharge for the next day. There were many people who worked on causes for a year or two and then moved on to pursuits more in line with everyday priorities and mainstream lives.

Bollard is an acolyte of Cal Newport's *Deep Work* and his thesis that several hours of focused work activity every workday trump grueling hours over time.[20] Bollard works for eight hours a day, with roughly five in the morning dedicated to focused, distraction-free work and three in the afternoon to email, calls, and meetings. He sleeps normal hours, is married, and has a dog named Hope who was rescued from a dog meat farm.[21] If those sound odd to mention, many people in the movement choose not to marry or have pets so they can focus more of their energy on affecting farm animal policy. Another risk for someone of Bollard's age suddenly being put in his uniquely powerful position was arrogance and hubris, but whether by nature or nurture, in his seven years at Open Phil, he has not yet succumbed to those temptations. Bollard was motivated by the images of suffering he witnessed, and he used them productively rather than destructively. He was as normal as a polymath giving away a Facebook founder's fortune to help farm animals could be.

Meanwhile, there were a number of advantages to entering the field of farm animal philanthropy. The problems are comprehensible and quantifiable. One could know, for example, how many chickens, pigs, and cattle there were in the United States, the market share of the largest food companies in the country, and therefore how many animals of each species were being bought by each brand of restaurant, grocery, or foodservice.

I caught up with Lewis at Burger Bach, an ersatz diner that is his favorite restaurant in Washington, D.C. It has served veggie burgers and coconut ice cream milkshakes since before Impossible and Beyond Burgers came on the market. On the walk over from Dupont Circle, I had to take two steps to each of his. Lewis is 6'6" while I round up to six feet. People who would never otherwise look at me gave me a glance and wrongly assumed I must be cool. We sat down to order.

So, how does one go about changing the world?

The oligopolistic American economy gives tremendous autonomy to decision makers at large corporations. It is not much of an exaggeration to say that the United States government does not have an animal welfare policy: it is written by merely a dozen or so corporations. These otherwise highly vertically integrated conglomerates do not actually raise their own animals but generally buy meat, milk, and eggs from farmers working on contracts for agribusiness giants like Tyson and Cargill.

A counterintuitive (and unfortunate) advantage to charitable giving in this space is that the low-hanging fruit had not been picked because of historic underfunding. Thanks to the dedication of thousands of grassroots activists working tirelessly for decades, the public already strongly supported the humane treatment of animals. Sympathetic consumers and media did not tolerate the rampant abuses in American agriculture when they were exposed. Consequently, brands reliant on positive consumer perceptions of Happy Meals and healthy animals were able to demand reforms in their supply chains and switch suppliers or standards to reflect consumer sentiments.[22] Industry well knows this. A survey by the National Chicken Council found that more than 70 percent of consumers were somewhat, very, or extremely concerned about how chickens are raised and housed.[23] Open Phil did not have to start a revolution. They just had to nudge it into the boardroom.

The first grants Bollard made were a window into the world he came from and where he was going. He understood from his past work the basic layout of farm animal welfare in the United States. The nation's largest animal charity, the American Society for the Prevention of Cruelty to Animals (ASPCA), did not yet substantially focus on farm animal welfare because of its perceived controversy, and People for the Ethical Treatment of Animals (PETA) supported strict veganism and thus opposed welfare reforms on principle. Activism on corporate reforms was dominated in terms of size, financing, and capability by a handful of organizations: Mercy For Animals and HSUS; growing nonprofits like The Humane League and Compassion Over Killing (now Animal Outlook); and smaller, incipient groups.

Like any good effective altruist, Bollard ran the numbers. In February 2016, he began to pursue the following strategy, with grants focused on securing corporate commitments to cage-free eggs totaling $2.5 million—to Mercy For Animals, The Humane League, and HSUS's farm animal department.[24] Why?

- "Battery cages cause severe suffering, and cage-free systems are much better.

- Corporate cage-free campaigns are tractable and high-impact, with a strong recent track record.

- The cost-effectiveness of these campaigns, in terms of animal suffering averted per dollar, looks better than any alternatives I'm aware of.

- I don't see these campaigns as representing a short-term—only approach. I see them as a logical step along a long-term path toward greatly reduced farm animal suffering, and I think they're competitive with other approaches when thought of in these terms.

- I believe our funding has made and will continue to make a tangible difference to the success of these campaigns."[25]

And that was just the first month. Within a year, Open Phil had donated $14.5 million, including more seven-figure grants to the preceding organizations and a multimillion-dollar venture capital investment in Impossible Foods. Prior to this, Bollard estimated that the movement was spending less than $1 million per year on cage-free campaigns and "fewer than seven advocates were working full time on the issue."[26]

There was, in 2016, already a natural Darwinism by which only the most astute advocates founded sustainable, successful organizations. Their being given the freedom to realize their visions was the best thing that could have happened to the movement. The strategists running these campaigns—Paul Shapiro and Josh Balk at the Humane Society; Nathan Milo Runkle and Nick Cooney at Mercy For Animals; Leah Garcés at Compassion in World Farming; David Coman-Hidy at The Humane League; and their many capable co-leaders and employees, too numerous to mention—had spent the past decade honing their tactics. They just needed money.

"I think the most important factor behind these campaigns is that they have never given up a campaign until they've won," Bollard said in an interview. He continued:

> So if you think about the proposition as a company when one of these campaigning groups comes to you and says, "Hey, you're doing this cruel practice. We're planning to campaign against you." As that company, you face a choice. If you know that they have never backed out of a campaign they have ultimately won every campaign even if it's taken them a year or longer, you face a choice of either we can do this right now and incur whatever cost there is down the line and possibly get a mild kind of positive halo for doing a good thing, or we can endure a brutal campaign where our brand gets trashed for weeks, months, or even a year, and then we can end up doing the same thing with the same costs associated to it.[27]

Within a year and a half, advocates secured pledges from the remainder of "all of the top 25 U.S. grocers and 16 of the top 20 fast food chains," representing "70 percent of the U.S. non-organic flock" compared to less than 5 percent of hens prior to 2015.[28] "These campaigns will spare about 250 hens a year of cage confinement per dollar spent," Bollard estimated.[29] This perhaps even understated the scope of the gains because it assumed these victories would have happened in a further five years without the intervention of Open Phil. From 2015 to 2018, the budget of The Humane League increased from $0.9 million to $7.2 million while its workforce grew from 11 to 71 people. Mercy For Animals saw its budget increase from $4.1 million to $10.3 million as its workforce grew from 39 to 101 employees.[30]

It is important to note that companies also realized they could make more money by selling cage-free eggs. While it may cost 35 percent more to raise chickens in a cage-free system, companies charged two or three times the conventional price. Conventional eggs themselves were subject to price fixing. This price discrepancy is less apparent in prepared foods and can be expected to decrease in the future as market competition increases.

Although companies would still need to be held accountable for their pledges, the rapid successes of American activists allowed Open Phil to export the corporate reform model to dozens of other countries, where 96 percent of the world's farm animals are raised. As of this writing, The Humane League's Open Wing Alliance, launched in 2017, has seventy-seven member organizations in sixty-three countries working to secure cage-free commitments.[31] Funding from Open Phil and other donors allowed the Alliance to give substantial grants in the range of thousands to tens of thousands of American dollars to nascent animal welfare organizations on six continents, in countries from Argentina to Kenya to Nepal to Ukraine. The money gives one or two formerly volunteer activists in each member country, typically the top farm animal activist, the financial freedom to work on helping farm animals full time and the campaign infrastructure to do it. This seed money is launching groups that hopefully one day will be as successful as The Humane League has been in America, though some will surely fail.

Grants from the Open Wing Alliance and the Effective Altruism Fund may not sound like much compared to the nine-figure annual budgets of some American animal organizations, but it is hard to overstate their importance for sustaining activists in countries that have little to no farm animal advocacy to speak of. It is a form of venture philanthropy with easily measured results. Grants can be increased or eliminated based on whether new organizations sink or swim after a year of trying to get corporate pledges; if they are successful, the media will report the commitments so funders can verify them.

The snowballing success of cage-free campaigns allowed American activists to shift focus on to the next big target. The suffering of caged hens is worse than that of broiler chickens; however, in the United States there are roughly 300 million laying hens but 9 billion broiler chickens killed each year. The sources of suffering were qualitatively different, as were the asks from animal welfare supporters. Broiler chickens are not raised in cages; their primary cause of suffering is their rapid growth. Broiler chickens do not suffer from cannibalistic pecking—they are killed long before they become mature enough to engage in that behavior—but the mortality rate of broiler chickens is nevertheless about 5 percent per flock. Since they are slaughtered at roughly 48 days, their yearly mortality is roughly 35 percent. Many broiler chickens die of heart attacks, their organs too weak to support their massive weights. Other welfare concerns include rough handling (6 percent of broiler chickens suffer from broken bones when they are thrown into transport truck cages), overcrowding, unsanitary litter, and lighting too intense for sleep.

Nevertheless, the industry rapidly embraced commitments to sourcing slower-growing chickens and providing them more space and cleaner farm conditions. Food service giants Aramark and Compass Group announced their support for broiler chicken welfare on November 3, 2016, followed by Sodexo in December and most major restaurant chains within the next six months.[32] However, McDonald's and Walmart, whose commitments to eliminating battery cages within the next decade were salutary to the industry, are still on the sidelines.

LESSONS LEARNED

Bollard made some mistakes. One error was spending $750,000 over three years to launch The Greenfield Project, which was billed as a think tank dedicated to finding out the full truth about how federal policy, and particularly subsidies, affected farm animal welfare.[33] (A "greenfield project" is an architectural term for a plan created without any constraints from past work.) It was led by two lawyers with Harvard pedigrees, with the misconception that they would research new solutions and lobby the USDA to implement them.[34] As the reader might discern, the problems were manifold. First, there was already a voluminous literature on the subject of federal farm policy that came from professors at agricultural colleges, not from animal advocates. This volume of academic work was not something that could be circumscribed or improved upon by two inexperienced attorneys. The assumption that research emanating from agricultural research universities was conflicted and suspect may have made some sense on the surface, but it was naivete masquerading as ideology. Hubris is a problem amongst effective altruist researchers; that overconfidence is compounded by vegan groupthink.

There were already experts on this subject in the federal bureaucracy and a large number of people who lobbied them. It is true that in federal politics, the coin of the realm is campaign contributions, but lobbying non-political agencies is entirely different from lobbying Congress. At the level at which The Greenfield Project wanted to be engaged, decisions are much more firmly based in facts and science, and relationships are formed over time based on trust and expertise rather than transaction. For example, Dena Jones of the Animal Welfare Institute is an animal advocate, but she has decades of experience as the leading expert in Washington on humane slaughter.[35] Regulators at the Food Safety and Inspection Service, the branch of the USDA tasked with enforcing the Humane Methods of Slaughter Act, do not always do what she or her organization hopes, but they take her work seriously. The well-meaning founders of The Greenfield Project had no such experience or relationships. Third, even if it were possible for a new policy organization to accomplish all of this, it would essentially require a unique individual. There were many extant animal organizations the founders could have worked for that had the staff and profile to help catalyze their vision. "It's not clear the animal welfare movement needs another nonprofit," Marc Gunther presciently warned in his article for *Nonprofit Chronicles*.[36] Finally, the bottom line was that federal subsidies did not have significant impacts on the price of meat. Some subsidies even slightly increased the price of meat through increasing consumer demand. Ignoring the politics, eliminating all subsidies would perhaps affect the price of meat by a few percentage points.[37] There is a definite role for government to play in farm animal welfare and for animal activists in influencing government, but think-tank advocacy is not it. After two years of work at $250,000 per year, one of the founders of The Greenfield Project already saw the writing on the wall and decided she was not going to continue full time. The other brought on volunteers and another staff member, who produced reports that few read.[38] None of this should reflect negatively on the motives of the people involved, who all care about animals. But the whole project was an unfortunate and costly mistake.

Another judgment call was more of a mixed bag. Although many animal activists may deny it, not least because it flies in the face of common sense, the welfare benefits of cage-free eggs come with the tradeoff of higher mortality as farmers learn how to care for hens in cage-free systems. Hens exhibit dominance behavior within their aptly named "pecking orders," first described by a Norwegian farm boy so enamored of chickens that he kept diaries of their behavior when he was ten years old.[39] An adult chicken can remember an impressive amount of socialization information, including her or his and each other chicken's position in a flock of up to dozens.[40] At a certain flock size, however, the pecking order breaks down and chickens attempt to dominate, or attack with their beaks, other chickens more or less randomly. In cage-free systems, the number of deaths due to pecking—up to and including cannibalism—and the spread of disease can rise to 10 percent. There are usually six to eight hens in a conventional battery cage; despite the worse suffering, mortality is lower, perhaps 2 percent to 3 percent. Mortality due to pecking aggression is diminished by beak trimming, or the slicing off of part of a chick's beak, which is not without its own welfare concerns.[41] Egg-laying hens live one to two years, while broiler chickens' far shorter lifespans and less advanced cognitive developments, debilitating size, and sexual immaturity mitigate pecking-order aggression. The largest study of the mortality differences between caged and cage-free hens shows that it has taken five to fifteen years in countries adopting cage-free egg policies for mortality levels to decrease to those experienced by caged hens. The authors also conclude that this transition to lower mortality is accelerating as technology and experience improve internationally.[42] Bollard initially dismissed studies demonstrating this higher mortality rate.[43] Despite its initial optimism about cage-free systems, the Open Philanthropy Project later published a report acknowledging the mortality tradeoff during the transition to cage-free housing that it was bankrolling.[44]

FISH FRONTIER

Improving the welfare of fishes, the most numerous farmed animal, has proven far more difficult. The main problem is that the science has not caught up to the activism. One reason is anthropomorphism: it is easier intuitively to understand and observe that a hen would like to sleep on her perch than it is to see what makes a fish happy. Another is history.

The exponential rise in farmed fishes since the 1990s has dovetailed with the economic fortunes of China.[45] Large-scale fish farming is a relatively new industrial phenomenon and is far more common in Southeast Asia, where more than half of all fishes are raised, than in the United States, where 2 percent of the world's farmed fishes are.[46] It is only in the past decade that the number of farmed fishes surpassed that of fishes caught in the wild. Thirdly, "fish" is a catch-all term. There are thousands of different species of fishes, more than four hundred of which are farmed. Even for a single species, the farming systems and genetics are not uniform.[47] Fourthly, the amount of time, money, and research energy dedicated to fish welfare is minuscule compared to more established career paths involving land animals. Lastly, the quantitative tools used on land animals, like blood tests to measure stress hormone levels, do not translate well to fishes. It is harder to do experiments on fish, so scientists are left with the most obvious indicator, mortality rate, which is better than nothing but far too blunt.

Though there are but a handful of fish welfare specialists in the United Kingdom and Europe in general, the fish welfare world in American academia is even smaller. The most renowned advocate was Penn State biologist Victoria Braithwaite, who made the case in her seminal *Do Fish Feel Pain?* that they do. That book, published not without controversy by Oxford University Press in 2010, shows how far behind that of mammals the study of fishes remains. Professor Braithwaite tragically died of pancreatic cancer in 2019 at the age of fifty-two as she was researching how to improve the treatment of farmed fishes.[48] Two other professors, Jennifer Jacquet and Becca Franks, were hired for tenure-track work on fish welfare at NYU's new Center for Environmental and Animal Protection, launched in 2018.[49] Before of activists can take the usual tactics to social media and the boardroom, Open Phil and other donors are funding policy and physiology work to try to determine the best standards for fish welfare. In other words, fish welfare is so nascent that philanthropists are still giving money to scientists to determine what the activists should ask the corporations.

What a Fish Knows, a sublime work by ethologist Jonathan Balcombe, brought the issue of fish sentience into the mainstream. Dedicated "to the anonymous trillions," *What a Fish Knows* reached the *New York Times* bestseller list in 2016. The stories and abilities of the fish species Balcombe describes are captivating. To pick just two: In less than a week, one of the eyes of young flounders migrates completely to the other side of their face. They change from normal, upright swimmers to those who camouflage themselves on the bottom of the sea floor. One researcher placed a black and white chessboard at the bottom of a flounder's tank, and the fish changed his skin to blend into the squares. As for the American eels who migrate nearly four thousand miles from North American freshwaters to the Sargasso Sea and vice versa, their sense of smell is so refined that they can sense "the equivalent of less than one ten millionth of a drop of their home water in [an] Olympic pool." "As we learn more about fishes, be it their evolution or their behavior, our capacity to identify with them grows, along with our ability to relate their existence to our own," Balcombe writes.[50]

Hope in the future notwithstanding, concrete progress is being made today. Mercy For Animals has released two undercover investigations of fish killing. In 2011, they documented fishes being knifed and skinned alive at Catfish Corner in Texas in a horrifying and bloody exposé.[51] MFA used all the tactics they had honed over the years: media, viral video, referral to prosecutors, activation of supporters. To put it bluntly, nobody cared.[52] Then, MFA did an undercover investigation of driftnet fishing off the coast of California in 2018, and people did care. The investigation garnered national media attention and led to California banning driftnets.[53]

An unheralded victory demonstrating the power of smart activism came from energetic millennial hedge-fund employee William Bench. He ran the numbers, saw where the movement needed to go, and founded the Aquatic Life Institute (ALI) with Dr. Becca Franks in 2019 to focus on fish welfare certification standards. Roughly one-third of fishes worldwide are already certified on sustainability or environmental metrics. His group lobbies the certifiers to amend their standards to include heightened fish welfare. In June 2020, ALI launched the Aquatic Animal Alliance, modeled on the Open Wing Alliance, to bring together all interested global animal welfare organizations under one coalition.[54] The coalition developed standards to submit to the major fish certifiers. By the end of the year, GLOBALG.A.P. (one word), certifier of 2 percent of the world's fishes, revised or amended its standards in a dozen areas, including environmental enrichment, staff training on humane handling, and the elimination of eyestalk ablation (blinding) of shrimp. ALI estimates these reforms will improve the lives of 2 billion animals per year.[55]

FUNDING THE FARM ANIMAL WELFARE MOVEMENT

Wealth inequality is a pressing problem in America, and that stratification is exacerbated when it comes to charitable giving. Fundraisers often rely on the 80/20 rule: 80 percent of donations will come from 20 percent of donors. An astonishing study from the Association of Fundraising Professionals finds that this even understates the impact of large donors: 76 percent of charitable revenues come from 3 percent of donors, and 88 percent of donations come from the top 12 percent of donors.[56] Open Phil characterizes the current funding sources of the farm animal movement as highly concentrated among bicoastal major donors.

Nearly as important as the entry of Open Phil's liquidity and expertise into the farm animal movement has been the organizing of much of the other three-quarters of philanthropic giving into a loose donors' circle called the Farmed Animal Funders Group. It is impossible to tell for certain, as its operations and membership are for the most part private, but most of America's and perhaps two-thirds of worldwide farm animal philanthropic funding comes from members of the group. The group launched with thirteen members in August 2017 as the brainchild of Bollard and Ari Nessel, a California real estate developer and philanthropist. It has no formal structure, but is constituted as "a learning community" of members, each of whom gives at least $250,000 per year to ending factory farming.[57] The membership has since grown to several dozen, most of whom choose not to be identified at this time.[58] Few of these donors have any staff, and those who do might have one or two.

One of the donors who do share their identity is Jim Greenbaum, who was an effective altruist before there was such a term. Growing up Jewish in Louisiana in the 1960s, he was struck by the incongruity

21

between his rabbis' "Never again!" sermons and the violence he saw on the news. "When something didn't seem reasonable, logical, or fair, I'd fight against it," he recalls. After a frustrated attempt at becoming a civil rights lawyer, he turned his energies to business and decided to make as much money as quickly as possible so he could give it away. Remarkably, it actually worked. He had the perspicacity and talent to found Access Long Distance in 1985 and sell the telecommunications company for $250 million at the height of the dotcom bubble in 1999. He walked away with $133 million at the age of forty-one.[59] His foundation has since donated about $100 million, and the balance will be spent down to zero during his lifetime. Current foundation assets are roughly $40 million. Greenbaum gives away about 8 percent of the assets per year, above the IRS' 5 percent distribution requirements.[60] Though some people are surprised by his informal personal style, I find it endearing that there is no pretense about him. You certainly cannot tell he is a millionaire by talking to him.

The Farmed Animal Funders Group currently has just two staff members: Executive Director Mikaela Saccoccio and Director of Research Kieran Greig, who were hired from The Humane League and Animal Charity Evaluators, respectively. There is no pooled source of funding from members; in fact, there is not even a legal organization. Saccoccio and Greig's salaries were initially split between Open Phil and Nessel's charitable vehicle, Mobius, and are now paid through membership dues that the majority of members contribute. Donors receive biweekly emails, and there are one or two Zoom meetings on select topics per month. It is a useful way for donors to keep abreast of the movement without having the same series of conversations with the leaders of each of the top organizations. "In 2017, the entire global philanthropic sector to help farmed animals amounted to roughly $150 million," Saccoccio and Greig write.[61] They add:

> Just four years later, this sector is fast approaching or now even surpassing $200 million. That's certainly a step in the right direc-tion—but it's not enough. Let's not sugarcoat it: our food system is broken. Animals are raised and killed in crowded, windowless, worse than prison-like conditions. People around the world are

starving and our planet is dying. All of this could be addressed by reforming industrialized animal agriculture. And yet of the $435 billion dollars that goes to charity annually, only ~0.05 percent goes towards fighting factory farming. Farmed Animal Funders exists because it has to. At FAF, doing our job well means putting ourselves out of business.

Some of the wealthier donors have family foundations and foundation employees, but, for whatever reason, farm animal nonprofits have not yet attracted large donations from the corporate community or establishment foundations like the Gates or Bloomberg philanthropies. The dearth of corporate funding is understandable, as few corporations have much interest in supporting national farm animal welfare. But the lack of donations from major foundations committed to climate change mitigation is more puzzling given animal agriculture's central role in the climate crisis. To be fair, until recently there were no grant writers at any farm animal organization in the United States. Thanks to recent growth, the Good Food Institute has a full-time grant writer and a staff person dedicated to corporate philanthropic engagement, Mercy For Animals has a contract grant writer, and The Humane League has tasked an employee with grant-writing as part of her duties.

Another successful model, run through the Center for Effective Altruism, allows ordinary individuals to donate to the world's most effective charities via the Effective Altruism Fund. All operating expenses are paid for by a generous donor. There are four funds individuals can donate to: improving farm animal welfare; mitigating extreme poverty and disease; controlling longer-term risks to civilization; and improving the infrastructure of the effective altruism movement. Donors can give to any or all of the four funds in whatever percentages they wish; the money is then distributed every four months by a committee of volunteer experts. Bollard was the first to chair the farm animal welfare group, a role now filled by Kieran Greig. The animal fund has distributed more than $9 million in cash, mostly in unrestricted five-figure grants to international farm animal organizations or American organizations working on underfunded priorities like insect sentience and wild animal suffering. Where do Greig and fellow Effective Altruism Fund board member Saccoccio recommend that large and small donors put their money? "With evidence-based interventions and neglected regions and species in mind," they write, "we'd point an effective-altruist-leaning donor to organizations like Sinergia Animal, The Humane League, Rethink Priorities, Global Food Partners, Equalia, Essere Animali, and the Good Food Institute."[62]

The lack of reliable and uniform nonprofit metrics that led to the founding of GuideStar and Charity Navigator plagued the animal movement. The neoliberal move toward quantification of results, as well as blunt metrics and ratings from GuideStar and Charity Navigator, addressed the right problems in the wrong way. The best attempt to shine light on the animal movement's nonprofits has been through Animal Charity Evaluators (ACE). ACE was founded in 2012 as a branch of the UK-based organization 80,000 Hours.[63] At the time, the farm animal movement was still in its infancy. Easily the most effective was the Farm Animal Protection department at the Humane Society of the United States. The entire organization had a total budget of about $140 million, of which department head Paul Shapiro estimated 5 percent to 10 percent went to farm animals, including for support staff and others not involved in full-time farm animal work.[64] PETA had a budget of about $30 million, with perhaps the same percentage of its budget focused on veganism and farm animals, though budget numbers are confidential.[65] The ASPCA had the largest budget of all but was not focused on farm animal activism. Mercy For Animals and The Humane League had $2 million and $0.3 million annual budgets, respectively. The total yearly budget for the movement, not including sanctuaries, was roughly $10 million to $20 million. ACE's mission was to optimize charitable giving to end the most suffering.

The naming and identity of Animal Charity Evaluators were clever. ACE adopted the assumptions of effective altruism and correctly concluded that the most effective charitable donations should go toward the amelioration of farm animal suffering. Thus, ACE was created as almost entirely a farm animal charity evaluator focused on welfare reforms.[66] Its first recommendations were published in 2014 based on standardized reviews of twenty-nine American charities.[67] The process is revised and updated each year, though many of the questions its researchers are asking have no perfect answers. One strength of ACE is its online publication of an array of resources, from reviews and blog posts to interview transcripts and podcasts, that employees, volunteers, and donors can peruse in as much or as little detail as they want in order to form their own opinions.[68] ACE is the best clearinghouse for information about the movement, and I used its database of academic articles to collect research for this book.[69] There is certainly a space in the movement for ACE, as the demand indicates. Through 2021, ACE estimates that it has directed $34 million to its recommended charities—likely a high estimate—and distributed another $3.1 million through the ACE Movement Grants, on a total cumulative budget of $4.1 million.[70] Within less than a decade, ACE was influencing more charitable funding than had existed at its founding.

The nature of farm animal philanthropy leaves it better equipped for growth and change than philanthropy for other causes. Farm animal donors are motivated by the right reasons: they do not get box tickets, their names on libraries, or their offspring into the college of their choice. Similarly, farm animal leaders—as opposed to some of those in the broader animal movement—are not motivated by prestige or money. Concern about misguided funders was a common theme in a detailed survey of thirty anonymous movement leaders by Charity Entrepreneurship. Unfortunately, the power dynamics between donor and grantee can be mitigated but probably never truly eliminated. Nobody likes fundraising, but when it comes to farm animal advocacy, the credulous symbiosis between movement donors and organizational grantees is a relatively healthy one. The reliance on individual donors is a double-edged sword: though the field is underfunded, donors provide a great deal of autonomy to organizations and the experts. "Philanthropists playing nonfinancial roles should stick to areas where they bring unique skills or relationships," caution two Bridgespan consultants in the *Harvard Business Review*.[71] Many, though not all, donors in the farm animal movement do what they should do: give money and get out of the way. To the extent that some donors have a comparative advantage over nonprofit employees, it is in the field of plant-based and clean meat investing, the subject of our last chapter.

2

POLITICAL POWER

Family Farmers Versus Big Meat

This chapter tells the inside story of the last major fight for federal farm animal legislation in the 2018 Farm Bill. The next Farm Bill will likely be drafted after the 2022 midterms, so political animals will need to learn and adapt. In my experience, few in the movement are politically savvy. This chapter profiles a few who are so we can all learn from their examples.

The end goal of any American social movement is the enshrinement of its values as the highest law of the land. Abolitionists ratified a constitutional amendment; civil rights advocates passed federal legislation; LGBTQ supporters won at the Supreme Court. It is impossible to predict how the fight for the humane treatment of animals will be won, but it is sure to travel through Washington, D.C.

Activists must understand the reality of farm animal politics, where the most important color is not black or white but green. For all its appeals to fundamental principles, the American political system reflects the values of monied interests.[1] Wedge issues such as abortion, gun rights, and political personalities may divide and motivate voters on Election Day, but there is a bipartisan economic consensus supporting animal agriculture in America today. Farm animal advocates are far ahead in public opinion but far behind in the money race. This alone is determinative in analyzing political strategies. Enormous integrated agriculture conglomerates ("Big Ag," or "Big Meat" for animal products) write and pass the laws they want in Congress because they help elect many of its members. Animal advocates are fighting on a battlefield their antagonists designed. It is straightforward but worth highlighting because of the misleading image of politics inculcated in many Americans as schoolchildren: members of Congress do not actually draft legislation. Members of Congress need money to get elected, and when they are, they let their donors' attorneys write the bills they pass. Broadly speaking, there are really two separate interest groups fighting the hegemonic power of Big Meat oligopolies. One group is largely older, Republican, conservative rural farmers; the other is largely younger, Democratic, progressive, urban vegan nonprofit activists. Both sides misunderstand or ignore the vital role the other plays. This chapter discusses farmers while the next discusses vegans.

CHECKOFF:

THE HIDDEN TAXES THAT SUBSIDIZE BIG MEAT AND HURT ANIMALS

Thomas Jefferson foresaw America as a democratic republic of family farms, though his words masked brutal hypocrisy the nation is slowly coming to terms with.[2] Self-evidently, Jefferson's vision has not come to pass. Small farmers have little say in a government purportedly established to represent them.

The financial power of Big Meat is heavily subsidized by checkoff taxes that few know about. Under federal law, every head of cattle sold in America incurs a one dollar tax. Fifty cents goes to the National Cattlemen's Beef Association and fifty cents goes to its affiliates in each state. Consumers pay a similar hidden tax for every egg, pig, and gallon of cow's milk sold in America. The National Cattlemen's Beef Association, American Egg Board, National Pork Board, and American Dairy Association thus each collect hundreds of millions of dollars in guaranteed income each year, which is controlled by and used to advocate for the interests of the most powerful corporate players in their industries. "Beef: It's What's for Dinner;" "The Incredible, Edible Egg;" "Pork: The Other White Meat;" and "Got Milk?" are all products of

Americans' taxes hard at work to increase beef, egg, pork, and milk consumption.

Checkoff taxes are the farm animal movement's most significant impediment to political change. A decade ago, animal advocates at the Humane Society of the United States (HSUS) were riding high with their victory in California's Proposition 2 (2008), a ballot initiative that would eliminate chicken battery cages in the state. They sought to leverage their state win into a national victory. In 2011, HSUS cut a deal with United Egg Producers, the main industry group, and agreed not to run similar ballot initiatives in Oregon and Washington if UEP and HSUS would go to Congress together and ask it to pass a bill requiring a nationwide phase-out of battery cages.[3] The other big checkoff tax-funded groups— the National Cattlemen's Beef Association, the National Pork Board, and the American Dairy Association—worried about what they felt was a slippery slope of national animal welfare legislation and united with their political allies to kill the egg bill.[4]

EGG CHECKOFF TAXES AND ANTI-COMPETITIVE MARKETS

Big Meat's heavy-handed political tactics can backfire. Egg checkoff taxes are collected by the American Egg Board, which in 2015 became enveloped in a scandal surrounding the rise of the plant-based mayonnaise Just Mayo, produced by Hampton Creek (now renamed Eat Just) in Silicon Valley. Like any government entity, the American Egg Board is subject to the Freedom of Information Act (FOIA). Ryan Shapiro, the brother of then HSUS farm animal department leader Paul Shapiro, was the "most prolific" FOIA requester in the nation, according to the Justice Department.[5] What could he find in these government documents?

The popularity of Just Mayo among young people troubled the egg industry trade group. "It would be a good idea if [PR firm] Edelman looked at this product as a crisis and major threat to the future of the egg production business," wrote Egg Board CEO Joanne Ivy in 2013. In another email chain, the executive vice president of an egg company asked, "Can we pool our money and put a hit on [the Hampton Creek

CEO]?" "You want me to contact some of my old buddies in Brooklyn to pay [the CEO] a visit?" replied the Egg Board executive vice president.

USDA investigators were not amused. Though the assassination discussion was a sick joke, the USDA found the American Egg Board had run a campaign designed to kneecap the startup in violation of its congressional mandate. It is one thing to promote egg consumption; it is another to use government funds to harm American industry. CEO Ivy took an early retirement.[6]

Conservative senator Mike Lee of Utah found this rogue agency's anti-competitive behavior so repellant that he joined with Senator Cory Booker of New Jersey, a vegan, to become the lead sponsor of a bill to reform checkoff programs in an electrifying political battle that reached its denouement on the floor of the Senate.

BEEF CHECKOFF TAXES AND LOBBYING CONFLICTS OF INTEREST

The National Cattlemen's Beef Association (NCBA) is the primary contractor of the beef checkoff, the one-dollar tax on each cattle sold in America. Up to 80 percent of the NCBA's budget comes from checkoff taxes. The NCBA uses these government funds to build its brand identity. It controls the funds to influence state and national policy makers and to advocate policies that work against family farmers. All the while, the NCBA claims it is the voice of U.S. cattle producers, though its membership represents only 4 percent of U.S. cattle producers.

Examining the purportedly independent legal structures of America's beef checkoff program, Qualified State Beef Councils (QSBCs), and their NCBA state affiliates shows a program rife with conflicts of interest, government and nonprofit organizations operating with dubious legality, and a web of influence peddling through which a private organization controls tens of millions of ostensibly independent taxpayer dollars in order to advocate an agenda that harms the very cattlemen and cattlewomen who pay those taxes.

Forty-four states had QSBCs listed on the NCBA's website as of June 2021.[7] Researching their corresponding state affiliates and key data could indicate conflicts of interest and potentially illegal behavior.[8] For each of the forty-four states' QSBCs and NCBA affiliates, I examined the following:

1. Organizational leaders, including chairmen, board members, and ex-officio members of the board
2. Organizational staff, including executive directors
3. Legally identifying information, such as mailing and shipping addresses and phone numbers
4. Each state's legislative code and language that is required to form a QSBC
5. Government affairs and lobbying activity
6. Public-facing websites and materials
7. Other relevant data, such as associated charitable foundations and PACs

To operate legally, QSBCs must be formed by state code and must be independent from state NCBA affiliates. At a minimum, in order to segregate public and private funds, independent QSBCs and state NCBA affiliates should not share board members, staff, or facilities.

Of forty-four states:

- Three states had *identical* QSBCs and NCBA state affiliates, an egregious violation of federal law (Alabama, Kansas, and Illinois)
- Five states had no evident state laws creating their QSBCs, though this is required by federal law (Delaware, Hawaii, Maryland, New Jersey, and Vermont)
- Thirty states had QSBCs and NCBA state affiliates with significant overlap in staff, boards, and/or facilities (Arizona, Arkansas, California, Colorado, Florida, Georgia, Indiana, Iowa, Kentucky, Louisiana, Michigan, Minnesota, Mississippi, Missouri, Nevada, New Mexico, New York, North Carolina, North Dakota, Ohio, Oklahoma, South Carolina, South Dakota, Tennessee, Texas, Utah, Virginia, Washington, West Virginia, and Wisconsin)
- Only six states met the minimal requirements for legality and good governance by having QSBCs that are formed by state law and do not share board, staff, or facilities with NCBA state affiliates (Idaho, Montana, Nebraska, Oregon, Pennsylvania, and Wyoming)

THE FIGHT FOR CHECKOFF REFORM IN THE 2018 FARM BILL

The closest the American farm animal movement has come to passing federal legislation since the Humane Methods of Slaughter Act in 1958 was in the 2017–2019 congressional session. The events are worth examining for advocates interested not in textbooks but in the real world of political change.

The political forces came to a head during the passage of the 2018 Farm Bill. Farm Bills are omnibus agricultural appropriations and policy vehicles passed roughly twice a decade in an extraordinary interplay of money, politics, special interests, lobbying, legislative action, and horse trading. The 2018 Farm Bill cost $867 billion. These bills shape the direction of the rural economy.

Animal advocates were led by Joe Maxwell, an energetic attorney and fourth-generation pig farmer who had served as lieutenant governor of Missouri from 2000 to 2005. From 2011 to 2017, he worked at the Humane Society Legislative Fund, at the time the nation's only 501(c)(4) political lobbying organization for animal welfare. He also served as the executive director of the Organization for Competitive Markets, a farmers' group. Maxwell's legislative goal was simple: put an end to Big Meat's use of checkoff dollars for lobbying purposes by amending the 2018 Farm Bill. He was working nineteen-hour days to do it.

Equally important was rancher Bill Bullard, a Sam Elliott doppelganger who led the Ranchers-Cattlemen Action Legal Fund United Stockgrowers of America, or R-CALF USA, an organization of 5,000 ranchers centered in Montana.[9] When I picture Bill Bullard, I picture a man in a yellow rain jacket carrying a calf tucked under his arm through a Great Plains rainstorm.

Maxwell's campaign came on the heels of an astonishing victory. In 2016, he led a hybrid coalition of "animal welfare activists, environmental groups, Native American tribes and family farmers" to defeat a right-to-farm ballot initiative in Oklahoma that would have forever knee-capped environmental and animal welfare regulations by enshrining prohibitions against them in the state constitution.[10] Oklahoma was not just the playground for the nation's wealthiest agricultural interests and the politicians they controlled: it was a hotbed of deregulatory fervor. And, in 2016, it was Trump country.

"You have to go meet [voters]," Maxwell says. "It's about who they are and showing them that you are like them, that you share their values. If you're in their coffee shop or barber shop or their synagogue or their church—if you're there, then they feel comfortable to express themselves."[11]

"What people may not realize about places like Oklahoma is, yes, there is a huge agricultural industry, mostly wheat and cattle," said F. Bailey Norwood, the agricultural economist whose work on animal suffering we examined in the previous chapter. "But ag is also a very popular hobby. . . . For a lot of kids growing up, their hobby was showing cattle or showing hogs. They show farm animals the way other people show dogs. So even when people don't farm for a living, there's a real connection with farm culture."

Maxwell proved that such a coalition can win when he and his allies beat the right-to-farm ballot initiative in Oklahoma, 60–40, in 2016, the year when every politician with a "D" next to their name got crushed in rural America.

"Me personally, I'm just a good ol' boy, not too sophisticated," says Wes Shoemyer, a corn farmer who served with Maxwell in the Missouri legislature. "Joe, he's a *sophisticated* good ol' boy. And that's something the Democrats lost."

"Democrats don't have to throw out their values," Maxwell says. "Democrats don't even have to abandon their issues." Likewise, America's family farmers—who are small, medium, and even large farmers, all at the mercy of **Big Meat**'s relentless monopolization—can use the votes and resources of urban politicians whose districts might not have a slaughterhouse but whose voters care about the way animals are treated before they die. Few Americans support Big Meat corporations' vacuuming up money from their communities to send to Wall Street or China.[12]

"The farm community is so much faith-based, I thought the idea of stewardship could really be a powerful message," Maxwell continues. "Stewardship of the animals, stewardship of the land." Maxwell is onto something. It is difficult to change people's minds. It was the brilliant insight of Roger Ailes, founder of Fox News, that people do not want to be informed, they want to hear they are right.[13]

An urban–rural agriculture coalition has been central to the passage of the Farm Bill since the 1970s, as the Great Society began to pour billions of dollars into supplemental nutrition (formerly known as food stamp) programs that benefit both farmers and metropolitans.[14] Such a strategy would come into play in the 2018 Farm Bill checkoff fight, with an added element of partisanship.

It is best to think of the Farm Bill, like any omnibus appropriations bill, as not one bill, per se, but legislation by committee. Omnibus bills begin as thousands of different bills and amendments that coalesce to form the whole. For many farm-state politicians, this is why they got elected—to bring home the green bacon. And there is plenty of money to go around for special interests, donors, and districts, and everybody else's special interests, donors, and districts—all paid for courtesy of a global financial system willing to give America free money by buying Treasury bonds at near-zero interest.[15] In the Farm Bill, everybody gets paid and everybody gets bought.

The legislative mechanics of the Farm Bill actually fairly resemble the version taught in school. Politicians are each at the heads of individual machines that pull the pieces together in the House and the Senate agriculture subcommittees and then the full agriculture committees, with up-or-down votes on scores of bills offered as amendments to the Farm Bill. Then, the overall bill passes each chamber's agriculture committees, followed by each chamber, inevitably by huge bipartisan majorities. Few politicians want to vote against a popular, money (or "pork") -laden, debt-funded bill that farmers either love or learn to live with, though some progressives and conservatives will usually symbolically vote against the other side's bill when they happen to be out of power.

For the fight to put checkoff reform in the Farm Bill, Maxwell had able help. Angela Huffman, his longtime lieutenant, is a sixth-generation farmer. She worked as the Organization for Competitive Markets' (OCM) director of research and communications out of her family's Ohio farmhouse, where her "huge white Great Pyrenees dog watches over a small flock of sheep."[16] The OCM had a politically sophisticated network of farmers and prominent allies, like former Oklahoma state senator Paul Muegge; Virginia Contract Poultry Growers Association president Mike Weaver; and leaders of the National Farmers Union, who could speak up in every farm state. But they did not have a presence in Washington.

Maxwell's other lieutenant, HSUS Director of Rural Affairs Marty Irby, had had a fascinating and unconventional career. A native Alabaman, he was an eight-time world champion equestrian who had become the youngest president of the Tennessee Walking Horse Breeders & Exhibitors' Association. In that archaic blood sport, horses' hooves are bound with heavy chains and weights, and the skin around the hooves is chemically burned to create an artificially high-stepping gait that for some reason is preferred amongst participants. During his presidency, Irby had a change of heart about his life's path, and made the decision to abandon it at great personal sacrifice. To share any more of his remarkable story would betray confidences. Suffice it to say Marty Irby is an exceptional human being and animal advocate.

Maxwell had a plan and two unique allies. The first New Jersey senator Cory Booker was perhaps the nation's most prominent vegan and the leading animal advocate in Washington. His agricultural staffer, Adam Zipkin, was an observant Orthodox Jew who had become the best and most knowledgeable advocate for farm animals on Capitol Hill. New Jersey voters and national animal groups rewarded and supported Booker's fight for animals. The second, Senator Mike Lee of Utah, a former clerk to Supreme Court justice Samuel Alito, was not the most likely advocate for animals or family farmers. But his staff got wind of the American Egg Board–Just Mayo "hit"-man scandal, and Lee decided he would use his political capital to reform a wasteful, anti-competitive government program run amok.

If either one had not signed on, the bill would have been one of the thousands of lonely one-cosponsor items that never see the light of day in any two-year congressional session. The bill would have met a similar fate if both represented the same wings of the same party. It would have come across as too partisan and would have required unanimity among Republicans, who at that time controlled Congress and the White House. A Republican-only strategy was mathematically, not politically, possible.

In fact, that is precisely what happened with the House version of the bill. The bill was led initially by Dave Brat, a telegenic Tea Party representative from Virginia who gained fame by knocking off entrenched House Majority Leader Eric Cantor in the most surprising congressional upset in a hundred years.[17] Brat agreed to be the lead sponsor of the bill (or, rather, his ag staffer convinced him after Irby convinced the staffer), but Brat was a show horse, not a workhorse. (My favorite story about Dave Brat comes from a cousin of mine who knew him before he was famous. My cousin said they were on a rec league basketball team together, and the only time Brat showed up was for the championship game, dressed in bright purple warmup pants as if he were playing for the Los Angeles Lakers.) The Democratic lead sponsor was Dina Titus of Nevada, but the lobbying was really done by the first Democratic cosponsor, Representative Earl Blumenauer of Oregon, the top animal advocate in the House. With Blumenauer's support and Brat's slothfulness, the bill started to garner cosponsor after cosponsor—the House's top animal advocates—until the tally was 11:1, liberal Democrats to the lone Brat.[18] Brat (or his staffer) did the wise thing, from a political perspective, and stopped advocating for the bill, though, to be fair, it is doubtful Brat ever understood the bill even in broad terms. With such partisan liberal Democratic support, the bill went nowhere in the Republican House.

But with Booker and Lee as lead Senate cosponsors, progressives and the Tea Party were on board. Unfortunately, neither senator was on the Agriculture Committee, where the Opportunities for Fairness in Farming (OFF) Act to reform checkoff programs would surely be killed. Their strategy was to have the final vote in the Senate come with a surprise amendment on the Senate floor. Then, if it passed, it would become part of the Senate's version of the Farm Bill. Because two different versions of the Farm Bill had passed—a common occurrence with any major legislation—a bicameral conference committee would be formed in which designated leaders from both parties and both chambers would iron out differences behind closed doors until one final Farm Bill emerged. This final Farm Bill could not be amended but would be given up-or-down votes in each chamber and pass with large majorities. Then, it would go to the president for his signature.

Assuming Lee would force the vote, how could they convince senators to vote for it?

Politicians may claim to represent certain people or groups, but some of that is more or less an act. Members of Congress generally make policy based on the input of three groups: their staff in D.C., who are always around them; their staff in their home districts or states, because they need to keep their constituents happy to win elections; and their donors, because they need money to win elections. In all fairness, not all of this is nefarious, and some of it just boils down to human nature.

Unfortunately, the farm animal advocacy community has few donors who are engaged at the federal level. While Maxwell was the leader, he did not have the money to manufacture a grassroots coalition—nor would he have done so ethically. The urban–rural coalition would have to be formed from his work with farmers in the Midwest and from his office at HSUS near Dupont Circle in downtown Washington. A national sign-on letter was drafted to garner support from a coalition of nearly two hundred groups ranging from farmers and ranchers to animal lovers, environmentalists, and labor and immigrant rights advocates. Then, a weekly call was set up in which Maxwell and one or two others would speak for five to ten minutes about the plan for the upcoming week.

Checkoff taxes are unpopular among rural family farmers who want the government out of their lives. Adding insult to injury, these checkoff taxes were not only taken out of farmers' pockets at the point of sale, but also given over to subsidize their powerful competitors who were driving them further into debt and bankruptcy. The government was taking money from them and using it to destroy their livelihoods and identities. The theme played well among many farmers and consumers: stop the checkoff abuses and stop the government from picking winners and losers. Who could disagree with that? Value-driven appeals backed by facts were Maxwell's specialty.

Maxwell created an action playbook for supportive groups to blast out to their national mailing lists. Few people take action when a group asks them to contact their legislator. But one in a hundred or one in a thousand do, and for each one, an intern at the congressional office makes a note of what the constituent wants. Maxwell created a short phone script so constituents could ask their representative to cosponsor the OFF Act.

He also drafted sample letters to the editor of one to two paragraphs each. Letters to the editor can be surprisingly impactful. Good weekly polls are prohibitively expensive for all but the most well-heeled statewide campaigns, so many politicians use letters to the editor in place of polls to gauge the pulses and priorities of their constituents.[19]

Maxwell compiled a similar playbook for people in key Midwest farm states whose senators' votes would be critical in the Farm Bill: Michigan, Kansas, Oklahoma, and Ohio. Michigan senator Debbie Stabenow was the leading Senate Democrat on the Agriculture Committee and reportedly hated the NCBA, which had called her a liar during the 2013 Farm Bill negotiations in which she tried to carry HSUS's egg bill. The other three states ran highly suspect and corrupt state beef councils that benefited from checkoff dollars. The playbook went one step further in those states by asking people to write their state's auditor, attorney general, and the chairs of the state House and Senate appropriations committees about the mysterious and unaccountable money passing through their beef councils' coffers.

The introduction of the OFF Act in the Senate was led by the senators, who issued press releases encouraging their colleagues to sign on. It was an esoteric bill, but Beltway media like *Politico* covered the news. The afternoon of the bill introduction, the conservative Heritage Foundation led a congressional briefing—basically a room reserved by a member of Congress for interested staffers and press to hear about an issue and eat free food—at which Senator Lee spoke. Then, farmers' and ranchers' groups joined in, voicing their support over the next several days, leading to coverage in agriculture publications and letters to politicians representing those organizations' constituents. At the beginning of the next week, the organizations that had signed the national letter blasted out their own releases to their listservs, and a trickle of local press releases, letters to the editor, and shareable social media infographics started to flow.

With the groundwork laid by late March 2017, it was time to start meeting with congressional staffers. Huffman was in Ohio, but Democrat Maxwell and Republican Irby were both in D.C. most of the time. Any animal organization that wants to influence federal legislation needs to have a presence in Washington and needs to pay people to walk day after day down Capitol Hill's hard marble halls. The national sign-on letter, press releases, and media reports were invaluable for lobbying. Maxwell and Irby put a few of the best articles into a packet with a one-page fact sheet and started scheduling as many meetings as they could. Few were successful. Congressional ag staffers know what their bosses' priorities are, and Humane Society lobbyists are not at the top of their list. In July, about a dozen leading farmers flew to D.C. from as far away as Oregon to lobby their members of Congress on the bill.

When the floor vote loomed, the play became pure inside-the-Beltway politics. Irby spent thousands of dollars to target the Capitol Hill zip code with social media ads urging passage of the amendment. Congressional staffers would see these ads on their phones and work computers and, the thinking went, believe the accurate messaging, or at least think there was a much larger national campaign supporting the issue. It was the best use of $10,000 at crunch time. There are less ethical but still legal and cheaper ways to do this through the creation of hundreds of fake social media accounts (bots) that link to and magnify each other's content, but Irby did not go that route.

Senator Lee forced a Senate vote by offering an amendment to the Farm Bill on the Senate floor. The amendment was merely the OFF Act in a different legislative form. Big Meat was completely unprepared for Lee's political play and had not lined up its favored politicians to kill it. The vote on what seemed like a minor technical amendment was nerve-wracking and extraordinary to witness: most senators had likely not given the issue any thought. C-SPAN footage of the vote shows dozens of them walking in and out of the chamber to find out what was happening and what they were voting on. It is a misconception that there is measured debate or that staffers read and understand everything that comes across their desks. That would be impossible. At this level, legislating is like drinking from a fire hose.

The effort united a more unusual coalition than Maxwell had in Oklahoma. On June 28, 2018, the Tea Party and progressives voted for the bill, while those in the middle voted against it. Lee and Booker each got their people on board: Senators Ted Cruz, Rand Paul, Kamala Harris, and Bernie Sanders all voted for checkoff reform. But the 38 Tea Party and progressive votes lost to 57 no votes from the broad middle, with 5 not voting.[20]

Irby later told me that with $50,000 more, he feels the amendment would have passed. If it had, it would have cut the strength out from under hundreds of millions of dollars for the taxpayer-funded organizations that push the priorities of Big Meat to the detriment of small farmers and animals. Farm animal advocates will have to learn from and improve upon this strategy for the next Farm Bill in the 2023–2025 congressional session.

It is vital that farm animal advocates understand why vegan animal groups did not lead this work. It was simple math. Vegans are politically toxic except among progressive Democrats who do not have agribusinesses in their districts. Voters rarely go to the polls to help farm animals, but wealthy agribusinesses donate a lot of money to keep pliant politicians in office. They do not give that money out of the goodness of their hearts: they give it to get a return on their investment. If farm animal advocates only preach to the choir, they will continue to find support among progressive urban politicians but never have the political power necessary to drive policy in America. It is equally naïve to pretend that allies, even true believers like Senator Cory Booker and Representative Earl Blumenauer, are not well aware of the financial benefits of the work they do for animals. Urging people to do the right thing for animals and the environment is not a winning political message. We all must face the reality of our transactional, money-driven political system.

Corporate Power in Animal Agriculture

If government is for sale to the highest bidder, then those with the deepest pockets and most corrupt intents will shape the law to their personal advantage. The larger and more concentrated agribusiness companies become, the more policy and political resources they have to hinder competition and prevent the free market from working.

How did the federal government come to support international conglomerates instead of American farmers? In Congress, the clearest way the government supports the interests of the powerful is via campaign contributions. In the executive branch, where policy makers are appointed rather than elected, the interests of Big Meat predominate when governmental appointees are "captured" by the industry. Such "private industries co-opt governmental power for their own competitive benefit."[21]

A quintessential example is the revolving door, through which decision makers cycle from government positions to the industries they regulate and back again. Along the way, these individuals naturally adopt the attitudes and beliefs that benefit their private position, which many will rejoin after completion of their putatively public service. This cycle is all the more insidious for the omnipresent promise of higher pay in the private sector. Personal self-interest morphs into the self-interest of private companies. Family farmers cannot compete for the attention of public officials who favor personal wealth over public service.

The USDA is inherently more prone to regulatory capture than are many other agencies because "the USDA provides grading, certification and verification services intended to improve agricultural companies' marketing of a variety of farm products."[22] This makes the agency, and especially certain oversight mechanisms, dependent on the industry it works with through user fees and a broader mission to promote agriculture. Moreover, there are relatively few specialists with the requisite technical skills to hold high-level regulatory jobs. One way to get such experience is through private industry, so the intertwining of the USDA with private industry is to some extent inevitable. Nevertheless, this does not excuse self-dealing.

From top to bottom, the USDA is rife with petty and personal corruption. An April 2019 investigation described a conversation with a USDA official about the Food Safety and Inspection Service (FSIS). The official, granted anonymity to speak freely, noted that "large meat producers like Cargill, Tyson, Smithfield, Swift (JBS) and Sanderson Farms are often given a 'pass' thanks to their high-paid lobbyists."[23] The whistleblower characterized the USDA as an old boys' club with a revolving door "between the USDA and FSIS, and the captains of the meat industry." On a smaller scale, every Friday, the meat industry sends batches of donuts to USDA offices in Washington, a minor but indisputably corrupt practice that is evidently widely accepted.

Agribusiness consolidation has led to market domination not seen since the Gilded Age. Concentration exacerbates regulatory capture that harms family farmers. The meatpacking industry is more concentrated today than it was during the days of the Beef Trust in the early 1900s, when the "big packers accounted for 45 percent" of the total slaughter nationwide.[24] The Sherman (1890) and Clayton (1914) Antitrust Acts gave the Federal Trade Commission the tools to counter the monopolization of the meatpacking industry. More importantly, the Packers and Stockyards Act (1921) ensured competition and fair prices that provided the underpinnings for a functioning open market.[25] By 1976, the four largest meatpackers controlled just 25 percent of the marketplace. However, with the weakening of antitrust and consumer laws beginning under the Reagan administration, they are no longer meaningfully enforced.[26] Antitrust law notwithstanding, the top four firms today "together slaughter more than 80 percent of feedlot cattle in the U.S."[27]

The consequences are evident. There has been an 83 percent increase in meat and poultry recalls in the United States since 2013, including 12 million pounds of beef sold by JBS under the eyes of FSIS chief Al Almanza.[28] Despite this, the USDA is moving forward with proposals to speed up pork and poultry inspection lines.[29]

As concentration has increased, so too has exploitation of small farmers through usurious contract farming practices. A masterful exposé found that most farmers can eke out subsistence wages at best, so small farmers are increasingly joined in their ranks by desperately poor immigrants from Southeast Asia.[30] In the poultry industry, companies like Tyson own both the birds and the feed, and farmers contract with them to grow chicks to market-weight broiler chickens.[31] The system is "worse in certain respects than sharecropping," says farmer Garry Staples. "A modern plantation system is what it is," concurs Robert Taylor, professor of agricultural economics at Auburn University.[32] Farmers take out million-dollar balloon loans to meet the conglomerate's specifications, but their paydays are dependent upon the company's good faith to provide suitable chicks as well as up on a byzantine "tournament system" that seems rigged to punish whistleblowers. With only a handful of conglomerates dominating the market, and entire regions with just one active company, there is no competition, and farmers who do not like working for a company are faced with no choice but bankruptcy, or worse. A heartbreaking study from the University of Iowa found that "suicide rates for farmers were higher than for *all* occupations in *each* of the 19 study years (1992–2010) [emphasis added]."[33] The American heartland, with its historic destiny as a beacon of Jeffersonian freedom, has come to resemble a "rural ghetto," says Mississippi cattle rancher Fred Stokes.

PERSONNEL IS POLICY:
BIG MEAT IN THE EXECUTIVE BRANCH

Personnel is policy. The following sections will illustrate how the system of regulatory capture works and profile the people fighting against it.

First, Big Meat has always found its personnel atop the USDA, as it did with President Donald Trump's agriculture secretary, former Georgia governor Sonny Perdue.

To guard against conflicts of interest, wealthy politicians usually put their assets in a blind trust. Not Perdue. During his first gubernatorial campaign, in response to a question about whether he would put his businesses in a blind trust, he said: "I am a small business owner; I'm in the agri-business. That's about as blind a trust as you can get. We trust in the Lord for rain and many other things . . . [A] blind trust is not functional for a small businessperson."[34]

Two contrasting events illustrate Sonny Perdue's true governing philosophy. First, in 2009, the Biotechnology Industry Organization, whose membership includes agribusiness behemoths like Bayer, Monsanto, Syngenta, and Cargill, named Perdue Governor of the Year for his support of the industry.[35] Secondly, Perdue faced 13 complaints at the state ethics commission during his years as governor, two of which resulted in findings that Perdue broke state ethics laws.[36]

Governor Perdue's actions demonstrated he was often working for his own, rather than the public's, interest. Before he left office, he was already cashing in on his government service by starting businesses like Perdue Consulting Group, which offered what it called public policy advice, and Perdue Partners, LLC, which helped private corporations lobby government.[37] His revolving door involved placing business associates in state government and giving his gubernatorial staffers jobs in his businesses. In a brazen show of nepotism, Governor Perdue appointed his cousin, David Perdue, to be on the Georgia Ports Authority in 2010. Then, in 2011, David Perdue became a co-founder of the Perdue Partners consultancy, and he later won election as a U.S. senator.[38]

Sonny Perdue also brought on key Georgia administration officials, such as Heidi Green and Trey Childress, to work at Perdue Partners to aid domestic and foreign corporate clients in navigating Georgia politics and government. Another abuse of power came in his final year in office when he used his position to question a Georgia Ports Authority official about what services would be of use to them in order to lay the groundwork for some of his businesses dependent on shipping exports.[39]

When Perdue was nominated to be U.S. secretary of agriculture, American family farmers who had believed in President Trump's promises to "drain the swamp" and protect domestic agriculture felt betrayed. Perdue continued his gubernatorial *modus operandi*. Before he even had a Senate confirmation hearing, Perdue installed Heidi Green, the former Georgia administration official and partner at Perdue Partners, as a senior adviser at the USDA. She subsequently became Secretary Perdue's first chief of staff.

The Obama administration promulgated regulations that sought to protect farmers trapped in the contract debt model and to level the playing field for other small and medium farmers through the Farmer Fair Practices Rules (FFPR). The rules would have "[made] it easier for poultry and livestock farmers to sue meat processing companies with which they have contracts" and "[protected] these contract farmers from unfair practices," like being forced to make costly and unnecessary upgrades.[40] However, when Secretary Perdue came in to lead the USDA, the rules were rolled back. This handout to agribusiness interests devastated independent farmers.

Even the largely unenforced safeguards set up after the Beef Trust era were targeted for dismantlement. Secretary Perdue reorganized the USDA to move the Grain Inspection, Packers and Stockyards Administration (GIPSA), the agency tasked with enforcing the Packers and Stockyards Act, under the control of Agricultural Marketing Service (AMS). This move is a coup for meatpackers: AMS works in concert with meatpackers, while GIPSA is supposed to regulate them.[41] Astonishingly, the USDA also purchased 62 million pounds of Brazil-based JBS's pork products in the name of a farmer trade war bailout.[42]

FROM PUBLIC HEALTH ENFORCER TO A CAPTAIN OF THE MEAT INDUSTRY: AL ALMANZA, THE FOOD SAFETY AND INSPECTION SERVICE, AND JBS

Public power also lines private pockets when industry lures career government officials away with lucrative employment offers, as was the case with Al Almanza. Almanza served as the head of the Food Safety and Inspection Service (FSIS), which is tasked with ensuring the safety of meat, poultry, and eggs. Almanza seemed to be different from Sonny Perdue: by all accounts, Almanza was a competent and ethical public servant during his tenure at FSIS. The reality would be borne out in a disturbing scandal.

Meat conglomerate JBS had been so successful in capturing the Brazilian government that a state-owned Brazilian bank gave JBS "favorable loan terms starting in June 2007 to acquire other meat companies around the world," facilitating its entrance into the U.S. market through the purchase of Swift later that year.[43]

In early 2017, Almanza helped approve the lifting of a ban on the importation of Brazilian beef that had been in place for 13 years.[44] That year, JBS was facing disaster as multiple corruption probes culminated in raids at Brazilian meatpackers that uncovered serious food safety issues as well as bribery. Almanza had the power to stop the importation of JBS's rotten Brazilian beef but took ninety painstaking days to do so, even as China and other countries immediately banned importation.[45] After 39 years at FSIS, he left in July 2017 to become the global head of food safety and quality assurance at JBS, now the largest meat seller in America.[46]

Just as Almanza was transitioning out of the USDA, the agency moved to suspend all importation of Brazilian meat in June 2017.[47] The timing of and circumstances surrounding this move were deeply troubling. For him to take his decades of government experience and training into the private sector certainly indicated that he had come to favor industry over the public interest by the end of his career. Almanza favored JBS to the point of allowing rotten meat to enter the U.S. food supply. This cronyism landed him a sweetheart job with JBS.

In a *Politico* interview, Almanza defended his actions by stating that he had recused himself from any discussions about the Brazilian rotten meat scandal. In his opinion, no rotten beef had gotten into the U.S. food supply, but his statements seem disingenuous.[48] As head of FSIS, Almanza should not have recused himself, but should have actively been protecting public health by banning the importation of unsafe food. This further indicates he was in talks with JBS about future employment during his public service to such a degree that he felt he had a financial conflict even during his tenure at the USDA.

FROM STEWARD TO SPENDER: CRAIG MORRIS AND THE USDA's AGRICULTURAL MARKETING SERVICE

Career bureaucrats little known to the public, like Al Almanza and Craig Morris, likely have more impact on farm animal welfare than do politically appointed cabinet secretaries. Morris started his career working for The American Meat Institute (TAMI), a trade organization of large meat and poultry companies. In his role with TAMI, Morris led an industry-coordinated effort to weaken FSIS-proposed pathogen reduction rules. He also spearheaded an industry project concerning Americans' ground beef consumption that was funded by the Cattlemen's Beef Board through beef checkoff tax dollars flowing through the USDA's Agricultural Marketing Service (AMS), a government body tasked with increasing Americans' food consumption.

Morris moved on to a twenty-year career with AMS overseeing cattle and pork checkoff dollars, split by an interim position working for private industry, and capped by a high-level job at the National Pork Board, an entity he had previously regulated.[49] Morris's two decades at AMS were interrupted for just ten months when he went to work for a company, Future Beef Operations, LLC, that soon went bankrupt. During his tenure at AMS, Morris worked within livestock, poultry, and seed programs during separate stints. Eventually he rose to deputy administrator and consolidated oversight of the livestock, seed, and poultry programs until his departure in October 2017 to become vice president for international marketing at the National Pork Board. Morris's insider knowledge of AMS was welcomed by the CEO of the National Pork Board, Bill Even. Even's appraisal was that Morris's "extensive knowledge of the pork industry, export markets and consumer preferences will elevate the [marketing and global promotion] role during this crucial time for [the] industry."[50] The entire cycle represents a head-spinning circuit of conflicts and shady deals.

The web is further complicated by the fact that the National Pork Board is a public–private entity responsible for collecting and spending pork checkoff tax dollars under a dubious legal scheme.[51] One executed while Morris was at AMS used taxpayer money to purchase the slogan "The Other White Meat" from a lobbying organization. The slogan itself has been out of use since 2011, replaced by "Pork: Be Inspired." As with any government funds, the taxes sent to the National Pork Board cannot be used for lobbying. How to get around this stricture? The National Pork Board struck a deal to "rent" the unused "The Other White Meat" slogan from the National Pork Producers Council, the lobbying organization that used to share office space with the National Pork Board, for $60 million, or $3 million per year for twenty years.[52] The National Pork Producers Council donates about half a million dollars per year to federal candidates, an enormous sum that buys influence sufficient to prevent farm animal advocates from winning votes in Congress. Indeed, this money helped kill the national egg bill a decade ago.

In 2015, TAMI merged with another industry trade group to create the North American Meat Institute (NAMI). Ironically, this merger was consummated under the guidance of Barry Carpenter, himself a nearly twenty-year USDA veteran who, like Morris, was a deputy administrator at AMS before becoming CEO of NAMI.[53]

The USDA has a revolving-door problem at its core. International conglomerates like JBS and organizations like the National Cattlemen's Beef Association and the National Pork Board end up controlling policy and tax dollars to serve Big Meat's whims over the public interest, whether it is Secretary Sonny Perdue showing a well-documented disregard of family farmers; the veteran regulator at FSIS, Al Almanza, going for a lucrative payday at the private company he failed to protect the public from; or the AMS marketing guru, Craig Morris, spending the pork checkoff taxes whose stewardship he was responsible for.

It is not necessary to memorize all the details of Perdue's, Almanza's, and Morris's conflicts of interest. Farm animal advocates interested in research, media, and legal strategies should expose the mishandeling of tax money and miasma of influence peddling surrounding checkoff programs to fight the source of factory farmers' political power.

WASHINGTON'S IMPACT ON FAMILY FARMERS

Big Meat's policies are carried out by people with names, faces, alliances, and agendas. The mosaic of American agriculture, too, consists of millions of individuals who work to feed our fellow citizens and the world. This section describes how decisions made by people in Washington, D.C., affect four farmers in the heartland: Sarah Lloyd, a dairy farmer in Wisconsin; John Boyd, a cattle farmer in Virginia; and Connie and Jonathan Buttram, contract poultry farmers in Alabama. Farmers and vegans should understand each other and work together politically; demonization is counterproductive.

FAMILY FARMING MEETS THE MACHINE:
SARAH LLOYD AND THE DAIRY INDUSTRY

Sarah Lloyd brought special insight into her service on the National Dairy Board. Lloyd has a Ph.D. in sociology from the University of Wisconsin and runs a 400-cow dairy farm with her husband Nels. His family has been dairy farming in Wisconsin for more than a century.[54] Even a business with as much longevity and a family with as much talent as theirs have faced intensifying headwinds. With losses mounting year after year, "we're really just digging deep into the asset base that the generations have built,"[55] Lloyd laments. "We're just going to have to go further and further in debt."[56]

More than 600 dairy farmers left the industry in Wisconsin alone in 2018, and thousands of cattle were lost in each month of 2019, victims of a rigged market that keeps prices low and encourages expansion rather than raising prices to make up for lost income.[57] The dairy business cycle that used to wax and wane has been stubbornly stuck at levels below the cost of production since 2015. At the state level, one of the macabre signs of the desperation among Wisconsin farmers is the substantial increase in funding for farmer depression and suicide prevention. At the federal level, President Trump's trade wars were "the crappy icing on the crappy cake," Lloyd says.[58]

The National Dairy Board, funded by checkoff taxes on small and large farmers alike, shows the conflicting prerogatives of farmers and national bureaucrats. Even as a board member, Lloyd found she could not alter the system. She quickly discovered during her term of board service that the checkoff funds were co-opted by industry and a "good old boy system" that did not have the interests of ordinary farmers at heart.[59] "I would often leave the meetings and weep on my way home," she remembers.

Dairy farmers are being forced to pay into a system that puts them out of business. Lloyd's farm pays about $16,000 per year in checkoff taxes. This government program has paid out millions of dollars to some of the world's largest food corporations, including McDonald's and Pizza Hut. It paid a staggering $25 million to the National Football League for a "partnership" that lasted just four years, from 2013 to 2017. "These high-priced marketing people sitting in fancy offices in suburban Chicago were driving up to the meetings in luxury foreign SUVs," Lloyd continues. "They were using my money and farmers' money when farmers' kids are on free and reduced lunch."[60] President Barack Obama's USDA secretary, Tom Vilsack, revolving-doored straight into a position as the head of the Dairy Export Council, funded by the checkoff, and earned a million-dollar salary, before revolving back to head President Joe Biden's USDA.[61]

"To cover this gaping wound, we have been offered Band-Aids," Lloyd writes of the Trump administration's response. What's the real solution? "We want a fair price in the market."[62] But at the National Dairy Board, "you're not allowed to talk about price," she states flatly. "They will honestly just say: 'We can't talk about price.' It's ridiculous."[63]

It does not have to be this way. "The Canadian system is protecting its family farmers," Lloyd notes. "It would be nice to have a U.S. system that did the same."[64]

PERSEVERANCE OVER DISCRIMINATION: JOHN BOYD AND THE NATIONAL BLACK FARMERS ASSOCIATION

Of all the indignities heaped upon farmers in America, the added burden of discrimination is hardest to stomach. "My dad is a farmer," Dr. John Boyd writes. "My dad's father was a farmer, his father was a farmer, and his father was a slave." Through charisma, grit, and movie-star looks, Dr. Boyd, founder of the National Black Farmers Association, has led the way to a fairer farm economy for all Americans.

The problems Black farmers face in America are daunting. The 45,000 Black American farmers today are disproportionately represented in the ranks of smaller farmers, with an average farm size of just fifty acres. In a study of the federal government's role in perpetuating such economic problems, the Government Accountability Office concluded that the USDA "has been addressing allegations of discrimination for decades and receiving recommendations for improving its civil rights functions without achieving fundamental improvements."[65]

Boyd has felt this sting personally. "I had a great winter wheat crop," he recalls. "When I got to the mill to sell it, I saw some of my neighbors receiving the going price, but then I got there with good grain, and they found a way to dock it. . . . It's getting harder and harder to get an operating loan from banks, too. I think some of that is race-related."[66] One time, "[w]hen he went to his county office seeking a USDA loan to help save his farm . . . a white farmer spit on him."[67]

The inability to access capital and acquire savings leads to a cycle of intergenerational debt bondage. "The most troubling part of the whole story was my great-grandfather was able to obtain land after the Civil War, keep it, pass it on to a generation, and here I am, supposed to be a free man. Why can't I live this life that my forefathers lived? Why can't I obtain credit?"[68]

Yet all is not lost. While problems remained at the USDA and with the banking system, President Obama continued the quest he had begun as a senator to help redress the hardships of thousands of Black farmers that mirror Boyd's. In a heroic trek, Boyd "hitched up two mules—40 Acres and Justice—and drove his wagon 280 miles to D.C., attracting news coverage and support along the way."[69] Just as individuals passing through the revolving door can harm the lives of millions of Americans, focused leadership in Washington can make a real difference. When President Obama signed a 2010 settlement to provide $1.25 billion to farmers who were victims of discrimination, Boyd attended to represent all of America's Black farmers.[70]

When one's own situation is so precarious, why dedicate such enormous time and energy to help others? "I'm haunted by the faces," Boyd concludes.[71]

INTEGRITY AND RETALIATION: THE BUTTRAM FAMILY AND CONTRACT POULTRY FARMING

What strikes one most about third-generation poultry farmers Jonathan and Connie Buttram is the kindness they exude—toward people, animals, and each other. Partners in both life and business, the Buttrams are people of considerable integrity—which is precisely why they ran afoul of the oligopolies that dominate the American chicken industry.

Like virtually all contract poultry growers in America, the Buttrams are beholden to the tournament system, an opaque payment structure that pits farmers against each other by rewarding those who produce the most chicken meat at the lowest cost and paying the lowest performers at rates that do not cover their expenses. The system is easily gamed by the companies that run it. Companies do not have to share information with farmers about payment calculations. All chickens are not created equal. If a batch of chicks are hatched and have health problems or are generally of lower weight, this is a perfect batch to send to punish whistleblowers.

"When I became president of the Alabama Contract Poultry Growers Association, JBS began a process of harassment that ultimately led to their terminating my contracts and putting my family in near bankruptcy," Jonathan says.[72]

From birth to slaughter, the chickens themselves are owned by the oligopolies, with ostensibly independent labor provided by contractors like the Buttrams. Fully half of American contract poultry growers live in regions served by just one or two chicken companies.[73] "The company has 99-and-a-half percent control over the grower," says Jonathan. "Then, they say we're not employees—we are employees, but they won't let us have any kind of benefits or insurance."[74]

"We have no rights," Buttram notes. "We're basically turned into sharecroppers."[75]

Larger farms with newer technology and higher upfront investments can produce chickens that outcompete those from farms with older technology and equipment. However, the initial costs are a hidden subsidy from farmer to monopoly. The economic imperative for small farmers to build larger, newer barns and farming systems finds people with little or no collateral taking out multimillion-dollar balloon loans, subsidized by government-backed Small Business Administration credit, that subject farmers to debt peonage.[76]

The pain and suffering of American farmers is so immense that Jonathan has been compelled to minister to friends driven to unspeakable desperation by Big Chicken. "I have counseled numerous farmers who have considered suicide because of JBS's continued harassment and abuses," he says.[77] "A grower called me and said he was going to kill his broiler manager and kill himself. I never thought that I would have to be talking people out of committing suicide or committing murder."[78]

The retribution visited upon the Buttrams became more severe when they appeared as the stars of Morgan Spurlock's documentary *Super Size Me 2: Holy Chicken!*[79] Jonathan was blackballed. The only poultry company in his area severed all ties with him.[80] Even more galling, the chicken cartel went after his children, denying them business "not because of anything they did but because their parents spoke out."[81]

Despite the retaliation, the Buttrams are moving forward with their lives. Organizations like the Alabama Contract Poultry Growers Association are powerful means to fight for change. Many of its members come together after experiencing firsthand the inequity of a broken system that commodifies humans and animals alike. The Buttrams joined with farmers from across the country, with legal help from the Organization for Competitive Markets and Democracy Forward, to file a federal lawsuit against the USDA regarding the Trump administration's withdrawal of one of the Farmer Fair Practices Rules discussed earlier. They have also exited the chicken business after watching their farm "over the past decade shrink from 360,000 birds and 1,000 brood cows to simply 80 brood cows."[82]

"We care about the food supply," Jonathan states. "These large packers and integrators do not care. The bottom line is the money, the dollar."[83]

For people of conscience like Dr. Lloyd, Dr. Boyd, and the Buttrams, the hope is that their whistleblowing and legal advocacy will lay the groundwork for a new generation of American farmers to be treated with the dignity and respect that Big Meat has denied so many. Vegan nonprofit activists will need to ally with farmers like these, and vice versa.

Animal advocates often ignore the people who work so hard to raise animals. Small farmers care for their animals every day, feeding them and mucking their stalls in every sort of weather. It is not easy labor. It is understandably difficult for vegans to feel much sympathy for those who make money by killing animals, or by the same token for farmers to want to work with young and often privileged people who have little knowledge about or respect for farmers' lives. But an alliance between rural family farmers and urban animal advocates is the only political coalition that can take on Big Meat and win. Such an alliance would be based, as Joe Maxwell proved, on the shared value of compassion for animals to achieve national political change.

3

Vegans Making Laws

From California to Capitol Hill

N early all Americans believe animals deserve to be treated humanely. Public opinion on farm animals is as close as one can come to unanimity in the political system. Just 3 percent of people feel that animals "don't need much protection," according to Gallup. In comparison, 62 percent agree that animals deserve some protection, while another 32 percent say that animals deserve the same rights as people. do[1]

Animal advocates should recognize that while their positions enjoy majority support, American politics is ruled by money. Few citizens vote for or against politicians based on their animal welfare records. "Animals are already in the political arena, except these representatives are allied with powerful commercial interests," famed animal activist Kim Stallwood writes.[2] It would be surprising if it were otherwise: if animals could hold $1,000-per-plate fundraisers, there would be no animal cruelty in America.

FEDERAL LAWS PROTECTING FARMED ANIMALS

Advocates can read through a bookshelf of material calling for animal protection laws without coming across a realistic suggestion of how they might come to pass. Similarly, "the bulk of animal law scholarship has ignored political and social forces that shape the outcome of animal law cases," writes law professor Steven Tauber.[3] America is not the democracy of *Schoolhouse Rock* songs, nor was it constituted as such. In the debate on the creation of the Senate, James Madison convinced the delegates at the Constitutional Convention in Philadelphia to secure the interests of wealth and privilege over popular government:

> In England, at this day, if elections were open to all classes of people, the property of the landed proprietors would be insecure. An agrarian law would soon take place. If these observations be just, our government ought to secure the permanent interests of the country against innovation. Landholders ought to have a share in the government, to support these invaluable interests and to balance and check the other. They ought to be so constituted as to protect the minority of the opulent against the majority.[4]

Few citizens could vote then, and state legislatures elected senators until the Seventeenth Amendment was ratified in 1913. Over a century later, the Senate remains a roadblock to democratic progress. Animal welfare legislation is routinely killed in the industry-captured Senate and House Agriculture Committees. The problems are similar in agriculture committees in statehouses across the country.

America has minimal legal protections for animals. There are only two federal laws that deal with the treatment of farmed animals: the Twenty-Eight Hour Law of 1873, which limited lengthy transport times, and the Humane Methods of Slaughter Act of 1958. There are no federal laws that govern how animals are raised on farms. State laws vary but are generally written by corporate agricultural interests to exempt "customary farming practices."[5] Thus: "In most of the United States, prosecutors, judges, and juries no longer have the power to determine whether or not farmed animals are treated in an acceptable manner. The industry alone defines the criminality of its own conduct."[6]

The Twenty-Eight Hour Law requires animals transported for more than twenty-eight hours to be "unloaded in a humane way into pens equipped for feeding, water, and rest for at least five consecutive hours," with the exception of sheep, who may be transported for thirty-six hours.[7] Token civil fines for violations are between one hundred and five hundred dollars.

The Animal Welfare Institute (AWI) used Freedom of Information Act requests to pursue a Sisyphean twelve-year investigation into the enforcement of the Twenty-Eight Hour Law.[8] Federal records show ten investigations into possible violations over twelve years; the AWI found another in the media. Of these eleven, six "found sufficient evidence for a violation of the law," yet just one was reported to the Department of Justice for prosecution. The AWI concluded that violations are likely common, especially involving animals shipped to or from Canada or Mexico, but there was no reliable enforcement of the law. In so many words, the Twenty-Eight Hour Law may as well not exist.

The Humane Methods of Slaughter Act (HMSA) applies to more animals and is better enforced. The law regulates the killing of livestock for food in the United States but exempts poultry and religious slaughter, such as halal and kosher rituals.[9] Industrialization and economies of scale actually benefit livestock welfare at slaughter. It costs more time and money to slaughter an animal while she or he is conscious than when unconscious.

It is a misconception that most American cattle die painful deaths. That reflects a deregulatory world of twenty years ago, documented in seminal works like *Slaughterhouse* and the *Washington Post* investigation "They Die Piece by Piece."[10] Congress responded to these reports by including a section in the 2002 Farm Bill calling on the USDA to fully enforce HMSA.[11]

Federal meat inspectors tasked with enforcing food safety laws, including HMSA, are present at all federally inspected slaughterhouses. Most slaughterhouses in America are under federal jurisdiction due to their products' entry into interstate commerce. State-inspected slaughterhouses participating solely in intrastate commerce must meet or exceed federal standards.[12]

The great secret of animal protection at the intersection of corporations' and animals' interests is that animal cruelty costs money. Laws like HMSA are pro-industry and pro-animal.[13] When animals are scared, bruised, cut, or conscious during slaughter, it disrupts production, adulterates meat, and leads to loss of efficiency and profit. It seems counterintuitive, but animals are often treated better at large plants due to the humane imperatives of mass production.[14]

Federal inspectors have powerful tools for compelling companies to fix problems affecting humane livestock handling or slaughter. Inspectors can order an immediate suspension of any area unsafe to animals in a slaughter facility, ranging from truck loading ramps to pens and chutes to the kill box, until the violation is rectified. A suspension of even a few minutes of production affects the bottom line as idle workers and equipment cost a company progressively more money. Repeated egregious violations can even lead to inspectors being withdrawn and facilities being permanently shut down, as was the case with Westminster Meats in Vermont in 2017.

Cattle have it the "best" at slaughter. Although mistakes are not uncommon and lead to animal torture, slaughter methods for beef cattle are thought to be *relatively* routine and painless for them. They are docile herd animals for whom slaughterhouse chute architecture has been optimized to minimize panic and suffering through the visionary work of Temple Grandin. Cattle follow the animal in front of them until they find themselves suddenly in a pen, where a worker applies a captive bolt gun to their foreheads. The pressurized bolt ejects through the skull and into the frontal cortex responsible for consciousness: they are shot painlessly and drop to the floor unconscious. A chain is placed around one leg, they are mechanically hoisted in the air upside down, the carotid arteries supplying the brain are cut, and they exsanguinate before they regain consciousness. Cattle benefit from their large size compared to chickens and the necessity to slaughter one animal at a time even at the largest abattoirs. It is easier for workers and inspectors to handle and observe an individual dairy cow or beef cattle than it is other kinds of animals. At the same time, young cattle skulls are thinner than those of larger and older animals like oxen or buffaloes. Captive bolt guns and even shotguns and rifles do not always pierce the skulls of the latter at first shot.

Pigs encounter more difficulties due to their biology. Pigs are fast prey animals instinctively wary of humans. Their natural response is to run from fright. Slaughterhouses are places of fear. Pigs are smaller and harder to corral than cattle. They do not benefit from the same carefully designed serpentine chutes that cattle do; thus, their foreheads are not as easy to shoot as those of cattle. They are terrified and recoil from the strange human form hovering above them with the captive bolt gun or electric stunner, so the bolt or voltage can miss the frontal cortex. Pigs are also commonly "stunned" in carbon dioxide chambers. Pig slaughterhouses are filthy from so many animals defecating in terror before they die.

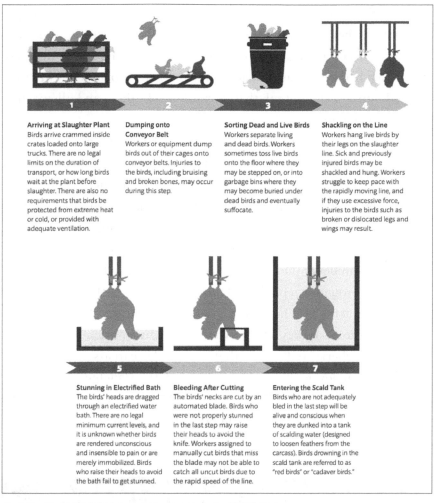

1 — Arriving at Slaughter Plant
Birds arrive crammed inside crates loaded onto large trucks. There are no legal limits on the duration of transport, or how long birds wait at the plant before slaughter. There are also no requirements that birds be protected from extreme heat or cold, or provided with adequate ventilation.

2 — Dumping onto Conveyor Belt
Workers or equipment dump birds out of their cages onto conveyor belts. Injuries to the birds, including bruising and broken bones, may occur during this step.

3 — Sorting Dead and Live Birds
Workers separate living and dead birds. Workers sometimes toss live birds onto the floor where they may be stepped on, or into garbage bins where they may become buried under dead birds and eventually suffocate.

4 — Shackling on the Line
Workers hang live birds by their legs on the slaughter line. Sick and previously injured birds may be shackled and hung. Workers struggle to keep pace with the rapidly moving line, and if they use excessive force, injuries to the birds such as broken or dislocated legs and wings may result.

5 — Stunning in Electrified Bath
The birds' heads are dragged through an electrified water bath. There are no legal minimum current levels, and it is unknown whether birds are rendered unconscious and insensible to pain or are merely immobilized. Birds who raise their heads to avoid the bath fail to get stunned.

6 — Bleeding After Cutting
The birds' necks are cut by an automated blade. Birds who were not properly stunned in the last step may raise their heads to avoid the knife. Workers assigned to manually cut birds that miss the blade may not be able to catch all uncut birds due to the rapid speed of the line.

7 — Entering the Scald Tank
Birds who are not adequately bled in the last step will be alive and conscious when they are dunked into a tank of scalding water (designed to loosen feathers from the carcass). Birds drowning in the scald tank are referred to as "red birds" or "cadaver birds."

Graphic of industrial chicken slaughter process in the United States
Source: Animal Welfare Institute

HMSA applies to livestock but not to poultry. While hog slaughter line speeds have been capped at 1,106 pigs per hour—18 per minute—poultry slaughter speeds are set at a maximum of 8,400 birds per hour, or 140 per minute.[15] Broiler (meat) chickens are typically touched by humans thrice in their lives: once when they are vaccinated as chicks, once when they are thrown into cages to be transported to slaughter, and once when they are hung upside-down in shackles at the slaughterhouse. They are mechanically dumped from the truck cages onto conveyor belts that lead them to workers at the shackles. After the chickens' legs are put in shackles, they are transported like dry cleaning through an electric stunner or electrically charged stunning bath to temporarily paralyze them, then between rotating blades that cut their throats. They are then dunked into a scalding tank that partially cooks them and allows their feathers to be removed.

Food inspectors have a little-known backdoor method to enforce minimal welfare standards for poultry at slaughter. Although not covered by HMSA, poultry are covered by "good commercial practices" regulations designed to protect the safety of the nation's food supply. There is a gratuitous way to ensure the chickens are slaughtered properly and to tell if their throats are not cut before they enter the scalding tank, as is commonly the case. Chickens can be hung by only one limb; or they flap around in a panic and miss the stunner or the blades; or the voltage is set too low. Their lungs are still working and blood congeals in the upper torso as they are drowned. This physiological effect creates nauseating "cherry red" meat that makes the carcass unsuitable for sale. Plant employees can see when to stop the slaughter line and fix problems when multiple "cherry red" chickens start coming out of the scalder. An estimated one million American chickens suffer this fate every year.[16]

Picture of chickens shackled upside down
Source: Animal Welfare Institute

There is a financial incentive not to engage in egregious animal cruelty. In addition to cherry red carcasses, broken bones and bruised meat are evidence of animal cruelty, and the bodies of these animals are condemned. Chicken products that are adulterated are unsafe for human consumption and must be discarded. They would look like exactly what they are under supermarket cellophane. Nobody would buy them.

The authority for good commercial practices regulation was promulgated by the USDA's Food Safety and Inspection Service in 2005 under the Poultry Products Inspection Act.[17] The USDA has the authority to fully bring poultry under the rubric of the HMSA, but it chooses not to.[18]

How Capitol Hill Actually Works

It is exciting to think about passing laws like they do in movies. That is unfortunately not how the real world of farm animal advocacy works. There are limited ways in which we as a movement can engage with politicians, because the farm animal movement has little realized financial or voting power. A movement could hardly pick a better spokesman than Cory Booker, the 6'3" vegan Rhodes Scholar and former Stanford tight end. But to focus on Senator Booker is to misunderstand the nature of federal legislative policy. Elected politicians have limited time and are necessarily most adept at campaigning rather than understanding the nuts and bolts of policies, though senators can spend more time legislating, given their six-year cycles. A town school board member may be able to read every bill or budget item that crosses her desk, but as issues become larger and more complex at the federal level, the staff act as the politician's eyes, ears, and brain and are entrusted to carry out the politician's broad vision with specific policies. The many issues a staffer may be tasked with may themselves be impossibly large, such as health care, agriculture, and the environment. To truly see the political power of the modern farm animal movement, you need to venture to a small office in the Ford House Office Building and meet twenty-six-year-old MacKenzie Landa. Bright, energetic, and five feet tall in heels, Landa seems too authentic to work on Capitol Hill. There is no mask or pretense when the former PETA lawyer talks about farm animals. She is from New Orleans, the foodie capital where, as she was growing up, one could not find a single vegetarian restaurant. Until two years ago, she was one of a handful of Hill staffers who worked primarily on animal issues—in her case, on behalf of Virginia Democrat Don Beyer. She is a member of the vegetarian congressional staffer association and a behind-closed-doors vegan dream team driving congressional policy for farm animals at the margins.

Much of the work done in Washington is done in the White House and through backdoor maneuvering, as exemplified by the federal hog slaughter line speed acceleration measure in the 2019–2021 Congress. The following is a snapshot of one moment in time: December 3, 2019.

CASE STUDY: ONE DAY OF RULEMAKING AND LEGISLATIVE TACTICS ON HOG SLAUGHTER LINE SPEED IN THE TRUMP ADMINISTRATION

The USDA increased permitted line speeds for hog slaughter through federal executive rulemaking. The House agriculture appropriations bill put a stop to this through an amendment delaying the rule pending further research, but the Senate's did not. Both bills have passed in their respective chambers as part of a larger appropriations bill. Farm animal advocates want to ensure the amendment currently in the House bill remains in the final appropriations bill negotiated between the House and Senate.

USDA Rulemaking on Increased Hog Line Speeds[19]

February 1, 2018:	FSIS proposes rule, "Modernization of Swine Slaughter Inspection."
April 2, 2018:	Public comment period closes.
October 1, 2019:	Final rule published.
December 2, 2019:	Final rule becomes effective.

Current Funding Status of USDA

Current appropriations status of USDA is under a continuing resolution (CR).

September 27 & 29, 2019:	CR passed House & Senate maintaining budget levels through November 21, 2019.
October 1, 2019:	End of USDA FY2019.
November 21, 2019:	Another CR passed maintaining FY2019 budget levels through December 20, 2019.[20]

A FY2020 bill will pass when the House and Senate compromise on the differences between their two bills.

Federal Ag Appropriations Bills for FY2020

*Note that the House and Senate versions of HR 3055, Division B (Ag Approps) are different.

House

House FY2020 Ag Approps is HR 3164.

May 23, 2019: House Appropriations Committee, Subcommittee on Agriculture. HR 3164 (FY2020 Ag Approps) introduced and approved by voice vote.

June 4, 2019: House Appropriations Committee, full committee. HR 3164 (FY2020 Ag Approps) introduced. Amendment offered by Reps. DeLauro and Price that would prevent implementing USDA hog line speed rule change pending OIG report passed by voice vote.[21] The substance of this amendment (incorporating USDA OIG study) was supported by animal groups in a sign-on letter. This amendment became section 779 of the HR 3164.[22] The House Appropriations Committee passed the entire appropriations bill by a 29–21 vote that day.[23]

June 25, 2019: The bill was rolled into a minibus ("small" omnibus bill) and passed as HR 3055, Division B. (HR 3055 is the entire bill, and Division B is the House Agriculture Appropriations bill, which includes the pig slaughter provision.)

Senate

Senate FY2020 Ag Approps is S2,522. This bill does not include the pig slaughter provision that animal groups support.[24]

September 19, 2019: This bill passed the Senate Appropriations Committee, 31–0.

October 31, 2019: The bill was rolled into a minibus ("small" omnibus bill) and passed as HR 3055, Division B by 84–9. (HR 3055 is the entire bill, and Division B is the House Agriculture Appropriations bill, which does not include the pig slaughter provision.)

Language of Rep. DeLauro (CT-3) Pig Slaughter Amendment[25]

Sec. 779. None of the funds made available to the Department of Agriculture shall be used to finalize, issue, or implement the proposed rule entitled "Modernization of Swine Slaughter Inspection" published in the Federal Register by the Food Safety Inspection Service on February 1, 2018 (83 Fed. Reg. 4780 et seq.), including insofar as such rule relates to converting establishments, until—

(1) the Office of the Inspector General of the Department of Agriculture has provided to the Food Safety and Inspection Service and the Committees on Appropriations of the House of Representatives and the Senate findings on the data used in support of the development and design of the swine slaughter inspection program that is the subject of such proposed rule; and

(2) the Food Safety and Inspection Service has addressed and resolved issues identified by the Inspector General in the findings referred to in paragraph (1).

Administration Position

The administration issued a veto threat for the House version of HR 3055. The White House listed DeLauro's swine slaughter amendment as part of 11 pages of objections.[26] This was likely an idle threat, as any bill would have to pass the Senate, and a veto would move the government toward a shutdown. In general, the White House wanted substantial cuts to funding levels, while both House and Senate appropriators have marginally increased funding.[27]

Next Steps

The rule became effective on December 2, 2019. The large appropriations bill, HR 3055, will need to pass the House and Senate. The differences between the two bills will likely be resolved in a conference committee. The conference committee will be a bicameral, bipartisan group of leading lawmakers who will agree on one bill. The agreements will then come to a full House and Senate vote with no possibility of amendments and will likely be voted into law.

Source: Congressional Research Service

BALLOT INITIATIVES

Ballot initiatives have been the favored tool of farm animal advocates, who recognize the political reality of a supportive population and recalcitrant politicians. Populism and progressivism against corporate control of state politics led many states to adopt mechanisms for direct democracy, beginning with South Dakota in 1898. Twenty-six states now allow popular initiatives or referenda, in which, very generally speaking, citizens may collect petition signatures to put a measure on the ballot that will become law if it receives a majority vote.[28] In many states, the legislature itself can, or sometimes must, in the case of constitutional changes, put a measure up for popular vote, with the theory that the authority for the constitution ultimately derives from the will of the people.[29]

Ballot initiatives have long been used to protect wild animals, beginning with Oregon's 1926 measure to ban fish wheels, gill nets, and other inhumane and indiscriminate fishing methods on the Rogue River. The success rate accelerated in the 1990s: Californians passed an initiative banning the trapping and sport hunting of mountain lions; "Colorado voted to prohibit spring sport hunting of bears with bait or dogs; Arizona voted to prohibit the use of leg holds and snare traps on public lands; Alaska voted to ban same-day airborne hunting of wolves, foxes, lynx, and wolverines; and Oregon and Washington voted to prohibit the use of dogs to hunt bears and cougars."[30] These Western states were hardly liberal bastions at the time, but each of these measures garnered majority support by wisely singling out particularly indefensible and unsporting wildlife killing methods.

The test case for farm animal protection was the banning of sow gestation crates in Florida in 2002. The political landscape was favorable: "surveys showed sufficient support for eliminating intensive confinement of sows; Florida had a relatively small pig industry, which was less likely to be able to fight back effectively; funding was available for that state; and it appeared to be a state in which the potential for success was high enough to take the risk."[31] Florida voters passed the initiative with a sizable 55–45 majority. Arizona followed and passed a gestation and veal crate ban in 2006. The pork giant Smithfield announced a phase-out of gestation crates in 2007. That year, Oregon's became the first legislature to eliminate gestation crates when activists threatened a referendum; this tactic was successfully used in Maine and Colorado's legislatures and to cut a deal with the Ohio Farm Bureau. "If you read *The Art of War*, the most important thing you have to establish is momentum," attorney and animal advocate David Wolfson writes. "Florida changed everything. Florida led to Arizona, to Smithfield, to Maine, to Washington, which led to Prop 2 [in California], which led to Colorado, then Michigan, then Ohio. That energy elevated the debate."[32]

CALIFORNIA'S PROPOSITION 2 (2008)

Since 2008, California has been the most important state for farm animal activism due to its large population, economy, agricultural sector, sympathetic voter and donor bases, and political climate. California's Prop 2 (2008) was the movement's first attempt to ban not just gestation and veal crates, which had a minor economic cost easily passed on to consumers, but also battery cages for egg-laying hens, which would noticeably increase the price of eggs and engender an industry counterattack. The California egg industry was the nation's fifth largest. HSUS campaign leaders recounted another issue:

> Among animal advocates, there was a prevailing concern that it would be difficult to get people to care about chickens; in previous pre-ballot statewide polling, a measure to protect hens alone was less popular than polling language on pigs and calves. However, [HSUS's Factory Farm Campaign] suspected that most people just never really thought about chickens. Investigations in the 1990s revealed poor welfare of hens in battery cages, but this was before the rapid dissemination of investigative footage (the early videos were distributed on VHS tapes). FFC's leadership reasoned that it was not that people did not care, they simply did not know, and when given the chance to help all three species at once, voters would approve such a measure, as polling in California later showed. They further wagered that if people could see for themselves, through video and photo evidence, the conditions in which hens in the egg industry were commonly kept, they would support reform.[33]

It was a bold gamble. The measure was timed for an anticipated blue wave presidential election year that turned out to be a blue tsunami due to the 2008 financial crisis and Barack Obama's popularity among Democrats and swing voters.

For the purposes of Prop 2, in 2008 the cameras were not rolling at the Iowa caucuses, but in Chino, California, where HSUS planted an undercover investigator at the Hallmark Meat Packing Company and Westland Meat Company. At the time, the Hallmark/Westland facility was "the second-largest supplier of beef to the National School

Lunch Program," according to an in-depth political history by HSUS litigators.[34] Among other horrors, the investigator's videos documented a dairy cow too disabled to walk being brutally jabbed and dragged by a pitchfork, and helpless cows' faces and eyes as they are mercilessly beaten with poles and shocked with stunners. Interestingly, "Farm Sanctuary had been conducting investigations since 1986, and thirteen previous complaints of animal mishandling at the same plant over the preceding decade by the Inland Valley Humane Society and the Society for the Prevention of Cruelty to Animals seemed to have hardly been noticed."[35] The talented advocates in the HSUS Farm Animal Protection division would break the logjam of inaction. HSUS attorneys turned the evidence over to the San Bernardino County District Attorney's office, then the national media. This and later undercover exposés were aided by nascent social media platforms that meant news media no longer held a monopoly on how and when recordings reached the public. It caused the nation's largest meat recall, drove Hallmark and Westland into bankruptcy, and led to a $317 million federal fraud settlement for the illegal sale of meat from abused animals to the federal government.[36] Two workers were convicted of animal cruelty under California law.

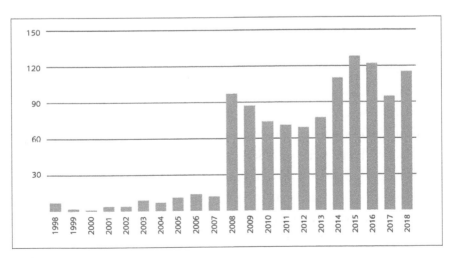

Timeline Graph of Federal Enforcement Actions for Egregious Violations of the Humane Methods of Slaughter Act, 1998-2018
Source: Animal Welfare Institute

The president of Hallmark was hauled in front of Congress, and the USDA issued regulations to prohibit downed cattle from entering the food supply in March 2009.[37] HMSA enforcement rose dramatically, according to records from the Animal Welfare Institute.

It is expensive to collect hundreds of thousands of signatures to put a measure on the ballot. It is possible to collect some signatures utilizing volunteers but unrealistic to collect a sufficient number without paying professional signature-gatherers. California signature-gatherers garner a premium. Furthermore, Prop 2 would be expected to face millions of dollars in opposition television advertising. Supporters of Prop 2 raised $10.5 million, with $4.1 million coming from HSUS, while opponents raised $9.0 million, mostly from the egg industry.[38] Two weeks before Election Day, Mercy For Animals released its own undercover investigation of a California egg farm with the help of fifteen-time Emmy Award–winning ABC reporter Dan Noyes.[39]

During this time, HSUS attorneys uncovered a brazen scheme to launder $3 million in federal funds to lobby against the referendum.[40] The American Egg Board, a USDA entity funded by egg taxes and tasked with increasing consumer demand for eggs, set aside $3 million in fall 2007 to oppose Prop 2. "The scheme was patently illegal because the American Egg Board is a federal commodity promotion program, and is consequently prohibited from spending any funds 'for the purposes of influencing governmental policy or action.'" It is a well-established American legal principle that the government cannot lobby itself. "HSUS's lawyers were less than fifteen minutes into their arguments against USDA's actions," husband and wife litigators Jonathan Lovvorn and Nancy Perry write of *HSUS v. Schafer* (N.D. Cal., filed August 12, 2008), "when Federal District Judge Marilyn Hall Patel enjoined the entire scheme from the bench—thus depriving opponents of millions in illegally funded television advertising."

Prop 2 passed by a landslide 63–37. It was a historic victory for animals. In some ways it would also signal the high water mark of teamwork and activism at an organization that would in the future be ripped apart by sexual abuse.

PROP 2 REDUX

The victory was not as resounding as it seemed. Critically, the measure did not include a sales ban; it applied only to animals raised within the state's borders. While hens in the San Joaquin Valley might have more space, more hens would be raised in tiny cages outside of Des Moines to provide the cheaper eggs demanded by Californians. The lack of a sales ban was due to a cautious approach to ballot measure–waging. Advocates calculated that Prop 2 would be the most far-reaching farm animal ballot measure ever and the first one to include chickens ever, all waged in the biggest agriculture state in the country. It was hard enough to go up against the California egg industry, but taking on the national industry was daunting. The national industry came in anyway, but at the time, advocates were focused on winning something historic for chickens, which they did.

A legislative fix, AB 1437, was passed in 2010 due in part to the exceptional work of then HSUS California state director Jennifer Fearing and Assemblyman Jared Huffman, now a congressman representing northwestern California.[41] Politically, the real reason it passed was because the California egg industry was lobbying for it. However, it applied only to eggs, not to pork and veal. Farm states led by Missouri sued California over this law, alleging it was an unconstitutional restriction on interstate commerce, but the suit was thrown out on standing grounds at the federal district level and then on appeal.[42]

Secondly, Prop 2 was perhaps not as clearly written as it could have been, although hindsight is always 20/20. All parties at that time, including the egg producers, argued Prop 2 required cage-free conditions. The entire argument of the egg industry before and during the campaign was that it would actually require free-range conditions, which advocates denied. But to suggest that it was confusing or that people at the time thought cages would still be allowed ignores the actual record of events in 2008.

The relevant language mandated that "a person shall not tether or confine any covered animal, on a farm, for all or the majority of any day, in a manner that prevents such animal from: (a) Lying down, standing up, and fully extending his or her limbs; and (b) Turning around freely."

Given California's ballot initiative rules, part of the impetus for this language was an emotional appeal to voters. However, these standards were open to a great deal of interpretation. If six hens are in a cage, do all six need to be able to freely extend their limbs and turn around simultaneously? Or can five hens cram themselves into one corner so one hen can spread her wings? It would have been far easier to explicitly define minimum space requirements. The issue was resolved after much litigation when the U.S. Ninth Circuit Court of Appeals ruled in 2015 that the language was intelligible and effectively set minimum space requirements.[43] However it was written, the legislation would always be subject to legal challenge and corporate attacks.

HSUS got a do-over a decade later when it ran Proposition 12, the ballot initiative it should have run in 2008. This campaign was ostensibly run by California state director Crystal Moreland, the ex-assistant to disgraced former HSUS CEO Wayne Pacelle. Promoting people based on physical considerations demeans women and hurts animals. Her campaign spent ten million dollars in after-tax money for TV and digital ads on behalf of a ballot initiative that was already guaranteed landslide passage, an identical measure (from voters' perspectives) having passed 63 percent to 37 percent in 2008.[44] Nobody needed polls to know that the outcome would be the same: there had already been a plebiscite. Millions of Californians who had already voted for the measure in 2008 were going to wake up on Election Day 2018 and do the same. Yet Moreland and the consultants and pollsters she hired were happy to spin their own narrative and take the money. The ads were irrelevant in the massive California media market, and the 2018 measure won 63 percent to 37 percent, exactly the same vote as in 2008, and by a greater percentage than Mitt Romney won Utah or Elizabeth Warren won Massachusetts. There was a lot of good that money could have done, and there are legitimately accomplished women who could have run that initiative. One of them, whom I will not name because she was an anonymous source for the *Washington Post*, rejected one of Pacelle's unwanted advances. We will discuss this more in Chapter 6.

However, this is all said only in retrospect. At the time, some advocates were truly concerned about a battle royale against Prop 12 with massive industry spending. Many at HSUS did not want to pursue it. It is true that Moreland worked on this and had dubious fundraising and polling, but she did not lead the effort, to my knowledge. Josh Balk, head of the farm animal department and perhaps the movement's most effective advocate, really was the main force on the campaign. He moved to California and worked on it full time. The landslide helped to propel the subsequent legislative victories in Oregon, Washington, Michigan, Colorado, Utah, and Nevada, again, all led by Balk. The reader can form their own opinion about the degree to which television ad spending was a justified use of limited after-tax resources.

BACKLASH TO FARM ANIMAL MOVEMENT SUCCESS

Twenty-five years ago, there was hardly an organized farm animal movement to speak of in the United States. Factory farming is a relatively recent phenomenon in American history, and corporate control over farm animal policy was absolute. But skillful nonprofit activism and its increasing economic and political power since the turn of the century have fomented two major areas of political backlash: the federal King Amendment and state ag-gag laws.

THE KING AMENDMENT

After the passage of California's Prop 2 and AB 1437, the egg industry fought back in Congress. Iowa has the most egg-laying hens of any state in the country. Reactionary Republican Steve King represented Iowa's Fifth District, and then the Fourth after its 2010 redistricting. King was easy for national media to caricature for his incendiary statements, but he was a good retail politician who kept his conservative constituents happy and had a prime perch on the House Agriculture Committee.

The one-page King Amendment, the Protect Interstate Commerce Act, was a blunt tool designed to scuttle California's egg laws by prohibiting any state from setting standards for "agricultural products" imported from other states.[45] Even notwithstanding the constitutional concerns of such legislation, the impact on states' rights would be enormous, according to a 255-page report released by Harvard Law School's Animal Law and

Policy Program.[46] State laws impacting broad regulatory areas—food safety and labeling; alcohol and recreational drugs; fire protection; fishing; wood and lumber imports; children's products; home goods regulations; and invasive pests—would be repealed at the drop of a hat. This did not stop House Republicans enjoying their majority from incorporating the King Amendment in their 2014 Farm Bill.

The King Amendment's inclusion in the House Farm Bill represented a true threat for farm animals. The amendment would not merely have to stay out of the Senate bill but would have to be actively scuttled in conference committee as leaders from both chambers ironed out their differences. Luckily, animal advocates had a champion who was willing to make this happen: Senator Debbie Stabenow of Michigan, chair of the Senate Agriculture Committee, who had a hardworking and capable staff and no love lost for Steve King. In conference committee, she flatly refused to include the King Amendment in the final Farm Bill despite lobbying by the leading Republican on the committee, Kansas senator Pat Roberts.

King would reintroduce his amendment in every subsequent congressional session, but in 2020, the Republican Party stripped him of his committee assignments and his voters kicked him out of office after he asked a *New York Times* reporter, "White nationalist, white supremacist, Western civilization—how did that language become offensive?"[47] Steve King was his own worst enemy, and self-destruction was inevitable. Ag-gag laws would be fought on a different battlefield.

AG-GAG LAWS

Undercover investigations have long been the most effective tactic at animal advocates' disposal. They cost perhaps $30,000 to $50,000 upfront and easily pay for themselves when media coverage brings new recruits and donors to the movement. They are also a smart use of money for raising awareness about the plight of animals and driving corporate and legislative policies to reduce suffering. Even in an age when mass media can have an indifferent relationship with truth, nobody can deny the reality of animal abuse caught on video. Activists can stage lonely stunts outside of McDonald's for years; corporations only change their treatment of animals when consumer opinion starts to threaten the bottom line. An undercover investigation can bankrupt a company, as we saw with the Hallmark Westland scandal in Chino. Undercover investigations have been a mainstay of the animal movement since Upton Sinclair obtained employment as a meat-packer under false pretenses to write articles that would become *The Jungle.*

Kansas, Montana, and South Dakota were the first states to pass ag-gag laws. Kansas's 1990 law did not merely target filming but "turned otherwise criminal offenses, like trespass, property destruction, and vandalism, into new crimes when committed against an agricultural facility."[48] A new wave of ag-gag laws began in 2012, starting with Iowa; over the next decade, the majority of state legislatures would have ag-gag bills introduced. They would pass in eleven states; federal courts would rule them unconstitutional in six. As of this writing, Iowa's initial law was ruled unconstitutional and another has been introduced and challenged.[49] Superb law review articles and litigation by animal advocates, which judges have found convincing, have parsed the constitutional arguments about infringement on free speech, strict scrutiny, and difficulties of proving malice. These articles are well worth reading for specialists.[50]

On the one hand, ag-gag laws have not proven to be the threat that animal advocates feared as they passed in state after state over the last decade. "Nationwide, there have been only two ag-gag prosecutions"—and even then, both were dropped.[51] On the other hand, there are few prosecutions because ag-gag laws likely prevent some groups that would do investigations from doing them in the first place. The degree to which limited resources should be spent playing defense against ag-gag laws is debatable.

Industry has responded both by improving conditions for farm animals, as advocates hoped, and by restricting access to the killing areas of slaughterhouses for all but the most experienced employees. Now, employees in some slaughterhouses might have to work a year dismembering dead carcasses before they are allowed access to the kill box. The fact that corporations specifically targeted undercover investigators in a nationwide campaign shows the power of that tactic and where to keep putting resources, in both the United States and other countries.

FARM ANIMAL POLITICS: MYTHS AND REALITIES

Hypothesis: *"We need to pass a federal law to help farm animals. There isn't much political support for farm animals in America, so we need to start a lobbying organization. Then if we spend enough money, we can pass a law in Congress."*

Myth 1: *"We need to pass a federal law to help farm animals."*

Reality 1: The farm animal movement has won many victories with its current effective altruist framework and strategies.

Myth 2: *"There isn't much political support for farm animals in America."*

Reality 2: There is widespread political support for farm animal welfare amongst the public. The problem is that few people vote for politicians based on farm animal policies: farm animal laws are written by Big Ag lawyers and Big Ag politicians to maximize profits.

Myth 3: *"We need to start a lobbying organization."*

Reality 3: The farm animal movement already has lobbying organizations. 501(c)(3) nonprofit organizations such as the Good Food Institute, Mercy For Animals, and The Humane League are allowed to spend a certain percentage of their budgets—in their cases, more than a million dollars per year—on lobbying.[52] Donations to 501(c)(3) organizations are tax deductible; donations to 501(c)(4) organizations and PACs are not. In this case, founding a 501(c)(4) organization would actually waste time and money.

Myth 4: *"If we spend enough money, we can pass laws in Congress."*

Reality 4: The farm animal movement does not have enough money to outspend Big Ag and pass a law in Congress. The movement cannot and will not pass a standalone law through Congress this decade and probably not for at least a generation.

Myth 5: *"We need to lobby Congress."*

Reality 5: The movement should focus on where it can win politically: ballot initiatives, liberal states and localities, and smaller federal issues that one or a handful of allied politicians and their staffers can influence individually, such as appropriations (e.g., money for clean meat research), enforcement (e.g., of HMSA), and procurement (e.g., ensure the National School Lunch Program purchases some "humane" meat). At this point, most farm animal laws have been passed through legislatures, not ballot measures. They pass because of the threat of ballot measures.

Myth 6: "We can convince people to support us."

Reality 6: Politics is not driven by rational arguments; it is driven by money, emotion, and tribalism.[53] There will be outliers, but vegan messaging may find sizable support only within the Democratic Party, and then, only in a minority of Democrats.[54]

What can we do?

1. *Move and communicate.* Talk to experienced political staffers and campaigners to learn what works.

2. *Be realistic.* Set one or two achievable short-term (one-to-two months) and medium-term (one-to-two years) goals. PACs are easy and are a good first step.

3. *Don't forget effective altruism!* Political work *might not* be a fruitful avenue.

4

BUILDING A MOVEMENT

Mercy For Animals and Emotional Intelligence

"I suppose it only makes sense that I would someday found an international animal rights organization, given that I was delivered by a veterinarian."

Nathan Milo Runkle's autobiography, *Mercy For Animals*, opens with this, one of my favorite epigraphs.[1] Born in a farmhouse and delivered by his father Mark, Milo had an instrant connection to animals. Later on, like many others, he was brought to the movement by the inescapable reality of animal exploitation captured on video—in his case, he, at eleven years old watched the six o'clock news with his family.

> Near the end of the broadcast, a short piece came on about a small group of local animal rights activists who were protesting the sale of fur coats at Dayton Mall. Bundled in scarves and winter jackets, they were willing to stand outside in the frigid air to speak up for animals. The segment featured graphic footage of a drowning beaver caught in an underwater trap, a mink dying in a leg-hold device, and a dog just like mine with her mangled leg trapped in one. My heart broke as I stared at the images, cringing at the pain and fear radiating from the animals' eyes as they struggled to survive. But I also felt excited.
>
> "Animal rights activist." There was a name for people who felt as I did! I wasn't alone.

He read everything he could on vegetarianism and animal rights and sent away for vegetarian starter packets from HSUS and PETA.

His focus narrowed to farm animals when, one morning in 1999, Steve Jenkins, a science teacher and local pig farmer, attempted to kill six newly born piglets for students at his school to dissect.

But things didn't go according to plan. When Mr. Jenkins arrived at school, one of the piglets was still alive—standing on top of the other piglets inside a plastic bucket. She was crying out—terrified as only a small, defenseless animal can be. After spotting the piglet, a senior student in the class, who worked part-time on the Jenkins farm, proceeded to grab the baby animal by her hind legs and, in full view of the other students, slam her head first into the concrete floor. Twice. The piglet still didn't die. Instead, she lay writhing in pain, blood pouring out of her mouth, still breathing. When this was brought to Jenkins' attention, he responded, 'It's just a pig. I don't care what you do with it.' Another, more compassionate student then grabbed the piglet—still alive but now suffering from a fractured skull—quickly left the class, and ran down the hall to the classroom of Molly Fearing. Molly, a first-year teacher, was a fellow vegetarian and animal lover. Molly cradled the piglet in her arms, ran to her car, and drove fifteen miles to the nearest animal hospital. The little piglet was still alive when they arrived, but the veterinarian had to euthanize her.

Mrs. Fearing documented the incident for the sheriff, who pressed animal cruelty charges on Jenkins for failing to properly euthanize the piglet in the first place. It became a local controversy of some import, but the judge dismissed the case, claiming the method of attempted euthanization both Jenkins and the student had used was "standard agricultural practice." That was true. The method is sickly called "thumping."

Milo and the organization he founded, Mercy For Animals, have always been strongest when documenting cruelty, whether through open rescues or undercover investigations. Covering up animal cruelty is a necessary part of the business model of factory farming. "If slaughterhouses had glass walls, everyone would be vegetarian," as

Paul McCartney said. Animal agriculture's systematic marketing, which at times amounts to propaganda, leaves it vulnerable to exposure and whistleblowing.

Seventeen-year-old Milo learned this when he and allies called a press conference on the steps of the Ohio Capitol. Surprisingly, TV news reporters actually showed up. Inspired by Compassion Over Killing's *Hope for the Hopeless: An Investigation and Rescue at a Battery Egg Facility*, Milo and allies had documented open rescues at Buckeye Egg Farm and Daylay Egg. In an act of civil disobedience, they trespassed football field-sized buildings holding tens of thousands of hens and filmed themselves breaking the law by taking several hens. Their footage proved the reality of the factory farm myth. Viewers witnessed the squalor and the suffering of the hens left behind. It led to follow-up reports around the state, including an exposé by the state's largest news station, hyped by weeks of commercials featuring MFA's footage.

While the news was breaking, Milo notified the sheriffs in the counties where Buckeye and Daylay were located. He received a callback from a detective investigating his farm trespassing and burglary. Milo could not exactly deny the charges. Milo talked his way into being represented by Paul Leonard, an animal lover and former Dayton mayor. Weeks later, the detective's calls stopped, the egg farms being wary of the media backlash that charges would foment and likely cognizant of the infamous "McLibel" case, which was still pending in the British press and courts.[2]

Milo started to be homeschooled to pursue his activism. Part of his adolescence was spent getting a real education under the tutelage of Bruce Friedrich, then a PETA strategist. Mercy For Animals was legally founded in 2002 and accepted its first donations in 2003, when it raised a total of $7,718.[3] It remained a fully volunteer organization until 2006, when it hired its first outreach coordinator at a salary of $22,000 per year.[4] Its tiny budget was smartly used in the days before social media to run TV ads on networks such as MTV and Animal Planet, which helped establish a modest but loyal nationwide donor base. One of the people who saw those commercials was real estate entrepreneur and vegetarian Ari Nessel, who volunteered to match gifts for the next month up to $3,000. In the late 2000s, MFA's budget reached the low six figures.

Meanwhile, MFA kept up the work that has been most critical to the virtuous cycle of helping animals and charitable growth: exposing the cruelty of factory farming in the media. Animal lovers owe a debt of gratitude to the nation's undercover factory farm investigators. They are heroic, but their sacrifices come with "a heavy price to the investigators' physical and emotional well-being," Milo notes. The incontrovertible success of open and undercover investigations in ending animal abuse "is why Mercy For Animals sends out our own versions of Upton Sinclair—undercover investigators like Pete—donning rubber boots and armed with pinhole-size cameras concealed in clothing, pens and electronics," he writes. "Their covert footage has captured images that shock consumers and corporations into action. If our government won't take action, then we will. Their stories represent some of MFA's most challenging moments, but they are also moments that have changed the course of history, leading to new laws, prosecution of abusers, and adoption of international policies."

In April 2010, Milo received a call from a private number and took it on a whim. Bob Barker was on the line.

"I've seen your undercover investigations, and I'm very impressed," Barker said. "Can I help?"

Milo said they needed $250,000 for more investigations and investigators. Barker not only wrote him a check on the spot but put his money where his mouth was. He narrated investigation videos, stood with Milo at press conferences, and wrote letters to corporations MFA was targeting. The TV host, whom the *Los Angeles Times* called "the dean of West Coast animal benefactors," lobbied his network of funders. Soon, MFA counted animal rights celebrity donor-activists like Moby, Sia, Ryan Gosling, Joaquin Phoenix, and others among its supporters. "It's a rare person who becomes aware of animal cruelty who doesn't want to help on some level," Barker said.[5] MFA's fundraising grew from $460,000 in 2009 to $1.3 million in 2010 and eclipsed $10 million for the first time in 2016.[6]

In the mid-2010s, MFA's national undercover investigations helped the organization to play the role of bad cop to good cop negotiators like Josh Balk at HSUS. The Humane Society, universally recognized and with an approval rating at nearly 90 percent among the American public, could negotiate and cut deals with industry. The lesser-known Mercy For Animals, The Humane League, and Compassion in World Farming could continue undercover investigations and social media campaigns. MFA and HSUS worked together with corporate leaders to end the worst cruelty in their supply chains. They won the most important animal welfare agreement in American history, Walmart's pledge to abolish gestation crates for sows, veal crates for calves, and battery cages for hens, and to stop performing such cruel mutilations as castration and tail docking without anesthesia.

MFA is now a movement leader in its own right. Its budget and staff are three times larger than those of HSUS's farm animal department. Animal Charity Evaluators rated MFA as one of the world's three best animal charities from 2014 to 2017, estimating that a $1,000 donation "would spare ~10,000 to 80,000 animals from life in industrial agriculture."[7] It has earned every word of its accolades.

Other than working in the field and becoming vegan, what is the best thing people can do for animals? "My first, foremost, and final answer is: donate!" Runkle writes in his book.

> At this point people's eyes usually glaze over as they try to move past my obvious response. "Yes, of course," they say, "I will donate. But what else can I do to make a difference?" Question posed, they wait with bated breath, hoping I'll let them in on the hidden secret of how a regular person with a job, a family, and personal obligations can still play a big role in helping spare farm animals from misery. I'll tell you that secret now, although the answer is not very mysterious: Donate even more!

This work took a toll on Milo. At thirty-three years old, he was no longer a young adult. He missed his adolescence. He never went to college. He put the world on his shoulders, and it did not destroy him. But he needed a break. In 2018, he announced he was stepping back from the day-to-day operations of MFA. The organization launched a search for the next president.

People who work to help animals are motivated by altruism, and empathy for animals is ubiquitous. I have heard the hypothesis that the animal movement draws broken people, but that theory seems tenuous. I agree that activists can neglect self-care and care for others. This is natural in any field of social justice, not to mention many other careers. The leaders of the farm animal movement are the best and most altruistic people I have ever met. But one quality we have a dearth of in our community is emotional intelligence.

According to Daniel Goleman,

> [t]he most effective leaders are alike in one crucial way: They all have a high degree of what has come to be known as emotional intelligence. It's not that IQ and technical skills are irrelevant. They do matter, but mainly as "threshold capabilities"; that is, they are the entry-level requirements for executive positions. But my research, along with other recent studies, clearly shows that emotional intelligence is the sine qua non of leadership. Without it, a person can have the best training in the world, an incisive, analytical mind, and an endless supply of smart ideas, but he still won't make a great leader.[8]

The power of emotional intelligence has benefitted the movement's other leaders. Luminaries like autistic savant Temple Grandin, philosopher Peter Singer, and labor organizer Henry Spira helped address some of the worst abuses of factory farming, but many of the successes of the current farm animal movement were dreamed up by a group of young friends who undertook a tactical shift in the early part of this millennium. Josh Balk, Matt Ball, Bruce Friedrich, Erica Meier, Miyun Park, Matt Prescott, and Paul Shapiro lived in the Washington, D.C., area and came of age practicing the tactics of an older, vegan activism. They had all been arrested for various forms of civil disobedience. Before he turned to animals, Friedrich was a Christian pacifist who served time as a twenty-four-year-old for sneaking onto an Air Force Base and bashing in the nose of an F-15E fighter jet with a hammer alongside Jesuit former priest Philip Berrigan.[9]

"Bruce made the point that getting people to eat less meat may be easier than getting people to eat no meat, and you could probably spare more animals doing that," Shapiro said.[10] "What if we convert two people to be vegetarian half the time? That's the same as converting one person to be vegetarian all the time, and it's probably easier."[11] Pragmatism was more moral than absolutism, they reasoned.

Hectoring people or performing other stunts not only does not work but is counterproductive. "When I think back to what I used to do, I am horrified because I think about the number of people that I turned away," said Park. "I don't have the luxury of pretending that screaming at people is helping animals. I grew up."[12] Today, these leaders can be found in leadership at the organizations changing humankind's most important relationship with animals: Balk and Prescott work at the Humane Society of the United States's farm animal department; Ball and Friedrich are at the Good Food Institute; Meier headed Compassion Over Killing; Park held leadership roles at HSUS, COK, and the Global Animal Partnership and now authors books on the movement; and Shapiro founded The Better Meat Company.

Compassion for animals is an inborn value, and the organizations launched by those visionaries are now winning victories once unthinkable. Advocates had begun with the smart tactic pioneered by Henry Spira: focus on those companies and institutions with the most humane brand images, whose customers demanded and paid for higher standards.[13] The natural target was Whole Foods, which fully committed to cage-free eggs in 2005.[14] Not a single other major grocer joined it over the next decade. Then, in early 2016, Walmart announced its pledge to sell only cage-free eggs by 2025, and within a year, all of the twenty-five largest grocery chains in America had joined them.[15] In 2016, Whole Foods led the industry in committing to more humane, GAP-certified treatment of broiler chickens.[16]

Mercy For Animals wisely brought on Leah Garcés to succeed Nathan Milo Runkle. There was some justified euphoria from MFA's bringing on a woman of color.[17] Certainly, this was important, but, in my opinion, people missed the point. Leah was not hired because she was a woman of color. She was hired because she was the most qualified candidate, who happened to be a certain gender and ethnicity.

"Women have always been the prime movers of animal causes in both influence and rank," presidential speechwriter and vegan author Matthew Scully notes. "Early animal charities were mostly the work of heroic women giving shelter to other women, children, and animals alike from the depravities of men. Women of similar inspiration carry the banner to this day. One thinks, too, of Jane Goodall, Cynthia Moss, Gail Eisnitz, and the shrewd philosopher Mary Midgely, who have produced some of the finest books about animals and our duties of charity and justice. Over at PETA, likewise, Ingrid Newkirk remains one of the cause's most formidable debaters, forever surprising interviewers who expect to brush off a caricature but encounter a sharp, calm mind that gets the better of them every time."[18]

Leah Garcés' autobiography is the best book I have read on the animal movement, though it is held back by an unlikely title, *Grilled: Turning Adversaries into Allies to Change the Chicken Industry*.[19] It recounts her experiences helping animals but also provides an inspiring tale of the people driving the movement today. Leah was hired to a campaign job at the World Society for the Protection of Animals (now, World Animal Protection) at the age of twenty. She ultimately rose to become CEO. Goleman identifies five characteristics of emotional intelligence: self-awareness, self-regulation, motivation, empathy, and social skills. Each of these qualities comes out in Leah's autobiography.

> People who work in social-justice issues often recall a moment when they found their calling. They can pinpoint an event or a person that catapulted them into an irreversible journey. They identify the moment their shoulders got heavy and they couldn't unknow what they had learned. For me, that moment was when I became a mother in 2007. That day was not just about Ruben being born but also about me becoming someone different—a mother—and the world shifting as a result. The world I lived in, what it offered, how I impacted it, and—especially—my time, meant something very different to me after him. Suddenly, there were very definite limits to time. Not only did working for a cause now mean sacrificing time with my son; I was also thinking of the world I wanted him to grow up in.
>
> It may not be obvious how someone could feel fulfilled by dedicating a life to changing the world for chickens. For me, it is ultimately about the way we relate to animals and to each other—which turned out to be exactly the life I needed to live in order to pursue my dreams of the future world in which my children would grow up.

Leah moved from London to Georgia when she was seven months pregnant after her husband was hired by the Centers for Disease Control. This turned out to be fortuitous: Georgia is home not just to former USDA secretary Sonny Perdue, but also to more broiler chickens than any other state. It is an epicenter of American factory farming. Half of the state's agriculture economy comes from the chicken industry. In some rural Georgia counties, chickens outnumber people a thousand to one.

When her former boss and mentor, Philip Lymbery, left to helm Compassion in World Farming, she convinced him to let her launch the American chapter. "Now that I had kids, I didn't want to waste any time doing anything else except helping farmed animals," she writes. "I didn't get an answer for about nine months. There were lots of reasons Philip could say no. There was no money, for one thing. But he was intrigued. And eventually he decided to take a chance and let me try to tackle factory farming from inside the belly of the beast."[20]

Leah's emotional intelligence made her not just a superior manager but also a more effective activist. Reuters reporter Brian Grow connected Leah with an anonymous source who had provided him with a treasure trove of documents on antibiotics in feed additives. The source, Craig Watts, was a Perdue contract poultry farmer who was deeply concerned for the well-being of his chickens. Consumer demand for antibiotic-free meat led Big Ag to restrict or eliminate antibiotics in much of its supply chain. However, the antibiotics had been there for a reason: whether in hospital wards or factory farms, all animals confined in tight spaces face higher risks of communicable diseases. When antibiotics were removed from Watts's chicken feed, the health of his flock suffered and more chickens died. Watts had a lot more to share.

It is worth highlighting the courage of Craig Watts's whistleblowing. He had more to lose than most activists are willing to risk. His livelihood and ability to provide for his family were at stake. Why would a chicken farmer trust a vegan activist?

"We would text, speak on the phone, and email over the weekend as we felt each other out," Leah writes. "We were not meant to be on the same side. The only thing we had in common was our kids. His twins were the same age as my oldest. It was enough for us to build some trust." Leah, the person who ran undercover factory farm investigations, eventually asked him if she could see his farm. "Sure, come on over," said Watts. "And bring your documentary filmmaker friend with you."[21]

What she saw horrified her, just as it horrified him. Watts's principal duty as flock steward was to execute young birds each day. He walked around his cavernous industrial barn that reeked of ammonia finding those chicks who were sick, dying, or decomposing, pulled their necks until he heard a pop, then threw them into a bucket. It got harder as the chicks swelled to 600 times their birthweight in a few weeks, so Watts would have to hunt down "hoppers," or birds so deformed they could not walk but could only use their little wings to hop around on their raw bellies. This flock, imprisoned in both physical and biological cages, was destined to be killed and packaged with Perdue's "humanely raised" label.

Over the next six months, Leah returned to the factory farm a half-dozen times, strategizing with Watts and the documentarian. At the time, Compassion in World Farming USA had just two employees, and the other was on maternity leave. The stress and enormity of their action kept both parties up at night. Leah recalls: "[We brainstormed] every angle where we might be wrong, where we might get sued or ignored, every place where we might have assumed something incorrectly. We prepared in such depth, gathered so much documentation on contracts and communications and letters from the company, it became an obsession."[22]

During their work, Leah got to know the Watts family. The children were astonished she was a vegan, but Watts's wife, Amelia, understood the deeper struggle they all faced. "Learn a trade," she told her children. "But not this." "I could see her love for her kids in her face as she spoke," Leah writes.

When they were ready to go to the press, they reached out to Bruce Friedrich, the perspicacious leader who has counseled or worked with virtually every movement elder at one time or another. Friedrich pitched the story to Nick Kristof, a Rhodes Scholar and two-time Pulitzer winner with a widely admired *New York Times* column. Regular readers know that Kristof now often gives voice to the voiceless in the nonhuman world, but this was not the case in 2014. Prior to his introduction to Leah, he had written about factory farming just once. The documentary went live on YouTube as Kristof's devastating column was published.[23] Within twenty-four hours, the short film had received a million views. The Kristof column dovetailed with the shift of the farm animal movement away from its successful corporate and legislative campaigns against sow gestation crates, toward ways of helping broiler chickens achieve their own modest measures of freedom.

Perdue retaliated against Watts for blowing the whistle on its sick chickens and tried to force him out of business, but *pro bono* counsel saved his farm.[24] More surprisingly, Perdue began to clean up its act. "I think there's a stereotype out there that we were used to back in the 1980s and 1990s that was just, there was no way you could come to any agreement because there was no common ground whatsoever," Jim Perdue would later tell Leah. "The fact that there were groups out there that truly had an interest in animal care, and you could actually have some areas of agreement, I think that was a big 'aha' moment. . . . It turned out 90 percent of what they were trying to do and what we were trying to do was in agreement," Perdue marveled.[25]

There was a key event that happened between the Watts story and Perdue's changing his tone. That was an MFA undercover investigation at a Perdue farm that resulted in criminal animal cruelty prosecution, major media coverage, and public outcry.[26] Leah recounted the story in an extraordinary May 2021 piece co-authored with Mark McKay, president of Perdue Premium Poultry and Meats, the company's chicken division:

> Perdue knew that what the video had shown represented not only an opportunity but also a responsibility to animals, customers, and consumers to uphold the company's standards. So Perdue picked up the phone and did something meat companies rarely do: It called Mercy For Animals. A stunned Mercy For Animals sat at the other end of the call. Here was Perdue thanking the organization for the investigation that had exposed animal handling contrary to the company's standards—and promptly acting to remedy it . . .
>
> Our conversations were challenging, especially in the beginning, but the tension felt reassuring. Tension is the sense of the gap between where we are and where we'd like to be. This tension facilitates conversation and drives change.[27]

This tension and creative praxis heralded a closer connection between Leah's work and that of Mercy For Animals. Perdue is now seeking to be the leader in transforming niche animal welfare practices into practices with a broader scope. Bloomberg reported that Perdue invested more than $20 million in a system wherein chickens will never be touched by human hands.

> Perdue is starting to use a catching machine, which slowly advances down the length of a barn, nudging birds onto conveyor belts and then into roomier crates than the company previously used. The crates are moved by a forklift onto a newly designed trailer, which protects the birds from the elements during the drive to the processing plant. After the truck arrives, the crates are unloaded and the birds allowed to rest before entering Perdue's controlled atmosphere stunning system, which uses a combination of carbon dioxide and oxygen to render them senseless over a period of five minutes.[28]

Perdue says this system results in 1 percent of birds with broken wings, compared with 6 percent under conventional handling and transport. In another example, in widely used electrical stunning systems in slaughterhouses, birds often errantly enter scalding water baths designed to remove feathers, and they drown while still conscious; blood coagulates in their carcasses, which causes characteristic cherry-red cadavers that cannot be used for human food. Controlled atmosphere stunning (CAS) is quickly becoming the preferred method of rendering chickens insensate to pain before slaughter.[29] This industry-driven effort avoids wasting meat, and animal advocates may support CAS as a way to prevent painful deaths.

Perdue is not alone in embracing humane technology. Tyson has adopted third-party remote video monitoring and analytics to oversee operations and reduce cruelty from the time of offloading to slaughter.[30] Meanwhile Cargill has worked with renowned humane expert Temple Grandin to develop a just-introduced robotic cattle driver that reduces cattle stress and improves worker safety.[31]

Another concern for both the industry and animal lovers is poultry dying from exposure during transport, which prevents them from being used for human food. Broiler chickens weigh about five pounds and are shipped for slaughter at just six weeks of age: they are too small and young to thermoregulate. It is not uncommon to see hundreds or thousands of birds in one truck die during transport. During a 2018 cold spell, an estimated 34,050 chickens showed up dead at the Pilgrim's Pride slaughter plant in Natchitoches, Louisiana.

Pro-industry, pro-animal scientific advances in the near future have the potential to save many millions of dollars and billions of lives. The birth of male chicks in the egg industry tragically leads to their death at just one day old. These "surplus" animals are typically dumped into a truly gruesome device called a macerator—essentially, a large blender—and pulverized into pet food or fertilizer. Unilever has been pursuing genetic sexing in order to avoid this unnecessary expense and inhumane end for male chicks, and United Egg Producers announced a goal of eliminating the culling of male chicks.[32]

When it comes to the treatment of farm animals, even McDonald's was subject to public opinion. *Fortune* reports: "Consumer sentiment . . . turned out to be the most important of all. The phrase 'enriched cage' means nothing to the average person. So if McDonald's had shifted to that option, it wouldn't get any credit from consumers. 'Science was telling us enriched, but when talking with the consumer, they had no clue what enriched was,' says Hugues Labrecque, who runs the egg business that serves McDonald's at Cargill. Once that became clear, cage-free became the inevitable consensus." "When they move, the industry moves," said Paul Shapiro.[33]

"Now, in the Year of the Chicken, broilers' fortunes may finally be looking up," wrote Lewis Bollard. He continued:

> At the end of last year, America's two largest foodservice companies—Aramark and Compass Group—committed within hours of each other to enacting major broiler chicken welfare reforms by 2024. Their pledges followed campaigns by Mercy For Animals, Compassion in World Farming USA, The Humane League, and the Humane Society of the United States. Since then, these and other groups have secured similar commitments from 27 major food companies, including fast food giants Burger King, Chipotle, and Panera. Five of these companies have committed to only buying

chicken certified under the Global Animal Partnership's (GAP) new broiler welfare standards, which will address everything from genetics to slaughter once finalized. But most companies have only pledged to adopt a more limited set of reforms.[34]

What is the world that Leah hopes for? "In 2050, Compassion in World Farming, Mercy For Animals, and other animal advocacy organizations will shut their doors."

The founding and operations of Mercy For Animals are a quintessential model for animal advocates. The organization now has over one hundred employees and a yearly revenue and budget of nearly $20 million. Thanks to the vision and will of people like Nathan Milo Runkle and Leah Garcés, humans no longer have to work for farm animals out of their parents' basement. These two sacrificed their young adulthoods to run an organization that will outlast them and, ideally, one day be so successful that it will no longer need to exist.

5

BETRAYAL OF TRUST

Inside the Humane Society's #MeToo Scandal

For many, the animal movement is a secular religion. Acolytes dedicate their lives to its ethic non-violently, while extremists are willing to go further. Believers, including veritably every rank-and-file staffer at the Humane Society of the United States (HSUS), are motivated by altruism. They only want to help mitigate the unconscionable suffering of the world's animals.

Let's take a trip down the rabbit hole at the charity everybody thinks they know.

Charity and religious cult scandals recur throughout American history when evil people learn to mouth the catechism before their house of cards falls. So many believed those who claimed they worked "for all animals." There are good and honest staffers at HSUS, which makes all the more abhorrent the conduct of the executives whom CEO Wayne Pacelle promoted based on who either had physical relationships with him or enabled those relationships.

Religion can serve any end. Most people at the Humane Society are truly good, but the world has seen what can fester when the imprimatur of trust of working for a charity or a church is put in the hands of abusers. There is no other explanation for why Pacelle was able to get away with abuse for decades as the most famous man in the American animal movement other than by erecting a façade to enable him.

My cubicle was twenty feet from Wayne Pacelle's office in 2017. This chapter is a window into how the Humane Society covered up sexual misconduct. I hope this serves as a cautionary tale for others.

PLAINTIVE WHISTLEBLOWERS

Carol Adams, renowned author of *The Sexual Politics of Meat*, posted a heartbreaking account in which an anonymous victim described the climate created by Pacelle's abuses.[1]

There's so much I've wanted to say watching the #MeToo movement unfold. But, like many women in the AR movement, it has been ingrained in me not to speak up "for fear of hurting the animals." I'm also a very private person. I'm an introvert, I don't like drawing attention to myself and most of all I don't want to be identified as a victim. I don't want my success in life to be diminished or reduced to my sexuality or because of what one man put me through. I don't want to talk about these things. I didn't want to experience them or their aftermath in the first place so I certainly don't want to talk about them!

But now it seems we have to. Reading article after article, story after story about the sexual harassment, abuse of power and worse by men has been shocking and emotional. I never understood fully the idea of "trigger warnings" until I started seeing stories about him appearing. Now I understand.

It is very difficult for anyone to believe he could do any wrong. But, he has done a lot wrong, for a very long time. And now he is being investigated.

Many are fearful of the industry using these stories to attack animal groups. But, if this unethical, unchecked bad behavior had not taken place to begin with, then they would not have ammunition for their stories. These are men who have put animal groups' brand and missions in jeopardy with their actions—NOT the women who are coming forward and who are participating in the investigation. If you want someone to be angry at, direct it at the perpetrators. Not at the women who are brave enough to come forward.

There is no witch hunt. No one makes these stories up for fun. This isn't fun for anyone, much less the victims/survivors. Calling an investigation a witch hunt before it is complete diminishes the severity of the issue and discourages women from feeling like they can come forward.

People want facts. They don't realize that there are a lot of us women out here who have facts of our own. Facts of our experiences of sexual harassment. Facts about how this CEO told us, as his colleagues and subordinates, that if we would travel with him and we could be his fuck buddy, texted us late at night trying to develop a relationship, asked inappropriate personal relationship questions, repeatedly asked for sex and gave graphic details about how he would please us to pressure us or try to persuade us to say yes, asked us to strip for him, asked if he could masturbate in front of us, told us not to tell anyone because it would hurt his organization and his job and our jobs . . .

Facts about how if you did sleep with him that you would get promoted, more money for your program area, a job at this org even if you had no qualification or prior experience . . .

Facts about how if you said no to him he might tell you that "No one has ever told me no before." Or if you declined because you didn't want to cheat on your partner or spouse that it's okay because "everyone cheats." Or that he "doesn't drink, or smoke or do drugs. That sex is my vice."

Some people are arguing that these relationships are no big deal because they are consensual. Put yourself in these women's shoes. The most powerful man in the AR movement is saying these things to you. He's your boss. You don't know what will happen if you say no—you don't know what will happen to your job and you don't know what will happen to you physically either.

The US Dept of Health and Human Services definition of sexual coercion includes being asked by your boss or a person with authority over you to have sex. This is an abuse of power. And it has been going on for decades.

Let us walk you through what this behavior creates as a work atmosphere:

- a place where when a woman gets hired/promoted/a larger budget people remark, "Oh, she must be sleeping with him" NOT because it's a snarky thing to say but because he sleeps with so many staff members that it's probably the truth
- a place where a woman's worth and accomplishments are reduced by male and female colleagues to her sexuality or if she had sex with the CEO
- a place where rumors run rampant because the person at the top is creating an atmosphere of speculation through his behavior
- a place where female and male supervisors dismiss women coming forward with their experiences because "He just has a soft spot for

women" or "If it doesn't involve animal abuse, I don't want to hear about it" or "You are lucky he likes you!"

- a place where toxic or unqualified or less than stellar workers are able to stay for years without getting fired because they are keeping the CEO's secrets and are protected
- a place where people fear for their livelihood because they know there will be a sex scandal one of these days because of the CEO's behavior
- a place where you never know if a volunteer, donor, legislative aide, or legislator you have to work with has also slept with him or been asked to
- a place where younger generations of men copy this behavior because they have seen the CEO get away with it for decades
- a place where, if you are lucky, someone warns you about him so you aren't completely blindsided
- a place you are forced to leave because you don't want to deal with the drama and/or harassment anymore
- a place where men's contributions are valued far more than women's

It does not create a professional work environment and puts an undue burden on all of the women and their confidantes carrying around these secrets.

These are stories from some of us.

There is so much more that we know and could say, but hopefully this is enough for you to finally understand that this needs to stop. This behavior does not help animals! Talented women leaving our movement or dealing with all of this while trying to do their work for animals does not help the animals! Women staying silent about the myriad other men in our movement does not help animals!

So, what do you want? Do you want women to stay silent? I'll tell you what we want.

We want to create a movement where current and future generations of men know that this behavior is not acceptable and will not be tolerated. We want men, women, and nonbinary people to be able to work together without being objectified, harassed, or bullied by their colleagues and fellow volunteers and activists. We want a movement where our emotional energy can be spent on work to help animals, not on covering up or dealing with sex scandals.

We want to save animals' lives and stop animal suffering, without all of this other bullshit that gets handed to us while we are trying to do it.[2]

TRUTH BEHIND CLOSED DOORS

Wayne Pacelle was both an animal lover and a man accused of multiple cases of sexual abuse. He was brought into the organization in the mid-1990s by then vice president David Wills. Wills was fired for harassment and embezzlement, spent six months in jail, and was sentenced in 2020 to life in prison for sex trafficking a nine-year-old child.[3] As "a telegenic figure in the movement," Pacelle traveled the country on college book tours to recruit young people into the movement.[4] Over the years, he installed a number of lieutenants who covered up and enabled his predation.

In December 2017, Pacelle came under internal investigation for sexual misconduct based on an anonymous tip. This purported investigation was conducted by Morgan Lewis, which had represented the Humane Society in a fourteen-year Racketeer Influenced and Corrupt Organizations (RICO) Act action alleging HSUS had engaged in obstruction of justice, perjury, and witness tampering, which HSUS settled for $14 million in 2014.[5] Though Pacelle publicly claimed the 2014 settlement was covered by "insurance," HSUS's tax return listed $4,475,000 and that of its affiliated Fund for Animals listed $1,200,000 for "settlements" in 2013. (There were no such items in the 2014 tax return.[6])

The Humane Society concealed the existence of the 2017 CEO investigation from most employees until courageous whistleblowers began leaking its details to the press. Since 2017, newsgathering from anonymous sources has been indispensable for informing the public about how a rogue leadership element within the Humane Society hijacked a beloved charity.

In January 2018, Marc Gunther at the *Chronicle of Philanthropy*, whose main office is three floors above HSUS's in downtown Washington, D.C., reported, based on an anonymous tip, that a secret investigation was underway.[7] That same week, an anonymous source leaked the investigation to Danielle Paquette at the *Washington Post*.[8] Paquette reported the guileless motive of the whistleblowers whom most Americans would recognize as the real Humane Society: "they wanted to come forward to repair the culture at the Humane Society, which they believe does important work to help animals . . . [but] they worried that money going to address Pacelle's actions was misdirected from protecting wildlife."[9] The investigation into the CEO found credible evidence he abused women. Paquette wrote:

> The investigation also found that Pacelle had maintained a sexual relationship with a female subordinate and exchanged more than 100 emails with her. The woman told the investigation that she became afraid of Pacelle after the relationship ended, describing him as abusive and controlling. . . . One woman said she received a settlement from the Humane Society after she complained about Pacelle's alleged girlfriend joining her team without proper qualifications and was shut out of work opportunities, according to the memo. Two more received payouts after they leveled retaliation charges against the organization, asserting they lost their jobs after speaking up about Pacelle's office romance and sexual behavior in the office.[10]

The board of directors called an emergency meeting to discuss the allegations. After a seven-hour meeting, they voted to end the inquiry. Board Chair Rick Bernthal explained his rationale that "a great unfairness resulted to Wayne" after the *Post* published the report.[11]

Credulous allies took up Pacelle's cause based on the board's stamp of approval. They dismissed and targeted the victims who had begun to come forward. Matthew Scully, the streetwise, vegan presidential speechwriter, summarized:

> There was the accusation that had started things just before last Christmas, one employee's claim of receiving, in 2005, an undesired kiss in a coffee shop. There was another employee's account [of an unrequited salsa dancing invitation in 2012]. And there was a third alleging a supposedly lewd proposal to a female employee [for oral sex], outside a hotel room, in 2006.[12]

Pacelle was forced to resign in February 2018 only after Julie Bosman, Matt Stevens, and Jonah Engel Browmwich at the *New York Times* reported that he had sexually assaulted an attorney in his office.

On more than one occasion after 2010, she said, Mr. Pacelle summoned her to his office and pressured her for sex. She said she refused and once tried to placate him with a hug. After hugging her goodbye, he turned her around, pushed her over his desk and rubbed his genitals against her, she said. "I said, 'I'm going to elbow you really hard right now if you don't stop,'" she recalled. "I stood up for myself, and then he just went and sat down. He never hit on me again."[13]

The investigators never got around to interviewing this lucid, named victim until after the *Post* reported on the investigation. Board Chair Rick Bernthal asked for the CEO's resignation only after he read about the assault in the *Times*.

Peggy Kokernot Kaplan told the *New York Times* that she "heard so many undercurrents from women afraid to speak up for fear of retaliation if they pursued work with another animal organization, or they simply didn't feel their voices would be heard if they did speak up."[14] The common thread in exposing wrongdoing and holding the rogue leadership element of the Humane Society accountable has been whistleblowers anonymously sharing information with journalists. If it were not for anonymous whistleblowers, an abuser who objectified idealistic animal lovers would still be at the helm of the nation's largest animal charity, grooming his victims. Attorneys who orchestrated settlements to cover up retaliation remain at the Office of General Counsel, the funnel through which whistleblowing still flows.

Rank-and-file HSUS employees and department leaders—some of the most altruistic and devoted people in the movement—are not naïve. They can sense when something is wrong, so they have been taking what few steps they can to continue to come forward.

A website was set up so other victims could publish anonymous narratives about the culture of sexism and abuse in the animal movement. One story from February 2018 read:

> I was a victim of the CEO and executive officers of a major animal nonprofit. I have signed an NDA and am unable to speak out. I'm feeling hopeless because the harassment case against the CEO

recently closed without his being terminated. When will there be justice for those of us that have been bullied and then blacklisted?[15]

According to an HSUS Glassdoor review from September 27, 2020:

Since the former CEO departed the organization has spent a lot of resources trying to redefine workplace culture. Unfortunately not much has changed. Zero transparency. Staff are afraid to speak honestly. Retribution is real.[16]

From January 3, 2021:

High turnover rates will persist if you don't believe your employees when they report mistreatment and stop blaming them for it. Stop throwing others under the bus to protect yourself. I was honest and no one wanted to hear it. Listen to the feedback that you ask for.[17]

From June 24, 2021, entitled "Do Not Think I'll Make My 19th Year Anniversary at HSUS":

The HSUS management fosters a dictatorship and rules via fear.[18]

There are many more such stories.

MOLE HUNT

How did the Humane Society employ a sex abuser as its CEO for fifteen years?

I did not sign an NDA. Let's begin with what I witnessed from my cubicle near Pacelle's office.

Six weeks after I was hired, I expressed concerns about the inappropriate relationship between the married CEO and a "special assistant" half his age. "I am also so appreciative of the tireless, intelligent work of my adviser Crystal Moreland," Pacelle wrote in his 2016 book, *The Humane Economy*. "She is everything you want in a right-hand person—loyal, responsible, and intuitive. She's got a bright future in the animal protection movement, and she's a joy to work with."[19] She would spend twelve hour days around Pacelle, walk his dog, travel all over the country with him, and he would often pick her up in the morning and drop her off at night.

I first told the special assistant herself I was concerned about their relationship, and then my supervisor's supervisor, Humane Society Legislative Fund president Sara Amundson. Amundson replied that she "dated Wayne." I expressed concerns about the CEO's sexist and inappropriate behavior toward women to a much larger universe. Knowledge of those complaints was not limited to the special assistant and President Amundson, but included executive staff, D.C. attorneys, the deputy head of HR, the head of HR, Deputy General Counsel Becky Branzell, General Counsel Kate Karl, Chief Operating Officer Mike Markarian and Pacelle himself, and the complaints were written down in their own internal documents.

What did they do?

The HSUS Office of General Counsel was already well aware of Pacelle's long history of alleged predation and abuse, having already paid out at least three settlements. It set up a companywide "Women@ Work" taskforce, ostensibly to address discrimination and harassment issues at the organization. The purported anti-discrimination taskforce gathered intelligence to report whistleblowers to the Office of General Counsel.

It was a mantra and urban legend when I was employed at the Humane Society that somebody who wanted to *destroy HSUS* would plant a *mole* to *hurt Wayne*. Beginning at orientation, employees were brainwashed with the anti-"mole" omerta. Chief Operating Officer Mike Markarian's assistant, Sarah Barnett, was the organization's designated mole hunter. The "mole" indoctrination helped cover up Pacelle's sexual misconduct through exposing whistleblowers.

The CEO and his lieutenants knew of my complaints in mid-April 2017. A week later, they scheduled a mandatory "Women@Work" presentation in the D.C. office and offered a place for people to voice complaints. After the presentation to the staff, I again reported my concerns about the CEO and his inappropriate relationship with his special assistant, this time to Women@Work attorney Amanda Hungerford and D.C. attorney Rebecca Cary.

Immediately after I complained, Hungerford texted special assistant Moreland that I was asking "some really probing questions about sexism at HSUS," and, "We know he's not [a 'mole'], right?" Moreland replied: "I showed your text to Wayne and asked that he, [General Counsel] Kate Karl and I find a few minutes to chat about it today. I am really worried."

Complaints about discrimination against women are protected under the D.C. Human Rights Act. It takes a lot of "worry" about a policy analyst's "really probing questions about sexism at HSUS" to scramble a closed-door meeting between the CEO, the general counsel and the "special assistant." After my complaints, Barnett, Markarian's mole hunter, began coming to the D.C. office and sitting in the cubicle behind me to watch as I worked.

In early May 2017, Pacelle called me into his office and said, "I heard you have some concerns about sexual harassment." The sex abuser assured me they were doing everything possible to protect women at the organization, such as setting up a "Women@Work" taskforce.

Texts between attorney Amanda Hungerford and CEO Wayne Pacelle's special assistant, Crystal Moreland, regarding an employee asking "probing questions about sexism at HSUS". Pacelle's assistant, who had a personal relationship with the CEO, responded that she would ask for a meeting between she, Pacelle and General Counsel Kate Karl.
Source: Humane Watch

RETALIATION

The racketeering charges involving perjury and witness tampering and settled for $14 million were allegedly perpetrated by, among others, COO Markarian and the Office of General Counsel.[20] According to a disturbing public case history, Ringling Brothers "allege[d] that Michael Markarian, an officer of Fund for Animals/HSUS, gave false deposition testimony to conceal FFA/HSUS's payments to" a fake witness in that case.[21]

The *Washington Post* reported in March 2018, the month after HSUS fired the CEO for alleged sexual assault:

> Melinda Fox, who worked as the senior director of outreach and strategic initiatives at the Humane Society from 2005 to 2008, said she was pushed out after expressing concerns about how Pacelle interacted with female donors. She wrote in a widely shared Facebook post that she received "calls and emails from donors— women Wayne had affairs with, and when he turned cold with them, called [me] crying and sent lengthy emails saying they felt 'used.'" She sent "the most disturbing one" to Pacelle and Mike Markarian. . . . "Markarian called me into his office to tell me my job 'was to protect Wayne.'"[22]

Even after this was publicly reported, Markarian was permitted to stay on for five months and resign on his own terms to begin "studying and pursuing a career in wine."[23] That year he was paid $335,237, including $126,000 in severance, according to HSUS's IRS 990.[24]

In retaliation for my complaints, the "special assistant" fabricated the accusation that I secretly recorded her phone conversations. Wiretapping is a felony under D.C. Code § 23-542. Nobody from HSUS ever has or ever will report these criminal allegations to law enforcement because they are well aware the allegations are false. Instead of investigating the CEO, HSUS leadership ordered innocent employees to monitor the office, secretly investigate and surveil me, and search my personal phone for "bugs." During the time the Office of General Counsel and COO Markarian were secretly investigating me, they were well aware of the sexual misconduct accusations, the many settlements they had paid, and the NDAs they were paying powerless victims to sign. To end the threat of whistleblowing on the CEO's serial predation on female animal lovers, the predators used charitable resources to rope in other people such as HR and IT employees, who unwittingly believed them.

One concrete example will suffice to show the behavior of Pacelle's enablers. Despite my declining repeated meal invitations from the special assistant, she and I ended up eating together, once. I was on bereavement leave in June 2017 because my mother passed away. The Friday after the funeral, the special assistant asked me again to eat with her, this time purportedly to offer a sympathetic ear for me to discuss my mom. She paid for the meal, the only time she and I ever interacted outside of the office, and I cried when I talked about Mom. Three months later, she reported to HR that I had repeatedly asked her to dinner, she agreed to go once, and I was crying because she supposedly ended the meal earlier than I wanted. Imagine the mindset required to do that to another human being. After I found out about this fabrication, I forwarded HR the email in which the special assistant had invited me to this dinner. I received no response.

"She's got a bright future in the animal protection movement," Pacelle wrote, "and she's a joy to work with."[25] I was fired, and HSUS concealed the "mole" and "wiretapping" false felony accusations. Imagine what they did to other people. Imagine what they did to female victims. That month, the "loyal, responsible, and intuitive" special assistant who was "everything [Pacelle] want[ed] in a right-hand person" was shipped to a dream job in Hollywood, California.

RECONCILIATION, DETERMINISM, OR NARCISSISM?

Nearly a year after the Pacelle investigation, the organization's toxic culture apparently had not been fixed. In October 2018, HSUS launched a "Reconciliation Process" in which more than a hundred people were interviewed. The first two summary recommendations were:

1. Professionalize the HSUS reporting, investigation, and resolution experience by training leadership and staff, adopting and implementing a clear, comprehensive, and transparent set of policies and protocols, and enforcing accountability at all levels within the organization.

2. Establish and maintain a culture of affirmative respect, where people are encouraged to raise concerns, the work for animals is grounded in humane treatment of one another, those who come forward with concerns and complaints are truly protected, and meaningful consequences are imposed for retaliatory or silencing behaviors.[26]

This has not happened. The Reconciliation Process was evidently designed to protect HSUS from liability. No consequences, so far as I am aware, have been imposed upon the attorneys who ordered a bug hunt in the D.C. office in 2017 in response to complaints about Pacelle rather than investigate Pacelle.

Supervisors and subordinates should not be having physical relationships at all, and such relationships are now purportedly against HSUS policy. Yet Humane Society Legislative Fund (HSLF) president Amundson was promoted.

Attorney Hungerford penned a revealing newsletter on "Gender Equity" recommending the following "anti-harassment policies":

- Clear reporting provisions, and multiple points of contact for reporting in case victims feel uncomfortable with the primary point of contact;
- Special provisions for when there are concerns about an organization's ability to conduct an impartial investigation (such as allegations against an Executive Director, or head of human resources);
- Mechanisms protecting victims from retaliation, as well as procedures for reporting allegations; and
- Bystander training.[27]

"When a small number of famous charismatic figures dominate movements, it can begin to seem that the rockstars are the movement, and that disciplining them for inappropriate conduct would mean harming the movement itself," Hungerford wrote, ignoring her own role in maintaining Pacelle's privileged position. "I know many of the women involved, and believe all of them."[28]

MOVEMENT SEXISM

Pacelle is not the only formerly respected person in the animal movement to be forced to leave their job as a result of credible accusations of sexual misconduct or abuse of power. Nor is he the only man in the movement to take advantage of the fact that women constitute three-quarters of animal activists in order to engage in inappropriate or exploitative behaviors toward those junior to him. Nor is he the only person, man or woman, in the animal movement to be accused of cultivating an atmosphere of bullying, intimidation, favoritism, and transgression in their organization. He's also not unique in leveraging a weak board, cowed HR department, craven enablers, and a culture of "sacrificing for the common good" to satisfy his own desires. And he is not alone in cultivating a "hero" or "rockstar" persona or being accorded that status by a movement in search of glamor, visibility, and respect. All movements are ecosystems, and so are the organizations, associations, and groups that constitute them. The distortions that occur when individuals are given license to behave badly because they get "results," raise a lot of money, are charismatic or maverick, or promise the moon result when we as a society elevate individual triumph, technological moonshots, and genius plays over the much harder work of capacity building, professional development, effective teamwork, strategic planning, coalition building, and maintenance of organizational health.

Sexism and the dehumanization and objectification of women are endemic problems in the animal movement. America is a patriarchal society, but American animal activism has long been the purview of upper-class, white, progressive women and thus, is to some degree, more meritocratic than many other fields. It is a small victory that farm animal organizations have not participated in the offensive and counterproductive stunts involving typically white, female nude models PETA is known for.[29]

Acolytes of effective altruism differ from the animal activists who came before them. While employees in the American animal movement are roughly three-quarters female, those active in effective altruism are about 70 percent male.[30] The most in-depth survey of the effective altruism movement found that 90 percent are millennials, 87 percent are white, 86 percent are not followers of a religion, and about half do not eat meat.[31] Interestingly, only 10 percent of more than two thousand respondents identified animal welfare as their top priority, though 37 percent said it was a top priority and 71 percent said significant resources should be dedicated to it.[32] Lack of funding was identified as the foremost problem affecting effective animal advocacy nonprofits in developed countries, while a lack of capable or qualified staff was the top concern for organizations in developing countries.[33] One benefit of the broad spread of effective altruism among millennials who are or will be wealthy is the likely increase in future funding. "As a movement, the intellectual and programmatic life of EA is anchored by a growing number of organizations and funding sources from across Silicon Valley and other strongholds of global finance and technology, at elite academic institutions, and through thousands of individual donors who connect and collaborate in online forums and real-world meetups," summarizes another study.[34]

Some provocative academic studies ruminate on why American women are more likely than men to help animals, pointing to an empathy gap, consumer marketing, and a carnivorous or dominant masculine ethos.[35] Some of this literature devolves into biological determinism— women as emotional nurturers, men as emotionless hunters—of dubious merit. The differences between American male and female eating habits began to be manufactured during the Industrial Revolution. A Yale professor of culinary history recounts that early Americans ate as families and food became gendered only when women dining alone became socially acceptable after the Civil War. Madison Avenue began to appeal to women through advertising what were described in women-targeted magazines as "dainty" foods, such as salads, sweets, white fish, and Jell-O. Skillfully playing off a backlash was the invention of hearty "men's" foods, such as corned beef hash. How to convince women what sort of food their husbands supposedly wanted? One tactic was on display in the cookbook *How to Keep a Husband, or Culinary Tactics* (1872), along with its imitators, which implored customers to follow its recipes or their husbands would leave them.[36] It is written in neither our genes nor the stars that men and women should feel any difference in attitudes toward food or animals; those differences are socially constructed.

Fundraising at HSUS and HSLF

After Pacelle was fired for sexual misconduct in a national scandal, year-over-year fundraising at HSUS declined by $26 million, or about one-fifth, according to its 2018 IRS 990.[37] This fundraising gap was filled with dubious tactics.

The Open Philanthropy Project granted HSLF, the 501(c)(4) political affiliate of the 501(c)(3) HSUS, $520,000 in 2017 to fight the King Amendment. The grant was split roughly 4:1 between HSLF and the HSUS farm animal team.

Unfortunately, HSLF has nothing to do with the talented leaders and employees of the HSUS farm animal department. HSLF did not have a farm animal lobbyist at the time. It had no intention of hiring one. Its commitment was to hire two organizers. Many qualified people applied. Yet HSLF did nothing to move any applications forward while the money to do so was sitting in HSLF's bank account. The King Amendment was killed in 2018, but the jobs remained posted for years afterward. It was only when the Open Philanthropy Project's Lewis Bollard repeatedly asked HSLF president Amundson what happened to the money that she eventually relented and returned $129,906. The remaining grant, running into the hundreds of thousands of dollars, was not returned.[38]

HSLF is a substantial financial drain on the movement. Donations to HSLF, a 501(c)(4) political nonprofit, are not tax-deductible. Using limited charitable dollars on it costs donors doubly.

HSLF has a presence on Capitol Hill, which it uses to fundraise based on emotional appeals. HSLF's splashiest legislative success in the 2019–2021 congressional session was passing the Preventing Animal Cruelty and Torture (PACT) Act. The bill was a solution in search of a problem. The cruelty the PACT Act purported to criminalize was already illegal in all fifty states. While drafting the bill, HSLF could not find a single animal in the country when its bill would have helped, and it looked hard. Animal law professor Justin Marceau, an expert on criminal procedure and cruelty statutes, called it "a high-profile palliative intervention that provides a sense of accomplishment without addressing any of the underlying causes of animal suffering." Marceau found the PACT Act was worse than nothing for siphoning off scarce resources from sincere problem solving. It was nothing more than "a grand mirage."[39]

The unethical behavior of HSLF leadership is all the more troubling for the brilliance and compassion of some of the staff who work under and are hamstrung by President Amundson. Director Mimi Brody, a Harvard Law graduate and beloved voice on Capitol Hill, gave up a prestigious job as Senator Edward Kennedy's legislative director because of her love for animals. Her boss, President Amundson, was promoted to that position in part because she had dated Wayne Pacelle.

WHAT SHOULD BE DONE?

The HSUS board needs to step in and should have long ago. The problem is that non-staff board members are checkwriters who have little idea about the organization's day-to-day operations. "We're not an association that investigates sexual harassment," said an HSUS board member.[40] "We didn't hire him to be a choir boy."[41] "Which red-blooded male hasn't sexually harassed somebody?" the board member said. "Women should be able to take care of themselves."[42]

The attorney Pacelle sexually assaulted in the HSUS offices resigned in 2018. She wrote in her resignation email that "the board's handling of the situation 'made it impossible for me to stay at HSUS and be in good health.'"[43]

HSUS terminated the investigation into the CEO after its existence was reported in the press.[44] Board Chair Rick Bernthal, who had written to the staff in January 2018 that truthful reporting of Pacelle's sexual misconduct was "a great unfairness to Wayne," stayed on for another year after the 2018 immolation.[45]

The part-time board is not equipped to handle a rogue Office of General Counsel. The legal machinations provide a window into how HSUS discourages whistleblowing.

One starting point for the board and staff would be a zero tolerance policy for those who retaliated against whistleblowers, orchestrated settlements, or otherwise covered up Pacelle's abuse. The board should closely examine the documents and conduct of the attorneys and other top executives in the D.C. office who were involved in paying settlements and punishing whistleblowers while keeping a predatory CEO at the helm for years.

HSUS is a public charity that should release the documents concerning the coverup of Wayne Pacelle's sexual misconduct. The staff deserve to know the truth. HSUS can hire as many consultants as it wants but will never solve toxic workplace issues as long as Pacelle's enablers are operating at the organization.[46]

Sunlight

It breaks your heart when your faith is shattered. At the same time, my pain pales in comparison with the suffering of the countless human female victims and the nonhuman victims whom Pacelle's sexual abuse prevented good people from helping. Wayne Pacelle never violated my body, nor do I live in a cage awaiting slaughter.

I have never met HSUS CEO Kitty Block. I know that she sued David Wills, Pacelle's mentor, for sexual harassment and got Wills fired in the 1990s. She wrote in 2019:

> It is impossible to quantify the harm suffered by so many individuals, many of whom were driven from HSUS and in some cases the movement as a whole. In turn, it is impossible to know how much more HSUS and the movement might have accomplished during that same time period had HSUS fostered and maintained a truly inclusive environment.[47]

"Accountability is key," Block told Marc Gunther.[48] She is right. The board must either fire the people responsible for retaliation or explain why attorneys secretly ordering a bug hunt rather than investigating complaints about Wayne Pacelle's mistreatment of women is not a terminable offense. Sunlight is the best disinfectant.

Executive staff, D.C. attorneys, the deputy head of HR, the head of HR, the deputy general counsel, the general counsel, the president of HSLF, the COO, and the CEO at a minimum were well aware of my repeated complaints about the CEO and his inappropriate relationship with his special assistant. My concerns were documented at length in their own internal documents. When the allegations against him finally became public in February 2018, I offered to help HSUS in its investigation. To this day, they have never responded.

Should I have done more? HSUS leadership for years paid settlements to cover up Pacelle's abuse. His lieutenants were richly rewarded. After a mild defenestration, Pacelle started a new group, Animal Wellness Action.

According to the creator of the FBI's diagnostic tool on psychopathy, corporate psychopaths are disproportionately found in those positions one might expect: investment bankers, corporate tycoons, race car drivers—and executives at charities.[49] The nation's leading animal journalists, Beth and Merritt Clifton at *Animals 24-7*, described the sycophancy around Pacelle as "a cult of personality."[50]

There is a mood to the Humane Society of the United States. I could not articulate it when I got there, but I could feel it. I understand now that feeling is collective trauma. There are two Humane Societies: the real one the public knows and most employees support, and the predatory HSUS. People cannot proclaim the highest ideal of helping all animals while objectifying human animals without paralyzing the soul with guilt and shame.

I cannot in good conscience recommend that any employee, volunteer, or donor have anything to do with HSUS. The executives at HSUS are the most dishonest group of people I have ever met.

Every person in the animal movement knows how many out there need our help: billions, all innocent. The movement is too important to squander on an organization that for fifteen years employed a sex abuser as its CEO.

6

"WE ARE HURTING SO MUCH"

Racism and "Color-Blindness"

R acism in the animal movement presents myriad challenges for animal activists. Social movements' successes are contingent upon increasing the popular support necessary to recruit staff, volunteers, and donors; to attract sympathetic media coverage; and to elect and lobby political actors to change policy. The contemporary animal movement in the United States largely consists of upper-class, white, progressive women.[1] A myopic or discriminatory social movement restricts its audience, recruitment, and potential; a broader, more inclusive movement helps achieve activists' goals.

Racism is a difficult issue for the American animal movement. The nation has a sordid past in which white supremacists used demeaning language to equate people of different ethnicities with disfavored nonhuman animals. Contemporary campaigns comparing animal abuse to slavery, the Holocaust, or other racial or ethnic atrocities are offensive and counterproductive.[2] They do nothing more than "reinforce the idea in the Black community that animal advocacy is white."[3] Americans of diverse races and ethnicities may be wrongly assumed to care about or have expertise in issues stereotypically affecting other countries, such as dog meat, dolphin slaughter, or cockfighting.[4] Tragic but quotidian animal cruelty practices like slaughter can become subjects of protest and vitriol when they are carried out by marginalized ethnic groups, as has been seen with Chinese live animal markets and Islamic rituals involving animals.[5]

The humane treatment of animals is a politically controversial topic that engenders a fierce and well-funded opposition. The maintenance of animal advocacy as the stereotypical province of urban, upper-class, white liberals inhibits the formation of political coalitions with farm state and non-white politicians that are necessary to achieve congressional legislation and other policy priorities. Consequently, racism in the animal movement is a problem that must be addressed to help politically advance the humane treatment of nonhuman animals in the United States. Mitigating racism in the U.S. animal movement would help nonhuman animals.

Single-issue advocacy groups are more effective when they build alliances with other social justice movements. Animal activism naturally falls into a progressive coalition sharing overlapping goals with poor people's and labor campaigns and with groups fighting racism and sexism.[6] This broader alliance has not yet happened, however. Racism within the animal movement restricts the range of political allies.

Further, racism creates employment bottlenecks that restrict talent recruitment and diversification within the movement. A foundational issue is the dearth of new jobs. The salience of climate change in millennial activism and the launching of animal welfare programs at top law and professional schools have conflated to create a situation where in applicants' demand for new jobs far exceeds the supply. Class inequalities reinforce racial inequalities through narrowed volunteering and internship paths. The classism of animal advocacy restricts the pool of potential candidates, thus reconstituting a largely privileged, white workforce.

Most importantly, discrimination of any sort is morally wrong. It is deeply troubling that individuals who have devoted their lives to mitigating nonhuman animal exploitation seem to be ignoring or recreating systems of race-based human exploitation, contributing to a homogenous social movement.

The United States' 2020 racial justice protests were a "triggering event" that brought overdue attention to the issue of systemic racism in the animal movement.[7] Black Americans and other people of color who might be sympathetic to animal activism have suffered a long history of loss of land, lack of credit, hazardous working conditions, and environmental racism.[8] For example, George Floyd's great-great-grandfather was born into enslavement in North Carolina. He achieved marked prosperity after Abolition and amassed five hundred acres of farmland during Reconstruction. His land was stolen from him by whites, while his "state-mandated illiteracy left him powerless to mount a legal defense."[9] There was a burst of white consciousness–raising after George Floyd's murder. The two leading national animal protection organizations, the American Society for the Prevention of Cruelty to Animals (ASPCA) and People for the Ethical Treatment of Animals (PETA), released statements of solidarity.[10] As measured by their public statements, it would seem they did little else. The lack of serious external inquiry is telling. We must turn somewhere other than one-off press releases to examine the issues discussed in this chapter. My chapter on sexual discrimination at HSUS necessarily took a personal approach to the problem, since my personal experience added something new to the discussion. Here, I do not have unique personal experience with the subject matter. I do, however, have the ability to read the scholarship on the matter and present its findings.

To begin to address the problem of racism in the American animal movement, we must ask two questions. First, what is the scope of the problem? Specifically, what is the evidence of racial discrimination in the movement? Second, what theoretical lessons can be drawn from the extant empirical evidence? This chapter will first examine the empirical evidence of racism in the American animal movement through a systematic literature review.[11] In the theoretical discussion, this chapter will examine this evidence through the frameworks of (1) bounded rationality and its two sub-theories, Narrative Policy Framework and Social Construction & Policy Design, and (2) critical theorist Dvora Yanow's theory of myth analysis.

The literature is characterized by the following five themes:
1. Theoretical linkages between racist and speciesist oppression
2. Social movement analysis
3. Personal stories from people of color
4. Empirical research
5. Class inequalities and workforce bottlenecks

THEORETICAL LINKAGES BETWEEN
RACIST AND SPECIESIST OPPRESSION

Interestingly, all the scholars examined for this chapter recognized the link between racist and speciesist oppression. Enslaved persons were historically considered and labeled by white persons as animals, an unscientific ideological categorization that facilitated subjugation. Caviola, Everett, and Faber found a significant association between speciesist and racist attitudes among 242 adults they surveyed in the United States (p<0.001).[12] Oppressors who willfully ignore that their victims feel pain can objectify, brutalize, torture, experiment on, and even kill their victims without remorse. Jones argues that, in the present day, people of color are disproportionately kept like laboratory animals in prison cages to control their bodies.[13]

Psychologists Monteiro, Pfeiler, Patterson, and Milburn sought to test the theoretical construct between racist and speciesist oppression. Most Americans and Western Europeans both care about animals and eat meat, according to public opinion surveys.[14] In the authors' view, there is a psychosocial "meat paradox" through which individuals mollify or suppress their cognitive dissonances and express compassion toward animals while consuming dead industrial animal flesh daily. In these authors' formulation, meat eating is supported by conventional notions of carnism not only as healthy, tasty, and normal but also as an expression of intraspecies hegemony and the right to oppress others. Thus, meat eating becomes a dualistic ritual of both dissociative "carnistic defense" and aggressive "hostile" beliefs of "carnistic domination" that, the authors hypothesized, would be associated with mistreatment of other humans.

The authors conducted an analysis of meat-eating ideology, or interspecies dominance, to assess its possible relationship to forms of intraspecies dominance, including the ideology of racism. They surveyed two large samples of individuals: two undergraduate classes at the University of Massachusetts–Boston (n = 302 and 173) as well as paid participants through Amazon's Mechanical Turk (n = 306 and 203). The first group was used to develop a model to measure participants' support for "carnistic defense" (e.g., "Eating meat is better for my health") and "carnistic dominance" (e.g., "I have the right to kill any animal I want"). The total sample size analyzed for the linkages of speciesism with racism using the previously validated Symbolic Racism 2000 Scale (e.g., "Over the past few years, Blacks have gotten more than they deserve") was n = 578. The authors found no significant association between a carnistic defense ideology and racism but did find a significant association between carnistic dominance and racism at the p<0.01 level.

SOCIAL MOVEMENT ANALYSIS

Rodrigues analyzes the racial normativity of three People for the Ethical Treatment of Animals (PETA) campaigns in the United States: "Are Animals the New Slaves," "Glass Walls," and anti-SeaWorld litigation.[15] In the first two, exhibits comparing animal cruelty to the lynching, torture, and enslavement of Black Americans were set up at the New York Natural History Museum and at a Washington, D.C., shopping mall. A spokesperson for the National Association for the Advancement of Colored People (NAACP) stated: "Once again, Black people are being pimped. You used us. You have used us enough." In the third campaign, PETA attorneys filed a frivolous lawsuit in federal district court in San Diego arguing that SeaWorld's confinement of five orcas violated the Thirteenth Amendment's ban on slavery.

These three campaigns were designed to offend as part of PETA's strategy of deliberately courting controversy for media attention. Such tactics are the brainchild of PETA founder and president Ingrid Newkirk, who conceived of them when animal rights was a fringe notion in the early 1980s.[16]

Rodrigues is hardly unsympathetic to the plight of animals. He contends that the enslavement of humans and that of nonhuman animals are comparable.[17] However, he takes great issue with the tactical wisdom of conflating Black people's and nonhuman animals' suffering on myriad counts. First, the "animalization" of other races has a long and shameful history. Any conflation of the two struggles, even in the context of helping nonhuman animals, resurfaces these painful, racist names and comparisons. Second, the tactics egregiously offend non-white people and have no realistic chance of persuading people in the non-white communities to join the ranks of animal advocates. On the contrary, such campaigns are more likely to cause them to turn against PETA, or animal activists generally. Third, comparing current nonhuman animal suffering to past suffering of Black Americans ignores and therefore elides the ongoing reality of other forms of racial oppression like mass incarceration and police violence.

In sum, it is not shocking that PETA engages in media stunts. What is shocking is the egregious racism on display in the three campaigns explored in Rodrigues's article. PETA is one of the largest and most influential animal organizations in the world. Rodrigues argues convincingly that its animal slavery campaigns serve to alienate people of color from animal activism.

Wrenn takes a more sensible tack to the comparison between human and nonhuman abuse.[18] He argues that instead of resorting to offensive stunts, twenty-first-century animal rights activists should study the strategies of mid-nineteenth-century abolitionists if they believe the key to animal liberation is the legal abolition of the property status of nonhuman animals.

The PETA lawyers who filed the SeaWorld *habeus* petition implicitly agree with Wrenn, but they go about their work not just blindly but in a way that seems destined to accomplish nothing other than obstinately hurting the animal movement and the animals they want to help.

PERSONAL STORIES FROM PEOPLE OF COLOR

The apparent lack of understanding and acknowledgement of the reality of historical racial discrimination offends Black Americans in the movement, as evidenced in some of the personal stories told by them.

Critical race theorist A. Breeze Harper recounts her experience growing up Black in a predominantly white midwestern town and school system.[19] Her love for animals, encouraged by her father, led her in eighth grade to rescue bugs from the school carpet. For her compassion, a white male bully lobbed racist taunts that were encouraged with laughter from her classmates. She criticizes what she views as the contradiction between the glorification or normalization of white male children killing animals for "sport" hunting and the calumny leveled at Black celebrity animal abusers like Michael Vick and DMX.

A Vegan Outreach organizer painfully recalls the double-consciousness faced by Black animal activists.[20] "Sister, you're out here telling people not to eat animals, but what are you doing for our Black community?" She recalls an older man saying while she was tabling in Leimert Park, Los Angeles. "Black men are being shot in the streets." "Our culture is hurting," she writes. She continues:

> We are hurting so much that it is often hard for us to show love and empathy for nonhuman animals because of the comparisons we grew up hearing—that we are lower than animals, an eighth of a human, "savages," "apes," "monkeys," and are subject to having dogs sicced on us during protests. Experiencing, watching, and reading about these experiences can cause resentment toward animals, when it seems like they are being shown more love, empathy, and kindness. It's like having a sibling who gets treated with special attention, while the other sibling is constantly being compared to the perfect sibling and never gets the same amount of attention. At some point, no matter how nice the praised sibling might be, resentment will inevitably creep in. That is why so many POC [People of Color] are triggered when they hear non-POC talk about animal rights and when animal exploitation is compared to human slavery.[21]

EMPIRICAL RESEARCH

Empirical analyses of racism in the American animal movement are rare. Wrenn analyzed the covers of the two most widely distributed animal rights magazines in the country, *VegNews* and PETA's *Animal Times*, from

2000 to 2012.[22] These magazines serve to recruit new members into the movement and also to signal its values. It is plausible to consider them as valid data points for the national public representation of animal activism. The study found that of 149 people on the magazines' covers, 87 percent were non-Hispanic white, 60 percent were female, 93 percent were thin, and 13 percent were sexualized. The first two categories were determined by Wrenn and an independent observer, while the latter two were coded using previously published classification methods. Breaking down the racial category further, the study found that 87 percent were white, 7 percent were Black, 5 percent were Asian, and 1 percent were Hispanic or Latinx. At the time, the United States population was 72 percent non-Hispanic white, 13 percent Black, 5 percent Asian, and 17 percent Hispanic.[23] The magazine covers thus grossly underrepresented people of color over more than a decade.

CLASSISM AND WORKFORCE BOTTLENECKS

The largest farm animal organizations—Mercy For Animals, The Humane League, and the Good Food Institute—have competent, altruistic leaders who do not suffer from such dysfunction. The movement has other workforce problems preventing it from achieving its full potential. By no means are these problems unusual in the nonprofit world, and many of them are likely destined to improve as the movement grows and professionalizes.

Twenty-five years ago, there was no farm animal movement in the United States; fifty years ago, there was hardly an animal movement outside of advocacy for horses and shelter animals. Sclerotic upper management is less of a problem with farm animal advocacy due to its nascency but is particularly acute in the broader animal movement and the older, established groups. Each generation of activists is trained in its zeitgeist, and current leadership at HSUS, PETA, and the ASPCA does not feel that farm animals are as important an issue as wildlife or companion animals, judging by these organizations' budgets. The younger generation is smarter than the older, many of whom need to retire. Paradoxically, this recalcitrance has bolstered the personnel and finances of nonprofits whose sole focus is farmed animal welfare.

As noted, the salience of climate change in millennial activism and the launching of farm animal welfare programs at top law and professional schools have conflated to create a bottleneck for job applicants. (It is important to note that a degree is merely a proxy and by no means a prerequisite to success in this or any field. Some of the best activists and philanthropists have no degrees.) As this book attests, there is now a viable career pipeline for farm animal advocates.

A foundational issue is the dearth of new jobs, even with the recent influx of funding. For many animal organizations, a precondition of hiring is experience. Unfortunately, the only way to get the necessary experience is to volunteer or intern, which can only be done by people of means or students at wealthy universities that subsidize such opportunities. Similarly, entry-level jobs do not pay well, and graduates whose top priority is paying off student loans or supporting a family are disadvantaged. Farm animal groups point to the hiring of senior people with experience as the most significant talent bottleneck, with fundraising and political work coming in second and third, respectively.[24] It is a vegan chicken-and-egg problem.

Animal Advocacy Careers surveyed twenty-seven charities in 2020 and found seven hundred and forty positions, about 10 percent of which were open. Seven hundred and forty employees may not seem like a lot, but this survey only reflected positions at twenty-seven effective animal charitable organizations, not government, academic, or industry jobs. Plant-based meat is a $20 billion industry, and Beyond Meat alone has seven hundred employees.[25] Furthermore, the farm animal movement has grown by a factor of ten in the last ten years.

Meghan Lowery, the tenacious staffer at Jim Greenbaum's foundation, has been able to straddle the worlds of funder and advocate better than most. She spent six months on a qualitative survey of the movement's workforce and talent pipeline. What she heard from advocates was telling:

> The overarching theme is that our movement as a whole has not yet been professionalized. Here is what I have found in many of our top-, middle-, and lower-tier funded organizations: a true lack of professional development opportunities; employees feel undervalued; and many have flat-lined in their current positions. This is why

we are having the lily pad effect of great people jumping from organization to organization. The current working environments are judgmental and cliquey. Many have limited space for those that are not fully vegan. Only a few groups have salary brackets, have done compensation analysis, or have 360 degree reviews so that employees can give feedback to their supervisors safely and anonymously. Many of the top leaders have had little or no management training. Their style is often micromanaging and complete control, which leads to severe burnout. PTO, benefits packages, and paid maternity leave are almost non-existent. Finally, there is a lack of management structure and no clear on-boarding process or check-ins after hire. To summarize, individuals that currently work in our movement are unsatisfied, individuals who applied to work in our movement were underwhelmed and I believe that addressing these foundational elements is key before we try and attract highly-skilled professionals coming potentially from the for-profit sector.[26]

Area of expertise the role seems to focus on?	Current roles		Advertised jobs (no duplicates)		Advertised jobs (with duplicates)	
	Total	%	Total	%	Total	%
Total	740	100	72	100	95	100
Campaigns, corporate engagement, or volunteer management	227	31%	15	21%	20	21%
Management and leadership	181	24%	18.5	26%	23	24%
Operations, administration, and HR	131	18%	20.5	28%	24.5	26%
Marketing or communications	122	16%	13	18%	17	18%
Fundraising	70.5	10%	12	17%	18	19%
Other technical skills, e.g. web or software development	54.5	7%	6	8%	6	6%
Research	51.5	7%	0	0%	0	0%
Government, policy, lobbying, or legal	37.5	5%	9	13%	12	13%
Other	17	2%	2	3%	3	3%
Natural sciences	12.5	2%	1	1%	1	1%

Table of roles available in the animal advocacy movement
Source: Animal Advocacy Careers

DISCUSSION

Examining the popular and academic literature reveals a dearth of serious inquiry into the problem of racism in the animal advocacy movement. At the same time, those analyses that have explored the topic have found strong evidence for the proposition that the U.S. animal movement suffers from racism. It is fair to argue that the limited nature of public statements and scholarly inquiry into an issue that major organizations and scholars admit exists is evidence that addressing racism is hardly a top priority for the movement. What is the purpose in claiming organizations and individuals will address a problem if they are not going to try to solve it?

The theory of bounded rationality can explain why past patterns of discrimination and perceived discrimination persist in the largely white animal advocacy movement and why there appears to be sudden interest in but relatively little strong scholarship or action on the topic. The theory of bounded rationality in contrast to comprehensive rationality acknowledges the necessary restrictions any person or group faces that prevent collecting infinite information and making flawless decisions. Two theories within bounded rationality may explain the motive behind actions to address racism, or lack thereof. Narrative Policy Framework recognizes the role of broad, archetypal storytelling in the implementation of public policy. Social Construction and Policy Design is similar but relates moral storytelling to stereotypical good and bad actors or targets that can lead to "emotional and superficial judgments, backed up with selective use of facts."[27]

Lindblom articulates several reasons why administrators may "muddle through" and focus on more discrete, "branch" problems instead of expending energy attempting to solve "root" problems.[28] It seems clear that there could be a purpose to a charitable movement professionally and philanthropically dominated by upper-class white liberals adopting a public-facing "branch" stance of racial solidarity while ignoring the "root" problems of racial discrimination. That is not to conclude there is any nefarious or even conscious intent in ignoring the root causes of racism in the animal movement, but it would be naïve not to consider the power inequalities based on race and class.[29]

The two sub-theories of bounded rationality, Narrative Policy Framework and Social Construction & Policy Design, elucidate potential motives that might explain these results. An outcome of "muddling through" would fit well within the theory of Narrative Policy Framework. Cairney identifies four narrative traits of this framework: setting, character, plot, and moral.[30] In this framework, the setting is the American animal movement. The characters are white employees and leaders of the movement who have discriminated against people of color, whether intentionally or structurally. The plot is that the evil of racism is being addressed and mitigated in the movement—ironically, by those who have long perpetrated it. The moral is that racism has been extirpated from the animal movement. Thus, the power system can continue largely as it was before with an artificial ethical balm.

Foucault recognized that in post-Enlightenment, ostensibly free societies, the coercive power of the state necessarily shifted from violence to thought control.[31] Critical theorist Dvora Yanow sheds light on how power inequities are propagated through the use of rituals and myths.[32] Rituals are bureaucratic performance art that serve mainly to keep the target population docile and subservient without effecting actual change. Myths, on the other hand, are the propaganda inherently necessary to control the minds of the people.

"We create myths as an act of mediating contradictions, such as those that arise when we are faced with accommodating in daily life the mandates of two (or more) irreconcilable values," she writes. "Myths create areas of silence in public discourse." Both the myth that racism does not exist in the animal movement in the United States and the myth that racism is being addressed reinforce the continued dominance of white people in the movement who can use ritualistic performances to pretend to change while maintaining the dominant racial hierarchy that benefits them.

An analysis using Social Construction and Policy Design would signal that the American animal movement's purported concerns over racism are largely self-unconscious performance theater for organizations and their largely white, liberal donors, who presumably sympathize with such narratives. The subjugators present a narrative whereby they become the heroes by purporting to solve the problem that they created and benefited from. In this paternalistic conception, the white characters undergo catharsis and are cleansed of their past sins. If racism is solved by privileged white people, the victims are still victims but their claims to victimhood have been diminished. Such policies "send messages, teach lessons, and allocate values that exacerbate injustice, trivialize citizens, fail to solve problems, and undermine institutional cultures that are supportive of democratic designs."[33]

The American animal movement is represented in the public imagination as the group of national charitable activist organizations e.g., ASPCA and PETA, promoting public policy regarding the humane treatment of nonhuman animals. Yet vegans are one of the most despised groups of people, less popular than atheists and a step above drug addicts, according to one poll.[34] So a different narrative is necessary to attain public support and sustain fundraising. The public framing of animal organizations as anti-racist seems to be one factor in a public relations operation rather than a seriously pursued policy outcome.

ASPCA and PETA are institutions with historical memories and policies. Discursive institutionalism suggests there will be a coordinative discourse articulating values within those organizations and a communicative discourse used for public consumption.[35] This echoes the rhetorical strategy of, for example, some politicians who may assert that discrimination no longer exists because the United States abolished *de jure* segregation. In reality, little has changed.

Some scholars have begun the work necessary to further the cause of anti-racism within the U.S. animal movement. But that work, if sincere, is still in its infancy. A more sober analysis finds a lack of much scholarship or effort to redress the pathology of racism. Critical theories examining the evidence reveal a troubling reality. It seems the leading scholars and organizations in the animal movement are not seriously concerned with racism. If anything, the status quo of inaction perpetuates racism. To move beyond the legacy of discrimination will require much more serious attention than is now being paid. To continue to let racism fester within the movement is morally wrong and ultimately harms animals by hampering the movement's workforce and political effectiveness.

7

ANIMAL LAW AND
LEGAL EDUCATION

Pathbreakers and Millennials

The movement needs lawyers to change laws or, in the case of farmed animals, to create and sow the field. There are only two federal laws that directly deal with farmed animal treatment in America: the Twenty-Eight Hour Law of 1873 (Amended 1994), limiting transport, and the Humane Methods of Slaughter Act of 1958 (Amended 1978). Creative advocates have had to adopt other approaches on the fly or to engage in state lawmaking by playing offense with ballot initiatives or defense against ag-gag laws.

Farmed animal law today is in the same stage as animal law was in the 1980s, according to an excellent history by Joyce Tischler, the Animal Legal Defense Fund's (ALDF) co-founder and general counsel.[1] "When I entered law school in 1974, there were no animal law courses or seminars, no student chapter, and no casebooks. . . . What we, as pioneers in a new field of law, had was a 'clean slate.'"

The first animal law course was taught at Seton Hall in 1977; it was canceled after one semester, and a second such course did not come along until 1983, taught at Penn State. Course materials and syllabi were thrown together on an ad hoc basis well into the 1990s.

Lewis & Clark Law School remains the leading incubator of animal law practitioners and pedagogy due to its close association with ALDF's Portland office. The school launched the first animal law student group in 1993 and *Animal Law Review* in 1995. The *Review* was a student-initiated idea, led by future ASPCA attorney Nancy Perry. It was met with skepticism by the faculty as to its sustainability, rigor, and funding. ALDF committed to funding the journal for three years, but even then, "there was enough ambiguity in the faculty's approval that for the first six issues of the journal the masthead read 'Students of Lewis & Clark Law School,' rather than 'Lewis & Clark Law School.'"[2] Now in its twenty-eigth year, *Animal Law Review* is the gold standard and required reading in the field. ALDF continued to dedicate resources to Lewis & Clark with its founding of the Center for Animal Law Studies. Many good attorneys in this field have matriculated from the program.

Lewis & Clark also launched the nation's first animal law clinic, as recounted in a searching, erudite essay by clinic director Kathy Hessler:[3]

> Before talking about the importance of an animal law clinic, it is important to surface the underlying question: Why animal law? This is a common question that has many answers, the most straightforward of which is that animals are suffering needlessly and without legal protection. In our legal framework, we tend to restrict one's ability to cause needless suffering. Seen from this perspective, lawyers have the capacity to do something to alleviate or eliminate that suffering.

The turn of the century saw animal law become established in the mainstream. Harvard and Georgetown both offered their first animal law courses in 2000. Announcements about the courses in 1999 were considered so momentous they made the cover of the *New York Times*.[4] "The occurrence of the class at Harvard gave legitimacy—in the broad readership of the *New York Times*—to the issue that had not been previously considered," writes David Favre in *Animal Law Review*'s twenty-year retrospective.[5] The first animal law casebook was published the next year. At the same time, ALDF decided "to focus a significant portion of its energy and financial resources on a comprehensive, long-term program to establish student chapters and introduce animal law courses into a broad range of law schools."[6] By the end of the next decade, the number of schools offering animal law courses jumped from twelve to more than one hundred, including all of America's top five law schools other than Yale, though the latter did offer a reading group with David Wolfson and Paul Waldau in the mid-2000s.

There is still little money to be made from practicing as an animal lawyer. The money for animal law must come from nonprofits. Tischler recounts that working for ALDF in 1981 "was a risky and not altogether rational career choice." The only two other full-time animal lawyers in the country at the time were the general counsels of HSUS and ASPCA. "No one in private practice or elsewhere self-identified as an animal lawyer. Animal law has not grown in the way the environmental law movement grew: while federal environmental laws provide standing to sue and attorneys' fees, animal protection laws provide neither."[7]

The watershed moment in bringing animal law into the legal academy was a series of prescient and generous gifts by Bob Barker. The first was given to Harvard Law School in June 2001 as a $500,000 endowment by Pearson Television, the producer of *The Price Is Right*, at Barker's suggestion to honor his thirtieth year as host. Barker himself soon matched that gift and followed it up with endowment donations of $1 million each to law schools at Columbia, Duke, Stanford, and UCLA (2004); Northwestern (2005); Georgetown (2006); and the University of Virginia (2009). "Animals need all the protection we can give them," Barker told *The Associated Press*. "We intend to train a growing number of law students in this area of the law in the hope that they will ultimately lead a national effort to make it illegal to brutalize and exploit these helpless creatures."[8] The gifts spin off 6 percent to 7 percent per year in perpetuity with the stipulation that funds be used in alternate years for an animal law course then a conference.[9]

The endowments fostered continuity that permitted professors and universities to devote part of their scholarship and pedagogy to the field. The first professors were lone wolves: David Cassuto at Pace Law School; David Favre at Michigan State; Gary Francione at Rutgers; and Taimie Bryant at UCLA. They were joined by regular adjunct lecturers such as Steven Wise, former president of ALDF and founder of the Non-Human

Rights Project; Jonathan Lovvorn, director of litigation at HSUS; David Wolfson, executive director of the Wall Street firm Milbank; and Paul Waldau, former director of the Center for Animals and Public Policy at Tufts and founder of the master's program in anthrozoology at Canisius College. In 2003, Professor Rebecca Huss at Valparaiso "became the first legal academic in the United States to be advanced to tenure with a scholarly portfolio consisting exclusively of articles about animal law."[10] The nation's first professorship in animal law was endowed by ALDF at the University of Denver Sturm College of Law in 2015. It is held by Justin Marceau, whose first exposure to animal law was at Harvard Law School in one of the first courses funded by a Barker endowment.[11]

Animal law journals were published and went defunct at Stanford and the University of Pennsylvania, but Lewis & Clark's *Animal Law Review* and Michigan State's *Animal and Natural Resource Law Review* both thrived. Legal luminaries ranging from Laurence Tribe, Richard Posner, Alan Dershowitz, and Cass Sunstein to Martha Nussbaum each have written scholarly works on animal rights, and *Animal Law Review* has been cited by the Supreme Court.[12]

As groundbreaking as this history is, one will notice in revisiting articles and achievements from a decade ago the dearth of legal education on farmed animals. "I was involved in various conversations with leaders of the animal rights/protection movement in the 1980s, in which we bemoaned the plight of farmed animals and felt helpless to effectively create change through the normal legislative process, either at the federal or state level," Tischler writes. "The reigning wisdom was that the agribusiness industry was too powerful and would defeat all proposed legislation at the committee level."[13] If animal law was a niche topic, then farmed animal law was a subspecies, too narrow and fruitless for much rumination. However, as this book has argued, farmed animal advocacy is a social movement in its own right that has transcended its traditional place as one of many areas within animal advocacy, further subsumed within environmentalism. As it did twenty years ago, Harvard Law School took the lead in launching a formal animal law and policy program. This time, it would be joined by Yale Law School.

FARMED ANIMAL LAW AT HARVARD

The Barker gifts present almost a controlled experiment for how animal law programs can succeed. It is clear after two decades that, by far, the most important factor in the success of animal law programs is faculty support. Even a million-dollar endowment can get lost in the shuffle. "Without an association with one or more programs at the Law School," writes UCLA law professor Taimie Bryant, "animal law becomes a bit of an orphan: students who might have interest in it may not be able to fit it into their schedules while also meeting track requirements and taking a certain number of bar-related courses."[14] However appealing to students' passions, one-off courses taught by adjunct faculty otherwise unconnected to the university can easily take a backseat to other obligations. Adjunct lecturers also typically do not have access to law schools' broader resources to host academic workshops or larger public events.

Furthermore, until recently, there was a dearth of entry-level jobs in the farm animal movement. Though the situation is improving, some of the relatively few that are open are filled by favoritism rather than merit. Students interested in service still have far more traveled paths in public service, or environmentalism and other social justice movements. How can young people realize their dreams without mentors? There is, regrettably, a vacuum in the movement wherein some talented young people still have to fight to carve out a path that should be welcoming and smoothly traveled. Part of this problem lies with older people in the animal movement who came to it when it was less established and the barriers to entry were lower. They fill the ranks of the older animal organizations and are, consciously or not, keen to hold on to power. I have witnessed such people deliberately not hire or support promising young people because of an unstated fear that applicants or interns are smarter than they are. I have seen gifted people marginalized and kicked out of the movement so less qualified leaders can maintain sinecures. To some degree, this is human nature, but it does not justify such behavior when the consequences are so great.

One critical insight the legal academy and its students have had in recent years is the marriage of farm animal advocacy with more established fields. "How humans raise animals for food in this country and around the world affects animal welfare, human health, food safety, workers' rights, as well as climate change and the environment," Harvard Law School's Dean Martha Minow noted in 2016.[15]

Professor Kristen Stilt was recruited to Harvard Law from Northwestern University in 2014. With a doctorate in history and Middle Eastern studies from Harvard and a law degree from the University of Texas, she directs both the Animal Law & Policy Program and the Program on Law and Society in the Muslim World. Her research focuses on Islamic constitutional law and halal slaughter law.[16] Stilt is no aloof theoretician. While researching her Ph.D. in Cairo, "she conducted undercover investigations at animal slaughterhouses."[17]

David Wolfson, the attorney who taught animal law at Harvard in 2004, introduced Minow, Stilt, and philanthropist Brad Goldberg at a meeting at Wolfson's New York office in the summer of 2014.[18] Goldberg grew up in Kansas City, where images of a steady stream of cramped farm animals being transported to their sad fates never left him.[19] After a successful career in finance, he founded the Animal Welfare Trust in 2001 and incorporated it with a provision unusual among foundations: a twenty-year sunset. He donated generously to establish an undergraduate minor in animal studies at New York University, one of his alma maters. What would an expanded Harvard Law School animal program look like?

The participants were all in. Goldberg agreed to give $1 million over five years to establish the Animal Law & Policy Program (ALPP), which would be led by Professor Stilt when she arrived on campus that fall. As academic matters tend to go, it would take another year to launch. "Now is the time for the resources of tort, property, family law, environmental law, constitutional law, and legal change strategies to make a crucial difference in the lives of animals," said Dean Minow.[20]

The program recruited Chris Green as its executive director beginning in the fall of 2015. Green had taken the first animal law course at Harvard as a student and was working as the legislative director for ALDF and the chair of the American Bar Association's Animal Law Committee. Stilt and Green put into place programs to host visiting fellows, put on academic and book workshops, developed new courses, and enhanced the student experience. In addition, Harvard hosted its first academic fellow in a two-year postgraduate program designed to establish future academic leaders. That fellow, Delcianna Winders, subsequently became a clinical professor of law and director of the Animal Law Litigation Clinic at Lewis & Clark, and now is an associate professor of law and director of the Animal Law Program at Vermont Law School.[21]

Faculty leadership and the Barker and Goldberg gifts had begun to establish a virtuous cycle around which a community of animal law scholars was forming in Cambridge. Such programs "give young people a moral compass as to how animals should be treated in society that will stay with them throughout their careers," says Goldberg.[22] The preceding history of animal law, still relatively encompassable in a handful of pages, demonstrates that the dedication and vision of "a small group of thoughtful committed individuals can change the world," to borrow from Margaret Mead, and have created something that will long outlast them, exactly as intended. Ideally, the programs will be so successful that one day there will no longer be a need for them.

A million-dollar grant to ALPP in 2016 drew praise from Harvard president Drew Gilpin Faust, who said: "[the grant] will support the critically important work of the Animal Law and Policy Program. I look forward to seeing how it will advance research and teaching to improve the welfare of animals."[23] It paid for a number of initiatives. First, it paid for HSUS litigation director Jonathan Lovvorn to come to Cambridge as policy director; among his responsibilities was teaching the school's first Farmed Animal Law & Policy course.[24] Second, Harvard funded three visiting fellows in farmed animal law and policy. Environmental scientist Matthew Hayek had just finished his Harvard Ph.D. and is now an assistant professor at NYU; cultural anthropologist Elan Abrell wrote an ethnography of animal sanctuaries and is now an assistant professor in animal studies at Wesleyan and an adjunct lecturer in animal studies at NYU; HSUS litigator Peter Brandt wrote his book, *Indefensible: Adventures of a Farm Animal Protection Lawyer.*[25] Third, fellow Ann Linder authored an ALPP report on the consequences of the King Amendment, which many credit with helping keep the harmful measure out of the final Farm Bill. Fourth, the school hosted "The Death of Factory Farming" at the Harvard Law School Bicentennial and its first policy summit, a Clean Meat Regulatory Roundtable.[26]

Experiential learning clinics are indispensable in establishing and maintaining a presence in a university's legal education department.[27] Animal law clinics meet four needs for the animal movement. First, clearly, the training of students in preparation for careers or *pro bono* advocacy in animal law is paramount. Clinics marry students' coursework with the real world under the supervision of experienced attorneys. Second, animal law clinics meet representation demands that would likely otherwise be unmet. Third, clinics are free from "the political or economic constraints faced by private and nonprofit attorneys." Given the dearth of laws to protect farmed animals, creative scholarship and novel litigation tactics can be incubated in animal law clinics with the aid of practitioners from related fields, such as environmentalism, food safety, and labor studies, or broader areas of history, philosophy, and science. "In animal law, strategy and policy also are implicated in every legal matter," Hessler writes. "Questions exist among the few animal law practitioners and professors about ideal approaches to each issue. There is no significant archive of learned wisdom from practice and no settled approach to any single question. . . . Animal law offers a rare opportunity for students to be learning the law while trying to change it." Lastly, animal law clinics train the next generation of not just animal lawyers but also of animal law professors and scholars. Fairly or not, elite universities tend to select faculty from the ranks of their peer institutions.

The founding of a clinic signals that a legal discipline has reached a new level of social and scholarly maturity. Brooks McCormick Jr., scion of the International Harvester family, passed away in 2015 and directed his $60 million estate to establishing the Brooks Institute for Animal Rights Law and Policy.[28] The Brooks Trust gave $700,000 to Harvard in 2018 so it could launch its Animal Law & Policy Clinic, headed by Katherine Meyer and Nicole Negowetti.[29] "Animal law is a vitally important and rapidly growing field," said incoming dean John Manning. "Our new Animal Law & Policy Clinic will give students real-world experience in this burgeoning field, build on Harvard Law School's long tradition of innovative pedagogy, and prepare future graduates to address significant societal challenges."[30] The Animal Law & Policy Program's 2019–2020 year-in-review illustrates that the Visiting Fellows program is rapidly hitting its stride, with scholars publishing dozens of articles in academic journals and a handful of upcoming books from Oxford University Press, Springer, and Routledge.[31] In late 2021, the Brooks Trust gave the Animal Law and Policy Program an extraordinary $10 million endowment.[32] In the 2021–2022 academic year, the program will host a dozen new visiting fellows and researchers.

This is just a snapshot of the state of animal law at Harvard and the developments behind its success. As is the nature of education, the primary benefits lie in the future as attorneys and leaders move on to successful careers. "I came to law school interested in legal academia and quickly found a fantastically rich niche in animal law," enthused Andy Stawasz, HLS '21. "The close mentorship I've received from Professor Stilt and everyone in the Animal Law & Policy Program has shown me that this path is possible and set me up to have the best shot possible at attaining it."[33]

As Chris Green describes:

> It has been so incredibly rewarding to return to my alma mater and join Kristen in building the Animal Law & Policy Program here at Harvard Law School. Not only are we able to devote our professional lives to the issues that matter most deeply to us, but we also gain the meaningful enrichment of providing guidance and training to some of the brightest minds and most passionate advocates as they prepare to embark on their own careers. It also would be hard to overstate the value of having one of the most prestigious academic institutions in the world as a platform to educate and inform broader audiences about the plight of animals and what we as a society can do to protect them.[34]

FARMED ANIMAL LAW AT YALE

Yale Law School's animal law program has grown much faster than Harvard's; five years ago, Yale did not even offer a course in animal law. Rightly or wrongly, Yale did not accept an offered gift from Bob Barker two decades ago, likely because of the school's smaller size and the field's perceived lack of intellectual rigor. Times have changed, in part due to the Barker gifts, and the legal community now recognizes the importance of the field. Student demand has also risen as climate change confronts the world with the problem of how to minimize carbon dioxide and methane emissions from animal agriculture. Climate change is the most pressing global issue for millennial students.[35]

The Law, Ethics, and Animals Program (LEAP) was founded in 2019 by Deputy Dean Douglas Kysar, a beloved teacher and scholar whom many universities would love to humanely poach. Kysar is one of the ten most cited American legal scholars born in the last fifty years.[36] His poetic volume, *Regulating from Nowhere: Environmental Law and the Search for Objectivity*, revealed the moral-intellectual drive he brought to Bentham's question:

> Although we will never know how to satisfy the infinite ethical demand of the unknowable other, *we do know how to fail it.* We fail the demand when we deliberately refuse to promote conditions that, in our best understanding, are necessary to support life. Accordingly, we should strive at present to ensure sustainable management of soil, forests, freshwater, and other natural resources, and we should seek to minimize destruction of the ozone layer, accumulation of greenhouse gases, and other actions that we believe will harm life. We should do these things not because our cost-benefit analysis demonstrates them to be optimal after having been properly stripped of conceptual prejudice, nor because our Kantian-inspired ethics posits them to be necessary to protect a newly expanded Kingdom of Ends, nor, finally, because our political theory identifies them to be the choice of hypothetical contracting agents, once those agents have been placed behind a veil of ignorance sufficiently opaque to mask whether they are called "man" or "cat" by man. Instead, we should do this because we have experienced what Levinas calls the "epiphany of the face," the recognition of a primordial responsibility for the mortality of the other, which is the beginning of all subjectivity and, by extension, all ethics and all politics.[37]

LEAP was unusual in being created in the minds of faculty rather than by activist students or donors. Indeed, the expansion of the Harvard program with Professor Stilt's strong support showed how far animal law had come since the lonely *Animal Law Review* and Barker endowments in the first decade of this century. LEAP showed the field was gaining in legitimacy by the year and similarly attracted the financial support of forward-looking philanthropists such as Brad Goldberg's Animal Welfare Trust, the Brooks Institute, and Chuck and Jennifer Laue's Stray Dog Institute.

Unlike the Harvard program, the Yale program was centered around farm animals and preventing industrialized cruelty. Kysar founded LEAP as an interdisciplinary "think and do tank" to develop new legal and policy strategies to mitigate suffering. "Our laws regarding animals are often outdated, insufficient, or nonexistent," said Kysar. "The past two centuries, and particularly the last two decades, have witnessed a massive transformation in human attitudes towards animals, underscored by fundamental shifts in scientific understanding of animals and ethical thought regarding our obligations to nonhuman creatures. At the same time, our power over animals has been amplified exponentially by industry and technology." We all remember teachers who have changed our lives. Besides the involvement of Dean Kysar, perhaps the most important factor for the pedagogical success of the program is its sponsorship of roughly three dozen fellowships for graduate and professional students, half from the Law School.[38]

The program began with a traditional animal law course but quickly adapted to more hands-on learning through the spring 2020 launch of its Climate, Animal, Food, and Environmental Law & Policy Lab (CAFE Lab), a mini-clinic dedicated to training legal advocates and solving problems. Other initiatives include a podcast and a speaker series with a widening array of scholars in the field.

The pandemic temporarily put life on hold in the spring of 2020. The new norm of remote learning altered teaching at all levels of academic life for the next year. Despite this, LEAP was able to put on its most important event yet in its young history when it hosted its Big Ag and Antitrust Conference in January 2021, shortly before President Joe Biden's inauguration. We saw in Chapter 3 how monopolistic economic power bends public policy against farm animal welfare. Enforcement of existing antitrust law is a potent weapon in the arsenal of regulators. It is the preferred tool of the New Brandeis school of antitrust scholars, such as President Biden's head of the Federal Trade Commission, Columbia professor Lina Khan.[39]

Yale was a fitting place for the incubation and exploration of such regulation. Unlike in the business world, academic conferences are fora where draft manuscripts and journal articles are subjected to scrutiny that improves them for submission and publication. The conference was cosponsored by the university's Thurmond Arnold Project, an initiative launched in 2019 in honor of the Yale law professor who headed the U.S. Antitrust Division from 1938 to 1943.[40] As part of a virtual conference, and in a year in which scholars could spend more time writing, these academic brainstorming sessions could prove a fertile ground for scholarship that moves public policy toward the humane treatment of animals. It may seem esoteric, but these events are where many well-conceived regulations originate, particularly in Democratic administrations. While politics is driven by money and personality, policy is written by lawyers.[41] For example, within the field of agriculture, President Biden's July 2021 executive order on competition targeted enforcement of the Packers and Stockyards Act and the contract poultry "tournament" system, both discussed in our chapter on farmers.[42]

It is far too early to gauge the effectiveness of this program until new scholarship and future graduates begin to make their mark on the world. "This is an opportunity that my classmates and I are genuinely ecstatic about," said Manny Rutinel, YLS '22.[43]

FAITH IN THE FUTURE

The imperatives of effective altruism, for those who believe in its tenets, are worth paying attention to and contemplating. Is donating to animal law programs the best action to take with limited resources? Brad Goldberg had an interesting take on measurement bias in effective altruism:

> The Effective Altruism movement is all the rage, and I have some concerns that it could be causing a misallocation of funding away from great organizations and projects where results cannot be easily measured on a short-term basis. Foundations and individual donors should be confident their philanthropy will best serve the

issues they are most passionate about, but that does not necessarily mean that those expected results can be measured in an evidence-based methodology. When I look back over our grant program, including our more recent focus on funding academic programs, I can find many examples of what I believe were great funding opportunities that would not have met the criteria of an evidence-based approach.[44]

The roughly one half of 1 percent of American farm animal philanthropy spent on law schools and legal education seems a path of high risk and high reward if one assumes those donations are fungible. There may well be instances when such gifts are non-fungible and would not be spent on other farm animal organizations, such as the support of the Brooks Institute for Animal Rights Law and Policy, university alumni, or other new donors attracted by the prestige of these institutions. Leaving non-fungible gifts aside, in my opinion, the effective altruism case for legal education is still open. It is hard to estimate the marginal utility of even one brilliant young mind dedicating their career to farm animal protection, but the value could be substantial. Those interested in animal law who do not enter the field can incorporate animal protection into their future careers through board membership, *pro bono* service, or charitable fundraising.

The vision of the Harvard and Yale leadership put those universities and Lewis & Clark at the forefront of animal law. In the short term, donations to other charities likely help animals more. Recall the words of Emily Dickinson's poem from our introduction. Education and writing are acts of faith and hope in the future. These institutions' graduates may help solve some of the movement's workforce problems.

If law schools continue to inspire a generation of scholars and leaders who would otherwise enter other fields, time and resources will have been well spent. In 2022, the previous century's questions surrounding the legitimacy of animal law have been made moot.

8

DREAMERS

The Good Food Institute and Clean Meat

If we want to eliminate farm animal suffering, there are only two options: every human on Earth must become vegan, which will never happen, or we must eat clean meat grown outside of animals. This thesis—actually, a tautology—has transformed the *avant garde* of the farm animal movement over the last five years. When the once unthinkable had been achieved through perspicacious campaigners pursuing corporate and legislative reforms, the drive to make clean meat a reality was the province of dreamers. Animal activists were not trained in hard science or competitive businesses, but the unavoidable logic of clean meat demanded a concerted moonshot.

In the middle of the last decade, clean meat was scientifically possible but too expensive for commercialization. To make it viable, dozens of new businesses would have to be catalyzed and several scientific breakthroughs in the esoteric field of animal muscle stem cell physiology would have to be realized.

Scientific revolution is historically the more conventional path to animal liberation. Consider the Tale of Two Henrys: Henry Bergh and Henry Ford. Bergh was perhaps the animal kingdom's foremost advocate in American history.[1] After returning from a diplomatic post in Russia, where he witnessed trolley horses beaten to death in the streets, "alone, in the face of indifference, opposition, and ridicule, he began a reform that is now recognized as one of the greatest beneficent movements of the age," the *New York Times* eulogized.[2] The tactics and risk appetite of the founder of the American Society for the Prevention of Cruelty to Animals would be recognized and lauded by today's most able public advocates and undercover investigators. On one fearless night, Bergh climbed "with a policeman to the roof of a bloody dogfighting den run by a Five Points gang leader." The officer then descended "through the skylight, catching the perpetrators in the act." "Notoriety is wanted," Bergh declared.[3] "Bergh's own approach was fiercer; he had less faith in human nature," notes a review of his biography. "He thought the fear of arrest was a stronger deterrent than moral suasion."[4]

The antisemitic Henry Ford was hardly an animal lover or humanitarian. Yet it was not the ASPCA but the Model T that liberated American equines. Napoleon said that "men are moved by two levers only: fear and self-interest." Bergh would likely agree.

The logic of liberating farm animals through clean meat demanded that animal advocates attempt to accelerate its commercialization. In 2015, Mercy For Animals provided seed funding of $500,000 to spin off a nonprofit venture think tank, the Good Food Institute, helmed by Bruce Friedrich, one of the movement's most effective leaders and strategic thinkers.[5] "We've tried to convince the world to go vegan, and it has not worked," Friedrich conceded.[6] It was a different Tale of Two: Bruce Friedrich, vegan activist, would try to become Bruce Friedrich, venture capitalist.

Friedrich pushed not only a different tack but a different mindset. "I don't care much if vegetarians or vegans are supportive," he told *New York Times Magazine*.[7] Friedrich was right—and it is one reason why this book's first chapter on politics focused on family farmers. As noted in the previous chapter, vegans are less popular than atheists and a step above drug addicts, according to one poll.[8] If someone wants to start an organization to help farm animals and not just preach to the choir, a good start for a name would be one that repels the most vegans. I write this as a decade-long vegan.

Friedrich had the requisite emotional intelligence. "He always had this ability to see potential friends and allies where others would only see enemies," Nathan Milo Runkle said of his mentor.[9] Friedrich's acumen and fundraising abilities catapulted the nonprofit to the forefront of the clean meat space. Before its 2015 launch, Friedrich had already secured commitments of more than $1 million. In 2016, the organization raised $3 million, followed by $5.3 million, $8.4 million, and an astonishing $21.6 million in the years 2017 to 2019, respectively.[10]

Though certainly not all of the field's successes can be attributed to GFI, its effect on the clean and plant-based meat worlds has been remarkable. We can even thank GFI for the term "clean meat," adopted after it conducted two consumer polls as one of its first initiatives in 2016.[11] Through 2019, there had been about $1 million invested in public clean meat research in history; by mid-2021, GFI alone had invested more than $7 million.[12] But that is not the real metric of success. "Cellular agriculture has been exclusively the practice of the academy for more than a decade, and it seems to me that leaving it there will guarantee that we don't have a product on the market for at least another decade," Friedrich says.[13] Whereas Impossible Foods, inventor of the Impossible Burger, had raised $9 million in 2011, the sector it helped create raised a staggering $5 billion in 2021.

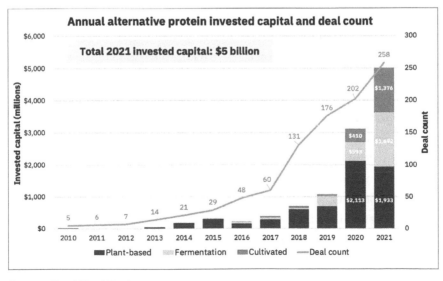

Source: Good Food Institute

Before this revolution, clean meat was a curiosity neatly summarized by two scientific events. First, NASA funded a proof of concept study purportedly assessing the viability of growing meat in space. More accurately, it was the type of moonshot basic government research that private industry would not fund. In 2001, a team led by Morris Benjaminson at Touro University in New York City cut strips of muscle from goldfish and placed them in fetal bovine serum, a conventional cell growth medium. After a week, the muscles had not died but had grown by 14 percent. "To get some idea whether the new muscle tissue would make acceptable food, they washed it and gave it a quick dip in olive oil flavored with lemon, garlic and pepper," a scientific journalist wrote. "Then they fried it and showed it to colleagues from other departments."[14] "We wanted to make sure it'd pass for something you could buy in the supermarket," Benjaminson noted. "They said it looked like fish and smelled like fish, but they didn't go as far as tasting it." This event was little noticed outside of a niche audience. But the researchers proved it could be done.

Authors of the most thorough historical review of clean meat delineate first and second waves of development.[15] The first was inaugurated with the NASA goldfish experiment and staccato research attempts at a handful of American, Western European, and Israeli universities. One artistic project, "initially developed during a residency at Harvard Medical School in 2000 [. . .] produced semi-living steaks from prenatal sheep cells, before later growing steaks from living frog cells, [which] were eaten at the world's first clean meat dinner party as part of their Disembodied Cuisine exhibition at L'art Biotech, Le Lieu Unique, Nantes, France, in 2003." The project "sought to engender discussion about the transgressive status of the tissue, as the frog muscle was consumed with the live frogs from which the cells were sourced also sitting at the dinner table." This stunt marked the historic first consumption of clean meat, but the optics would not exactly endear it to gastronomes or a broader audience. Other researchers deserve credit for working on the subject, as does PETA for offering a $1 million prize in 2008 for the first team demonstrating commercialization of clean chicken meat. The visionary behind that campaign was then PETA vice president Bruce Friedrich.

The biggest challenge facing the first wave of clean meat was funding. Many research proposals were submitted to governmental funding bodies in multiple countries, but met with no success. One core barrier was that clean meat remained a fundamentally novel concept that blurred existing categories. It did not fit well with funders that usually support tissue engineering research, because it was aiming to produce food. Equally, it did not fit well with funders that usually support food research, because it was tissue engineering. The ambiguity over its status meant it sat uncomfortably along the established disciplinary lines of university funding mechanisms. While we cannot evidence this, we hypothesize another barrier to attaining government finance was that the funding bodies may simply not have believed clean meat was a viable technology, more akin to science fiction than science fact, and possibly even that clean meat was stigmatized as an oddball science.[16]

The stigma of the "oddball science" would continue to hamper scientific development until advocates with better public relations skills joined the fray. *New Yorker* science journalist Michael Specter had profiled Peter Singer in 1999 and PETA founder Ingrid Newkirk in 2003. In 2011, Specter, who now also holds an adjunct professorship in bioengineering at Stanford, turned his attention to clean meat for his longform "Test-Tube Burgers."[17] Specter's feature made the ethical and environmental arguments for clean meat that have since become mainstream.

Specter interviewed Mark Post of Maastricht University in the Netherlands. Post, a respected surgeon and researcher who had been a professor at Harvard Medical School, had in recent years become an acolyte for the possibilities of clean meat. "I am a scientist, and my family always respected me for that," he remarked wistfully. "When I started basically spending my time trying to make the beginning of a hamburger, they would give me a pitiful look, as if to say, 'You have completely degraded yourself.'" His lamentation was followed by a paragraph that caught the eye of a far-sighted reader who would help launch the second wave of clean meat. "If what you want is to grow muscle cells and produce a useful source of animal protein in a lab, well, we can do that today," Post said.

The first hamburger will be incredibly expensive. Somebody calculated five thousand dollars. The skills you need to grow a small amount of meat in a laboratory are not necessarily those that would permit you to churn out ground beef by the ton. To do that will require money and public interest. We don't have enough of either right now. That I do not understand, because, while I am no businessman, there certainly seems to be a market out there.

The reader was a very good businessman: Google co-founder Sergey Brin.

Brin provided initially anonymous funding to Post to grow the first clean meat hamburger. More importantly, they orchestrated a masterful public relations event. The invited global media was veritably seduced by the demonstration, as exemplified by the *Washington Post*'s tantalizing coverage:[18]

> The scene in Riverside Studios in West London, where the event took place, looked like something you might see on a TV cooking show: There was a fake kitchen counter, a tiny sink, a single burner and, of course, a chef—Richard McGeown, who has worked with such culinary stars as Gordon Ramsay. The five-ounce burger patty—which cost more than $330,000 to produce and was paid for by Google co-founder Sergey Brin—arrived under a silver dome and was promptly put onto a pan to sizzle with a dab of butter and a splash of sunflower oil. The smells that drifted off toward the audience (a few invited journalists and scientists) were subtle but unmistakably meaty. Next came the tasting. Besides Post, only two people were allowed to have a bite of the test-tube burger: Josh Schonwald, the American author of "The Taste of Tomorrow," and Hanni Rützler, an Austrian nutritional scientist. Both said the burger tasted "almost" like a conventional one.

The tech mogul helped scientists previously dismissed as quacks seize the imagination of Silicon Valley.

> It provided what remains the defining moment for the emergence of clean meat technology, setting in place a coherent vision for what clean meat is and what it can accomplish that has remained

the robust and dominant account within the clean meat collective imagination. By staging the public eating of clean meat, the burger event asserted its realness, and realness as food. It set the template for making sense of making meat, as meat as we know it, and a technology designed for environmental, human health, and animal welfare benefits. The PR sensibility of the event brought a new aesthetic to the field, focused on style, slickness, and confidence. It was also significant in signaling a shift toward funding from commercial but mission-based Silicon Valley and Bay-area sources. In this regard, it sowed the seeds for the vision and economic underpinning of clean meat's second wave.[19]

Since then, we have seen a third wave inaugurated by the most momentous event in the history of clean and plant-based meat: the launch of the Beyond Meat IPO in 2019. On its first day, share price increased 163 percent and led global coverage as the largest percentage increase for any IPO that year.[20] As its stock surged in two months from $25 to nearly $250 per share, the financial press was agog. A Bloomberg researcher confirmed it was the most lucrative IPO for any American company going back to "at least 2008."[21] "Meteoric success," rhapsodized the Motley Fool in paradigmatic coverage.[22] Reflecting Napoleon's maxim, the Beyond Meat IPO proved that, regardless of individuals' ethics or politics, there were billions of dollars of opportunity. The plant-based foods sector had $14 billion in sales globally in 2019. Barclay's forecasts this will increase to $140 billion by the end of this decade.[23]

An interviewer asked Friedrich in 2009 about his dreams for the future. "If you had the power to change one person's stance on animal rights, whose would it be, and why?" "I'd change Bill Gates into a hardcore animal rights activist," Friedrich responded. "So that he would dedicate most of his billions to promoting animal rights."[24] Within a decade, Gates would be one of the lead investors in numerous plant-based and clean meat startups.[25] In 2021, Gates flatly stated that "all rich countries should move to 100 percent synthetic beef."[26] Even better, Cargill, Perdue, and Tyson all launched plant-based products and invested venture capital in this space, which will help with cost, distribution, marketing, and consumer acceptance.[27] Support from Big

Meat can move the needle not just economically but politically: Tyson alone has spent more than $25 million lobbying Congress since 2000.[28] It is a strange and welcome turn of events for animals who need all the help they can get.

EVANGELISTS

The promises of clean meat have often been a double-edged sword. On the one hand, boosters sell a dream that appeals to humanity's sensibilities for technological solutions to global problems. Dietary behavior change can work to reduce meat consumption, but affordable clean meat means that people will not have to change their behavior.[29] Depending on one's viewpoint, it is the promise, or the false idol, of neoliberalism: society can solve problems through capitalism; individuals can solve them through consumption. "We need to change the meat, because we aren't going to change human nature," Friedrich states.[30] On the other hand, business advocates can downplay or ignore the enormous technical barriers, from lipocytes to scaffolding to serum and other hurdles covered in the scientific press and academic literature.[31] Readers following the progress of clean meat over the past decade have seen that rose-colored thinking has often crossed the line into promises that cannot be kept. We saw in the chapter on the Humane Society of the United States that the failure to confront reality for what leaders insist is the greater good of helping animals can end up doing the opposite. The movement cannot subsume facts to wishful thinking or worse.

Billion Dollar Burger author Chase Purdy forthrightly recognizes this paradox. He describes Hampton Creek/Eat Just founder Josh Tetrick as what he is: a world-class evangelist. "He's a marketing maven with a skimpy science background who somehow found his way to the top of a relatively tiny field in the world of food," Purdy writes. "His success is undeniable, even to his harshest critics. And one thing is for sure: He talks a good talk."[32]

Tetrick may be overly enthusiastic about some of his claims, but critics should at a minimum give the University of Michigan Law School graduate and former Fulbright scholar and his company their due for inventing a successful consumer product, which is no easy feat.[33] Eat

Just credibly claims to have displaced the purchase of 100 million eggs with Just Mayo, and thus prevented 100 million days of battery-cage hens' suffering.[34] The latest funding round valued the company at $1.2 billion. If Tetrick ever decides to cash out, he will likely find himself a centimillionaire, perhaps more. It is an astonishing arc for the son of an itinerant laborer and a hairdresser.[35]

Pat Brown, founder of Impossible Foods, is another evangelist. Like many of his fellow travelers, the former pediatrician and Stanford biochemistry professor came to his epiphany after other career milestones. By age forty, he had invented the DNA microarray, an indispensable tool for scientists to study genomes. That invention would likely have made him a multibillionaire had he privatized it. His public spirit then led him and other eminences to co-found the Public Library of Science in 2001 to provide free global access to scientific papers.

Instead of resting on either of these laurels at the university, company, or on the island of his choice, he contemplated how to best use his limited time remaining on Earth. Brown took an eighteen-month sabbatical in 2009 and 2010 to address what he saw as the world's most dire environmental problem: animal agriculture. Brown used his contacts to organize a major conference in Washington, D.C., in 2010 on "The Role of Animal Agriculture in a Sustainable 21st Century Global Food System." The conference had all the trappings of a milestone event, but Brown saw that it "caused not a ripple." "I started doing the typical misguided academic approach to the problem," he realized.[36] "But the most powerful, subversive tool on Earth is the free market. If you can take a problem and figure out a solution that involves making consumers happier, you're unstoppable."

And so, in 2011, and nearing sixty, he launched Impossible Foods. First, he needed investors. "My actual pitch, if you showed it to a business school class, would've had people rolling in the aisles because it was so amateurish," he admits. But he could tell potential investors, with complete conviction: What I am proposing is going to make you even more obscenely rich than you already are. "I didn't say it in quite those words," he notes, "but I knew that this was something that was going to be incredibly successful. And that worked."[37]

His key scientific insight was that hamburger meat got its taste mostly from heme, the iron-affixing molecule in red blood cells.[38] He solved the taste problem that had long bedeviled veggie burgers. "This is not a product for vegetarians," he proudly announced.[39] He presciently turned down a purported $200 million to $300 million acquisition offer from Google in 2015.[40] By April 2021, the company's market cap was estimated at $10 billion.[41] "Pat Brown can't walk down the street without tripping over a venture capitalist," an employee marveled.[42]

REALITY CHECK

Animal advocates should dream big. Perhaps we must in order to stay sane. So it is no surprise that the best reporting on the technical barriers to clean meat landed with a thud.[43] The experts said it was impossible, yet that word does not reflect the magnitude of the impossibilities.

> A sequence of as-yet-unforeseen breakthroughs will still be necessary. We'll need to train cells to behave in ways that no cells have behaved before. We'll need to engineer bioreactors that defy widely accepted principles of chemistry and physics. We'll need to build an entirely new nutrient supply chain using sustainable agricultural practices, inventing forms of bulk amino acid production that are cheap, precise, and safe. Investors will need to care less about money. Germs will have to more or less behave. It will be work worthy of many Nobel prizes—certainly for science, possibly for peace. And this expensive, fragile, infinitely complex puzzle will need to come together in the next ten years.

The exposé is a hard read for those who care about animals. The numbers do not work. Taking GFI's own commissioned report, which, the author notes, should be taken with a shaker of salt, a clean meat factory producing 0.0002, "or one fiftieth of 1 percent," of all the meat in the United States annually, would cost $450 million. "If cultured protein is going to be even 10 percent of the world's meat supply by 2030, we will need 4,000 factories like the one GFI envisions, according to an analysis by the trade publication *Food Navigator*. To meet that deadline, building at a rate of one mega-facility a day would be too slow. All of those facilities would also come with a heart-stopping price tag: a minimum of $1.8 trillion." Again, this is merely using GFI's assumptions.

The author accuses Open Phil, albeit unfairly, of "burying" a feasibility report that the organization posted on its web page. Nevertheless, the report states in no uncertain terms that the economic barriers are insurmountable.

The author, quoting Open Phil's and others' independent experts, points out the difficulties in ensuring bioreactors do not become contaminated. Clean meat cannot be grown at industrial scale in breweries, as the conventional, avuncular image holds. It must be grown in pharmaceutical-style clean rooms.

> "Bacteria grow every 20 minutes, and the animal cells are stuck at 24 hours," says Dr. David Humbird, Open Phil's consultant. "You're going to crush the culture in hours with a contamination event." Viruses also present a unique problem. Because cultured animal cells are alive, they can get infected just the way living animals can. "There are documented cases of, basically, operators getting the culture sick," Humbird said. "Not even because the operator themselves had a cold. But there was a virus particle on a glove. Or not cleaned out of a line. The culture has no immune system. If there's virus particles in there that can infect the cells, they will. And generally, the cells just die, and then there's no product anymore. You just dump it."[44]

The clean rooms necessary for growing industrial clean meat triple the cost of GFI's estimates.

Growing clean meat without fetal bovine serum is also currently impossible. One analysis found that doing so increases the cost of production to $10,000 per pound, though GFI claims it would cost $8. "They say, 'Oh, but these costs are just going to go away in five years or ten years,'" Huw Hughes, a former Pfizer scientist, said. "And there's no explanation as to how or why."

The pharmaceutical industry has itself been dealing with related issues of cell-growth efficiency for decades. It has invested many billions of dollars for far more lucrative products than clean meat and still cannot get around the fact that cells excrete waste, and there is thus a physical limit to the size of bioreactors. "It would be a David and Goliath story of the most gripping and impactful kind: A fledgling industry musters an unthinkable scientific breakthrough that entrenched power players have been chasing for years, and in a shorter time period, with just a fraction of the cash."

Such skepticism, or acknowledgement of reality, does not come from just top independent researchers. The equipment necessary to scale up clean meat has not been invented. "I can't go to any company that engineers bioreactors and say, 'Can you please deliver a 100,000-liter reactor to this location in Doha in three months?'" Josh Tetrick says. "What they would say to me is, 'We have never, nor has any company in the world ever, designed and engineered a 100,000-liter reactor for animal cell culture. This has never happened before.'"

"To me this sounds like the story of the Emperor's Clothes," says Paul Wood, the former executive director of global discovery for Pfizer Animal Health. "It's a fable driven by hope, not science, and when the investors finally realize this the market will collapse."

Clean meat does not have to outcompete conventional meat, nor should we ignore the real successes of plant-based meat. But animal advocates taking the promise of clean meat on hope should seriously consider the science.

ECONOMICS

Pat Brown does not believe clean meat holds much promise.[45] "Some of the entrepreneurs I interviewed told me about issues they had getting funding in Silicon Valley explicitly due to Pat Brown's negative views," writes Jacy Reese in *The End of Animal Farming*.[46] "I'm glad Pat Brown is working hard on plant-based meat, but his sweeping dismissal of promising alternative technology is unwarranted." Progress over the last few years seems to have proven Reese right.

However, Brown is correct insofar as proselytizers envision a future of clean chicken breasts underselling and ultimately replacing conventional meat at Walmart. Chicken meat is too efficient, and growing 3D tissue is not yet possible. Even if it were possible, it would be too costly to compete. While the holy grail may be to replace Chick-fil-A with clean filets, given the numbers and suffering of that species, any other animal product is more expensive and thus has better economic prospects. Chickens are just too efficient, as a trip to the grocery store attests. Eat Just reports that one of its clean meat chicken nuggets costs about fifty dollars to produce, or a pound costs a thousand dollars.[47] Nevertheless, consumers are already willing to pay a substantial premium for plant-based meat, so commercial success need not rely on cost parity.

The path to success for clean meat may follow that of the Tesla model. Elon Musk understood that he would not be able to outcompete hydrocarbon Fords and Toyotas with his prohibitively expensive electric batteries. In 2006, he released his "Master Plan," summarized as: "Build sports car; Use that money to build an affordable car; Use *that* money to build an even more affordable car; While doing above, also provide zero emission electric power generation options."[48]

Two restaurants in the world have served cultured chicken meat. The Chicken, an Israeli startup, launched in fall 2020 during the COVID-19 pandemic.[49] The upscale restaurant near Tel Aviv offers its chicken burger, made with half cultured chicken cells and half plant-based meat, for free. (It cannot charge customers for food that has not yet been approved by Israeli regulators.) Meals are served in a chic bar with a glass wall adjoining the production plant, which produces about five hundred pounds of meat each week.[50] How much does it actually cost to produce? Thirty-five dollars per chicken burger, according to vegan CEO Ido Savir.[51] This is pricey but would not be out of place on menus in any global city.

The other restaurant is in Singapore, whose government granted the first-ever regulatory approval to sell clean meat. In December 2020, Eat Just partnered with the trendy 1880 restaurant to offer, over three days, a special meal with three types of clean chicken tapas, each "influenced by a top chicken-producing country in the world: China, Brazil, and the United States," *Food and Wine* reported. "The Chinese-influenced dish will feature a bao bun, crispy sesame cultured chicken, spring onion, and pickled cucumber; Brazil will be represented by phyllo puff pastry, cultured chicken, black bean purée, crispy garlic, and lime; and the U.S. dish will have Southern flair with a crispy maple waffle and cultured chicken with spices and hot sauce."[52] "This chicken, it's just chicken, but it's the most amazing thing I've ever seen or ever tasted," said one of the first tasters, a twelve-year-old epicurean with a bright future as a clean meat spokesperson.[53] "It's definitely made me see how small things, like changing the way we eat, can literally change our entire lives." The price? Just $23, reportedly sold at cost.[54]

Clean meat is currently expensive, but so are many other kinds of animal products. Kobe beef and shark fin meat each cost a few hundred dollars per pound.[55] A pound of bluefin tuna costs about two hundred dollars.[56] Science fiction possibilities at a higher price point could appeal to a tiny audience with limitless resources. For example, famed Harvard biochemist George Church, who successfully inserted woolly mammoth DNA into Asian elephant cells, suggests that woolly mammoth clean meat is a possibility.[57] You could eat meat grown from your favorite celebrity.[58] In theory, science can use CRISPR gene editing to produce "unicorn meat," or a unique meat optimized for human taste buds or even individual palates. To borrow from Ford and Musk, "sports car" meat with higher price points can provide the capital for "even more affordable" clean meat for mass consumers.

The "sports car" furthest along is clean foie gras, which holds a number of advantages over other high-end animal products. First, at a hundred dollars or more per pound, it has one of the highest price points of any food. Gourmey, a French company pursuing this idea, raised an additional $10 million in venture capital in July 2021.[59] Gourmey reports its current cost of production is five hundred dollars per pound. Second, avoiding a technical hurdle faced by Kobe beef and other muscles or organs, foie gras is often thinly served on toast, so it does not need to be grown in a 3D tissue. Third, foie gras has faced a major public backlash based on animal welfare concerns. Its production or sale has been banned by dozens of countries and corporations, as well as in New York City and California. Clean foie gras thus would enjoy a monopoly where "dirty" foie gras is banned.

POLICY

Three policy battlegrounds are shaping the future of clean and plant-based meat in America.

Rearguard labeling laws have seen by far the most action. The initial business and marketing successes of plant-based milk and the Beyond and Impossible Burgers spooked Big Meat and engendered a political backlash. Andy Berry, executive vice president of the Mississippi Cattlemen's Association, said they "looked at where dairy was twenty years ago and there's a consensus that no one wants to end up where dairy is with these alternative products."[60] Plant-based milks have undergone a Cambrian explosion of innovation over the last twenty years. The category, encompassing almond, cashew, coconut, oat, rice, soy, and other indulgences, has taken a 15 percent market share of the milk market and is growing at twice the pace of cow's milk.[61] Big Meat's strategy, which found a welcome constituency in the co-opted legislatures of agricultural states, was to prevent plant-based meat companies from labeling their products as "meat." The National Cattlemen's Beef Association has been the primary driver of this legislation.[62] Similar bills, many with identical language, have been introduced in twenty-four states and quickly passed in fourteen.[63] All were midwestern or southern farm states, from Montana to Georgia, with the exception of Maine.[64] These laws have not, so far as can be determined, had any effect whatsoever outside of the courtroom.[65] They are a sideshow, in my opinion, and take energy away from more fruitful avenues. It actually seems to increase sales if plant-based meat products' labels explicitly state they are plant-based and not animal meat. As noted, Big Meat has become an investor in this space; consequently, some of the legislative pressure has attenuated over the last two years.

On the regulatory battleground, clean meat opponents and advocates were married when an interesting political compromise was reached. The federal government has anticipated the rapidly approaching commercialization of clean meat and solicited comments as to a regulatory framework from 2017 to 2019. I attended the joint USDA–Health and Human Services conference in the autumn of 2018 as an observer. Animal advocates wanted the Food and Drug Administration to regulate clean meat and Big Ag wanted the USDA's Food Safety and Inspection

Service to regulate it; both sides felt that either of those agencies would be more amenable to their own viewpoints. In 2019, FDA–FSIS agreed to jointly regulate clean meat.[66] The Food Safety Modernization for Innovative Technologies Act was introduced on December 16, 2019, with two cosponsors: Senator Mike Enzi (R-WY) and Senator Michael Bennet (D-CO).[67] Their bill codifies the compromise agreement regulating clean meat manufacturing and sales and is essentially a copied-and-pasted version of the extant framework agreement. It was left on the table in subcommittee, the agreement having already been accepted at the agency level.

The final and most important area for clean meat public policy is appropriations. The entry of state agricultural universities and wealthy factory farm corporations into clean meat innovation over the last five years is a promising development. "I want Tyson Foods and other meat companies to be a part of this movement," says New Harvest's executive director, Isha Datar.[68] The Good Food Institute and New Harvest gave initial grants for clean meat research at the University of California–Davis in 2019.[69] In 2020, the National Science Foundation provided UC Davis with a $3.55 million grant over five years for research and training in clean meat.[70] Meanwhile, avian muscle physiologist Paul Mozdziak leads clean meat research at North Carolina State's Department of Poultry Science, thanks to a grant from New Harvest.[71] Clean meat public research can produce scientific breakthroughs that private companies can use to bring products to market. This is precisely how the agricultural, military–industrial, and pharmaceutical industries work: we can thank public scientific research for developing cell phones, computers, GPS, the internet, cheap chicken meat, and many other foundations of our dynamic economy.

The most fertile battleground for clean meat advocates is in the area of federal appropriations. Unfortunately, the political capacity of the farm animal movement was not yet deployed effectively at the congressional level in 2020. The organizations that should be driving change had not yet scaled up their lobbying teams to be able to address issues successfully in Washington. Because of the pandemic, the writing was on the wall by early summer of 2020 that Joe Biden would win the election and enact a massive stimulus bill during his honeymoon period. The time to begin lobbying for clean meat basic research was then.

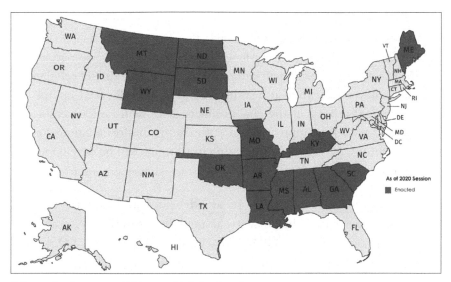

US map showing status of "fake meat" labeling laws by state
Source: National Ag Law Center

The opportunity to tap into the gusher of stimulus money has passed, but leading politicians, like Senators Cory Booker and Richard Blumenthal and Representatives Earl Blumenauer and Ro Khanna, along with staff at GFI and MFA and a network of donors led by Ari Nessel, have begun to work together to give farm animal welfare a seat at the negotiating table. Representative Rosa DeLauro, chair of the House Appropriations Committee, was a committed proponent of clean meat research funding by the Department of Agriculture as President Biden's first budget was negotiated during the 2021–2023 congressional session. "We should pursue parity in research funding for alternative proteins," she said in an April 2021 hearing with Agriculture Secretary Tom Vilsack. "The United States can continue to be a global leader on alternative protein science, and these technologies can play an important role in combating climate change and adding resiliency to our food system."[72] DeLauro's work achieved extraordinary results. She inserted a $10 million rider for the USDA into a House appropriations bill that ultimately passed. This funding will be used over five years in a joint, open-access partnership led by Tufts.

Virginia Tech will be carrying out research in many of the same areas as Tufts, such as cell isolations from other species, improvement of the meat in terms of authentic flavor and texture, nutritional analysis, and consumer acceptance. The University of California at Davis will be focused on food science, while the University of Massachusetts, Boston will gather data on sustainability of cellular agriculture. Research at Virginia State will be focused on the nutritional aspects of the new products. MIT will be focused on AI and modeling approaches to optimize media formulations for cell culture. All of our collaborating institutions will be developing educational programs to facilitate workforce development, too.[73]

Focused energy from clean meat advocates and donors speaking with one voice can achieve a great deal in Congress. A concerted federal political strategy is still in its early stages, but this single-line item dedicated more public funding to clean meat research than had ever been donated by all philanthropists in history. And this research is all public. Given that most politicians are transactional, money spent on lobbying and campaign contributions for politicians supporting clean meat research funding is probably the best investment the movement can make.

REALIZING THE DREAM

We saw in the previous chapter that pursuing animal law was once considered limiting, or not something that people with fancy degrees should do. Clean meat is for dreamers. "I'd been building this career toward a professorship," recalled an Impossible Foods convert who was hired away from a postdoctoral fellowship at the University of California–San Francisco. "But when I interviewed here, the culture and the scientific questions were so compelling that I actually walked away from everything. I spent a long weekend torturing over it, and the thing that tipped the scales was that I realized this was the one thing I could do as a scientist that would make the biggest impact on the world."[74]

"There's a big phenomenon of people self-censoring, worrying about the imposter syndrome," says Pat Brown. "There's no road map for what we're doing. But someone has to solve this problem."[75] Gifted people have even more reason to dedicate themselves to solving impossible problems. The creative entrepreneurs highlighted here come from fields as diverse as biochemistry, business, food service, journalism, law, philanthropy, politics, and vegan activism. For college students, the quickest path that can make the most difference may well be business school. "We were always raised with this false choice," Tetrick notes. "You can either work for a nonprofit and do a lot of good and not make any money, or you can work for a company and not do a lot of good, but maybe you can donate."[76] Those who have the scientific or financial talents to help make clean meat a reality should consider devoting themselves to it. "It really is a way that you can save the world," says Friedrich.[77] Clean meat, along with plant-based meat, is saving lives and minting billionaires. It is the most high-risk, high-reward field of farm animal welfare for any who wants to accept the challenge.

The clean meat wing of the animal movement has transcended its humble beginnings in the imaginations of proselytizers. Economic success has lured the genie out of the bottle, and the language and framing of the American farm animal movement can shift from regulation and cost to freedom and profit.[78] This is the riveting denouement of the moral revolution spurred by visionaries who saw defenseless animals tortured on local farms and sought to do everything they could to stop it.

There can never be one history of the farm animal movement in America. Many courageous personal histories constitute a transcendent collective journey. The farm animal movement shows human potential at its most altruistic. The stories of people like Leah Garcés are ones we should teach our children.

Ending innocent beings' suffering is your responsibility. How you help achieve the dream is what only you can know. "The things to do are: the things that need doing, that *you* see need to be done, and that no one else seems to see need to be done."[79]

What will you do to change the world?

SELECTED FURTHER READING

Abate, Randall (ed.). *What Can Animal Law Learn from Environmental Law?* Environmental Law Institute. 2015.

Adams, Carol. *The Sexual Politics of Meat: A Feminist-Vegetarian Critical Theory* (25th ann. ed.). Bloomsbury Revelations. 2015.

Animal Law Review. Available open access at https://law.lclark.edu/law_reviews/animal_law_review/past_issues/.

Animals24-7. https://www.animals24-7.org/.

Babiak, Paul, and Robert Hare. *Snakes in Suits: When Psychopaths Go to Work.* Harper Business. 2007.

Balcombe, Jonathan. *What a Fish Knows: The Inner Lives of Our Underwater Cousins.* Scientific American; Farrar, Straus and Giroux. 2016.

Ball, Matt, and Bruce Friedrich. *The Animal Activists' Handbook.* Lantern. 2009.

Baur, Gene. *Farm Sanctuary: Changing Hearts and Minds about Animals and Food.* Touchstone. 2008.

Eisnitz, Gail. *Slaughterhouse: The Shocking Story of Greed, Neglect, and Inhumane Treatment Inside the U.S. Meat Industry.* Prometheus Books. 2006.

Freeman, Carrie. *Framing Farming: Communication Strategies for Animal Rights.* Brill Rodopi. 2014.

Garcés, Leah. *Grilled: Turning Adversaries to Allies to Change the Chicken Industry.* Bloomsbury Sigma. 2019.

Greger, Michael, and Gene Stone. *How Not to Die: Discover the Foods Scientifically Proven to Prevent and Reverse Disease.* Flatiron. 2015.

Hawthorne, Mark. *Striking at the Roots: A Practical Guide to Animal Activism.* Changemakers Books. 2007.

HBR's 10 Must Reads on Emotional Intelligence. Harvard Business Review Press. 2015.

Hiddema, Krista Valerie. *Always for the Animals: Findings and Recommendations for Organizational Governance and Regenerative Practices in the Animal Advocacy Movement as Informed by the Stories of Women Vocational Animal Activists.* DSocSci dissertation. Royal Roads University, Victoria, B.C. 2022.

Imhoff, Daniel (ed.). *CAFO: The Tragedy of Industrial Animal Factories*. Watershed Media. 2010.

Kysar, Douglas. *Regulating from Nowhere: Environmental Law and the Search for Objectivity*. Yale University Press. 2010.

Lencioni, Patrick. *The Five Dysfunctions of a Team: A Leadership Fable* (20th anniv. ed.). Jossey-Bass. 2002.

Leonard, Christopher. *The Meat Racket: The Secret Takeover of America's Food Business*. Simon & Schuster. 2014.

Michelson, Brittany (ed.) *Voices for Animal Liberation: Inspirational Accounts by Animal Rights Activists*. Skyhorse Publishing. 2020.

Nestle, Marion. *Food Politics: How the Food Industry Influences Nutrition and Health* (2nd ed.). University of California Press. 2007.

Norwood, F. Bailey, and Jayson Lusk. *Compassion, by the Pound: The Economics of Farm Animal Welfare*. Oxford University Press. 2011.

Purdy, Chase. *Billion Dollar Burger: Inside Big Tech's Race for the Future of Food*. Penguin. 2020.

Reese, Jacy. *The End of Animal Farming: How Scientists, Entrepreneurs, and Activists Are Building an Animal-Free Food System*. Beacon Press. 2018.

Runkle, Nathan Milo. *Mercy For Animals: One Man's Quest to Inspire Compassion and Improve the Lives of Farm Animals*. Avery, Penguin Random House. 2017.

Scully, Matthew. *Dominion: The Power of Man, the Suffering of Animals, and the Call to Mercy*. St. Martin's Griffin. 2003.

Shapiro, Paul. *Clean Meat: How Growing Meat Without Animals Will Revolutionize Dinner and Save the World*. Gallery Books. 2018.

Singer, Jasmin. (ed.). *Antiracism in Animal Advocacy: Igniting Cultural Transformation*. Lantern. 2021.

Singer, Peter. *Ethics into Action: Henry Spira and the Animal Rights Movement*. Rowman & Littlefield. 1999.

Singer, Peter. *The Most Good You Can Do: How Effective Altruism Is Changing Ideas about Living Ethically*. Yale University Press. 2015.

Stallwood, Kim. *Growl: Life Lessons, Hard Truths, and Bold Strategies from an Animal Advocate*. Lantern. 2014.

Sunstein, Cass, and Martha Nussbaum (eds.). *Animal Rights: Current Debates and New Directions*. Oxford University Press. 2004.

Tauber, Steven. *Navigating the Jungle: Law, Politics, and the Animal Advocacy Movement*. Routledge. 2016.

Wagman, Bruce, Sonia Waisman, and Pamela Frasch. *Animal Law: Cases and Materials* (6th ed.). Carolina Academic Press. 2019.

Westen, Drew. *The Political Brain: The Role of Emotion in Deciding the Fate of the Nation*. PublicAffairs. 2008.

NOTES

Introduction: Ending the World's Worst Suffering

1. Cohan, Jeffrey. "*How Not to Die*: A Plant-Based Diet, the Ultimate Life Saver." *Pittsburgh Post-Gazette*. March 20, 2016.
2. Animal Charity Evaluators. "Why Farmed Animals." https://animalcharityevaluators.org/donation-advice/why-farmed-animals/; Engber, Daniel. "Save the Chicken." *Slate*. August 18, 2016. https://slate.com/technology/2016/08/animal-activists-crunched-the-numbers-to-learn-that-the-creature-most-in-need-of-their-support-was-the-lowly-chicken.html.
3. World Wildlife Fund. "Wildlife: African Lions." https://www.wwf.org.uk/wildlife/african-lions. 2023.
4. Garcés, Leah. *Grilled: Turning Adversaries into Allies to Change the Chicken Industry*. Bloomsbury Press. p. 9. 2019.
5. "The Toni Morrison Interview." *Word: The Soul of Urban Culture*. March 27, 2016. http://wordmag.com/the-toni-morrison-interview/.
6. Ruskin, John. *Sesame and Lilies*. 1865. Paraphrased by Leslie Noelani Laurio. 2013. https://amblesideonline.org/sesame-paraphrase.
7. Marchese, David. "Why Jane Goodall Still Has Hope for Us Humans." *New York Times Magazine*. July 12, 2021.
8. Robbins, John. *The Food Revolution: How Your Diet Can Help Save Your Life and Our World*. Conari. 2010.
9. Eisnitz, Gail. *Slaughterhouse: The Shocking Story of Greed, Neglect, an Inhumane Treatment Inside the U.S. Meat Industry*. Prometheus Books. 2006; Warrick, Jo. "They Die Piece by Piece." *Washington Post*. April 10, 2001.
10. Cassidy, John. "Me Media." *The New Yorker*. May 7, 2006.
11. Open Philanthropy Project. Farm Animal Welfare Organization Revenue, 2010–2019. https://docs.google.com/spreadsheets/d/1P9L5npjtv_cFu0iiddzOyH6pa2510UjMHIO7rlef-rc/edit#gid=1760212531. 2023.
12. Open Philanthropy Project. "Cause Selection." https://www.openphilanthropy.org/research/cause-selection. 2023.

13. Murphy, Mike. "Beyond Meat Soars 163% in Biggest-Popping U.S. IPO Since 2000." *MarketWatch*. May 2, 2019. https://www.marketwatch.com/story/beyond-meat-soars-163-in-biggest-popping-us-ipo-since-2000-2019-05-02.

14. Stone, Zara. "The High Cost of Lab-to-Table Meat." *Wired*. March 8, 2018.

Chapter 1: Numbers Don't Lie:
Effective Altruism and Venture Philanthropy

1. Singer, Peter. *The Most Good You Can Do: How Effective Altruism Is Changing Ideas about Living Ethically*. Yale University Press. 2015. pp. 117–118.

2. Ibid.

3. EffectiveAltruism.org. "Introduction to Effective Altruism." https://www.effectivealtruism.org/articles/introduction-to-effective-altruism/. 2023.

4. Ball, Matt, and Bruce Friedrich. *The Animal Activists' Handbook*. Lantern. 2009. pp. 15–16. This number is in the billions if we include fish.

5. Singer, Peter. *The Most Good You Can Do: How Effective Altruism Is Changing Ideas about Living Ethically*. Yale University Press. 2015. p. 139. The other sources quoted in this paragraph come from ibid, p. 138.

6. Norwood, F. Bailey, and Jayson Lusk. *Compassion, by the Pound: The Economics of Farm Animal Welfare*. Oxford University Press. 2011. Some in the animal movement have criticized their methodology. *See*, e.g., http://www.mattball.org/2014/07/part-1-analyzing-numbers-to-optimize.html.

7. Friedrich, Bruce, and Stefanie Wilson. "Coming Home to Roost: How the Chicken Industry Hurts Chickens, Humans, and the Environment." *Animal Law*, 22(1), 2015. pp. 103–164. If insects warrant consideration, these numbers would change drastically.

8. Leonard, Christopher. *The Meat Racket: The Secret Takeover of America's Food Business*. Simon & Schuster. 2014.

9. Ramstad, Evan. "Perot Sharpens Attacks on Clinton; Renews Criticisms of Bush." Associated Press. November 1, 1992.

10. National Cooperative Extension. "How Long Does It Take for Broiler Chickens to Be Ready for the Market." USDA. https://animal-welfare.extension.org/how-long-does-it-take-for-broiler-chickens-to-be-ready-for-the-market/.

11. Shahbandeh, M. "Global Feed Conversion Ratio of Selected Meat and Fish." Statista. July 9, 2021. https://www.statista.com/statistics/254421/feed-conversion-ratios-worldwide-2010/.

12. Honig, Esther. "JBS Sells U.S.-Based Cattle-Feedlot Business for $200 Million After Brazilian Scandals." *Harvest Public Media*. March 20, 2018. https://www.harvestpublicmedia.org/post/jbs-sells-us-based-cattle-feedlot-business-200-million-after-brazilian-scandals.

13. Harari, Yuval Noah. "Industrial Farming Is One of the Worst Crimes in History." *The Guardian*. September 25, 2015. https://www.theguardian.com/books/2015/sep/25/industrial-farming-one-worst-crimes-history-ethical-question.

14. National Agricultural Statistical Service. "Milk Production 02/20/2020." USDA. February 20, 2020. https://www.nass.usda.gov/Publications/Todays_Reports/reports/mkpr0220.pdf.

15. Royal Society of New Zealand. "Edward George Bollard." July 9, 2012. https://www.royalsociety.org.nz/who-we-are/our-people/our-fellows/obituaries/fellows-obituaries/edward-george-bollard/.

16. Bollard, Lewis. "Animal Atrocities: How Will History Judge Our Treatment of Animals?" *Harvard Crimson*. April 28, 2009. https://www.thecrimson.com/article/2009/4/28/animal-atrocities-i-could-hear-the/.

17. Ibid.

18. Yale Law School. "Lewis Bollard '13 Wins Hogan/Smoger Access to Justice Prize for Essay on Ag-Gag Laws." *YLS Today*. September 12, 2012. https://law.yale.edu/yls-today/news/lewis-bollard-13-wins-hogansmoger-access-justice-prize-essay-ag-gag-laws.

19. Karnofsky, Holden. "Incoming Program Officer: Lewis Bollard." GiveWell. September 11, 2015. https://blog.givewell.org/2015/09/11/incoming-program-officer-lewis-bollard/.

20. Newport, Cal. *Deep Work: Rules for Focused Success in a Distracted World*. Grand Central Publishing. 2016.

21. Bye, Lynette. "Lewis Bollard on Self-Experimentation, Zero Distractions, and Hyper Focus." *Lynette Bye Coaching*. April 27, 2020. https://effectivealtruismcoaching.com/blog/2020/4/27/lewis-bollard-on-self-experimentation-zero-distractions-and-hyper-focus.

22. Wilbin, Robert. "Ending Factory Farming as Soon as Possible." *80,000 Hours*. September 27, 2017. https://80000hours.org/podcast/episodes/lewis-bollard-end-factory-farming/#transcript.

23. National Chicken Council. "US Chicken Consumption: Presentation to Chicken Marketing Summit." July 18, 2017. https://www.nationalchickencouncil.org/wp-content/uploads/2017/07/US3002925_NCC_Consumption_Presentation_Final_170713.pdf. p. 16.

24. Brulliard, Karin. "How Eggs Became a Victory for the Animal Welfare Movement." *Washington Post*. August 6, 2016.

25. Bollard, Lewis. "Initial Grants to Support Cage-Free Reforms." Open Philanthropy Project. March 31, 2016. https://www.openphilanthropy.org/blog/initial-grants-support-corporate-cage-free-reforms.

26. Ibid.

27. Wilbin, Robert. "Ending Factory Farming as Soon as Possible." *80,000 Hours.* September 27, 2017. https://80000hours.org/podcast/episodes/lewis-bollard-end-factory-farming/#transcript.

28. Bollard, Lewis. "Why Are the US Corporate Cafe-Free Campaigns Succeeding?" Open Philanthropy Project. April 11, 2017. https://www.openphilanthropy.org/blog/why-are-us-corporate-cage-free-campaigns-succeeding.

29. Bollard, Lewis. "Initial Grants to Support Cage-Free Reforms." Open Philanthropy Project. March 31, 2016. https://www.openphilanthropy.org/blog/initial-grants-support-corporate-cage-free-reforms. It is important to emphasize that there is a *de minimis* level of giving sufficient to outweigh the cost of and staff time of processing a donation. In practice, although no charity would turn down one dollar, a donation would have to affect what a charity does to make a difference.

30. According to these organizations' yearly 990s tax returns.

31. Open Wing Alliance. "Grants." The Humane League. https://www.openwingalliance.org/grants.

32. Welfare Commitments. "Broiler Commitments." https://welfarecommitments.com/broiler/.

33. Gunther, Marc. "A Think Tank to Benefit Farm Animals." *Nonprofit Chronicles.* September 26, 2017. https://nonprofitchronicles.com/2017/09/26/a-think-tank-to-benefit-farm-animals/.

34. Bollard, Lewis. "The Greenfield Project—General Support." Open Philanthropy Project. July 2017. https://www.openphilanthropy.org/focus/us-policy/farm-animal-welfare/greenfield-project-general-support.

35. Animal Welfare Institute. *Humane Slaughter Update: Federal and State Oversight of the Welfare of Farm Animals at Slaughter.* April 2020. https://awionline.org/sites/default/files/uploads/documents/20HumaneSlaughterUpdate.pdf.

36. Gunther, Marc. "A Think Tank to Benefit Farm Animals." *Nonprofit Chronicles.* September 26, 2017. https://nonprofitchronicles.com/2017/09/26/a-think-tank-to-benefit-farm-animals/.

37. Bollard, Lewis. "Why Is Meat So Cheap?" Open Philanthropy Project. October 2019. https://us14.campaign-archive.com/?u=66df320da8400b581cbc1b539&id=d20cd35b72.

38. The Greenfield Project. "Work." https://www.thegreenfieldproject.org/work/.

39. Flank, Lenny. "Chicken Behavior: The Politics of the Pecking Order." *Hobby Farms.* September 8, 2017. https://www.hobbyfarms.com/pecking-order-chicken-behavior-history-science/.

40. D'Eath, Richard, and Linda Keeling. "Social Discrimination and Aggression by Laying Hens in Large Groups: From Peck Orders to Social Tolerance." *Applied Animal Behavior Science*, 84, 2003. pp. 197–212.

41. Cheng, Heng-wei. "Laying Hen Welfare Fact Sheet: Current Developments in Beak-Trimming." USDA Animal Research Service Livestock Behavior Research Unit. Fall 2010. https://www.ars.usda.gov/ARSUserFiles/50201500/beak%20trimming%20fact%20sheet.pdf.

42. Schuck-Paim, Cynthia, Elsa Negro-Calduch, and Wladimir Alonso. "Laying Hen Mortality in Different Indoor Housing Systems: A Meta-Analysis of Data from Commercial Farms in 16 Countries." *Scientific Reports*, 11(1), 2021. p. 3052.

43. Bollard, Lewis. "Initial Grants to Support Cage-Free Reforms." Open Philanthropy Project. March 31, 2016. https://www.openphilanthropy.org/blog/initial-grants-support-corporate-cage-free-reforms.

44. Bollard, Lewis. "How Will Hen Welfare Be Impacted by the Transition to Cage-Free Housing?" Open Philanthropy Project. April 2017. https://www.openphilanthropy.org/focus/us-policy/farm-animal-welfare/how-will-hen-welfare-be-impacted-transition-cage-free-housing#The_transition_cost_hypothesis.

45. Torrella, Kenny. "The Next Frontier for Animal Welfare: Fish." *Vox.* March 2, 2021. https://www.vox.com/future-perfect/22301931/fish-animal-welfare-plant-based.

46. Sengupta, Somini. "That Salmon on Your Plate Might Have Been a Vegetarian." *New York Times.* March 24, 2021.

47. Ibid.

48. Dean, Cornelia. "Victoria Braithwaite, Researcher Who Said Fish Feel Pain, Dies at 52." *New York Times.* November 1, 2019.

49. New York University. "NYU Launches Center for Environmental and Animal Protection." April 16, 2018. https://www.nyu.edu/about/news-publications/news/2018/april/nyu-launches-center-for-environmental-and-animal-protection.html.

50. Balcombe, Jonathan. *What a Fish Knows: The Inner Lives of our Underwater Cousins.* Scientific American; Farrar, Straus and Giroux. 2016.

51. Mercy For Animals. "Fish." https://fish.mercyforanimals.org/. 2023.

52. Clifton, Merritt. "Mercy For Animals Exposes Cruelty at a Texas Factory Catfish Farm." *Animals 24-7.* March 3, 2011. https://www.animals24-7.org/2011/03/03/mercy-for-animals-exposes-cruelty-at-a-texas-factory-catfish-farm/.

53. Hugo, Kristin. "Graphic Undercover Footage of Dead Dolphins, Sharks Could Make This Fishing Net Illegal." *Newsweek.* May 3, 2018; Gibbons, Sarah. "Shocking Video Shows Impacts of Controversial Fishing Method." *National Geographic.* April 27, 2018; Green, Miranda. "California Passes Bill to Ban Controversial Drift Net Fishing." *The Hill.* August 31, 2018.

54. Aquatic Animal Alliance. https://aquaticanimalalliance.org/.

55. Aquatic Life Institute. "Our First Major Victory: Billions of Lives Improved." February 4, 2021. https://ali.fish/blog/our-first-major-victory.

56. Association of Fundraising Professionals. "80/20 Rule Alive and Well in Fundraising." 2021. http://afpfep.org/blog/8020-rule-alive-well-fundraising/.

57. Farmed Animal Funders. https://farmedanimalfunders.org/. 2023.

58. Rowan, Beth. "How Animal Welfare Fundraisers Pivoted to Meet the COVID-19 Moment." *Inside Philanthropy.* May 7, 2021.

59. Singer, Peter. *The Most Good You Can Do: How Effective Altruism Is Changing Ideas about Living Ethically.* Yale University Press. 2015. pp. 39–41.

60. Greenbaum Foundation. 2018 IRS Form 990.

61. Email on file with author.

62. Email on file with author.

63. Animal Charity Evaluators. "Our History." https://animalcharityevaluators.org/about/background/our-history/. ACE was founded in 2012 as Effective Animal Activism and rebranded under its current name in 2013.

64. Open Philanthropy Project. "Conversation with Paul Shapiro." July 15, 2013. https://www.openphilanthropy.org/sites/default/files/Paul%20Shapiro%20July%2015%202013%20%28public%29.pdf.

65. Open Philanthropy Project. "A Conversation with David Byer of PETA." May 23, 2014. https://www.openphilanthropy.org/sites/default/files/David%20Byer%2005-23-14%20%28public%29.pdf.

66. Charity Entrepreneurship. "How to Make an Impact in Animal Advocacy: A Survey." EA Forum. August 26, 2018. https://forum.effectivealtruism.org/posts/jR2LKoXoL4Aq9T2MQ/how-to-make-an-impact-in-animal-advocacy-a-survey.

67. Smith, Allison. "Our Thinking about the Process Leading to Our December 2014 Recommendations." *Animal Charity Evaluators.* December 1, 2014. https://animalcharityevaluators.org/blog/thinking-process-leading-december-2014-recommendations/.

68. Animal Charity Evaluators. "Conversations with Advocacy Leaders." December 2019. https://animalcharityevaluators.org/charity-reviews/charity-conversations/.

69. Animal Charity Evaluators. "Research Library." https://animalcharityevaluators.org/researchlibrary/#/. 2023.

70. Animal Charity Evaluators. "Financials." https://animalcharityevaluators.org/transparency/financials/. 2023.

71. Foster, William, and Susan Wolf Ditkoff. "When You've Made Enough to Make a Difference." *Harvard Business Review.* January–February 2011.

Chapter 2: Political Power: Family Farmers Versus Big Meat

1. Ferguson, Thomas. *The Golden Rule: The Investment Theory of Party Competition and the Logic of Money-Driven Political Systems.* University of Chicago Press. 1995.

2. Gordon-Reed, Annette. *The Hemingses of Monticello: An American Family.* W.W. Norton. 2008.

3. Simon, Michele. "Who Really Benefits from the Egg Industry Deal?" *Food Safety News.* July 12, 2011. https://www.foodsafetynews.com/2011/07/who-really-benefits-from-the-egg-industry-deal/.

4. Shields, Sara, Paul Shapiro, and Andrew Rowan. "A Decade of Progress Toward Ending the Intensive Confinement of Farm Animals in the United States." *Animals* 7(40), 2017.

5. Potter, Will. "Meet the Punk Rocker Who Can Liberate Your FBI File." *Mother Jones.* November 13, 2013. https://www.motherjones.com/politics/2013/11/foia-ryan-shapiro-fbi-files-lawsuit/.

6. Mohan, Geoffrey. "The Egg Industry Launched a Secret Two-Year War Against a Vegan Mayonnaise Competitor." *Los Angeles Times.* October 7, 2016.

7. National Cattlemen's Beef Association. "Qualified State Beef Councils." https://www.beefboard.org/qsbc.asp. The following states had no listed QSBCs: Alaska, Connecticut, Maine, Massachusetts, New Hampshire, Rhode Island. These states' programs were administered at the national office in Denver. Their beef taxes were collected at a P.O. Box in Nashville.

8. National Cattlemen's Beef Association. "State Affiliates." http://www.beefusa.org/stateaffiliates.aspx. 2023.

9. Bullard, Bill. "Group Responds to Latest Round of NCBA's False Claims." Ranchers-Cattlemen Action Legal Fund United Stockgrowers of America. July 25, 2017. https://www.r-calfusa.com/group-responds-latest-round-ncbas-false-claims/.

10. Carter, Zachary. "While Trump Was Dominating in Deep-Red Oklahoma, This Democrat Won a Landslide." *Huffington Post.* March 9, 2017. https://www.huffpost.com/entry/democratic-party-future-rural_n_58b7089ee4b019d36d0fecb4.

11. For a discussion of value framing, *see* Freeman, Carrie. *Framing Farming: Communication Strategies for Animal Rights.* Brill Rodopi. 2014. pp. 67–99.

12. Wilde, Renee. "'American Soil' Is Increasingly Foreign Owned." National Public Radio. May 27, 2019. https://www.npr.org/2019/05/27/723501793/american-soil-is-increasingly-foreign-owned.

13. Sherman, Gabriel. *The Loudest Voice in the Room: How the Brilliant, Bombastic Roger Ailes Built Fox News—and Divided a Country.* Random House. 2014.

14. Nestle, Marion. *Food Politics: How the Food Industry Influences Nutrition and Health* (2nd ed.). University of California Press. 2007. p. 98.

15. Siripurapu, Anshu. "The Dollar: The World's Currency." Council on Foreign Relations. 2020. https://www.cfr.org/backgrounder/dollar-worlds-currency.

16. Wilde, Renee. "'American Soil' Is Increasingly Foreign Owned." National Public Radio. May 27, 2019. https://www.npr.org/2019/05/27/723501793/american-soil-is-increasingly-foreign-owned.

17. Thomas, Jeff. *Virginia Politics & Government in a New Century: The Price of Power.* The History Press. 2016. pp. 52–54.

18. H.R. 1753. "Opportunities for Fairness in Farming Act of 2017." 115th Congress. https://www.congress.gov/bill/115th-congress/house-bill/1753/cosponsors?searchResultViewType=expanded.

19. Hawthorne, Mark. *Striking at the Roots: A Practical Guide to Animal Activism.* Changemakers Books. 2007. p. 33.

20. United States Senate. "Roll Call Vote 115th Congress—2nd Session. Lee Amdt. No. 3074." https://www.senate.gov/legislative/LIS/roll_call_lists/roll_call_vote_cfm.cfm?congress=115&session=2&vote=00142.

21. Lindsey, Brink, and Steven Teles. *The Captured Economy: How the Powerful Enrich Themselves, Slow Down Growth, and Increase Inequality.* Oxford University Press. 2017. p. 5.

22. Perkowski, Mateusz. "USDA: A Captive Agency?" *Capital Press.* December 18, 2014. https://www.capitalpress.com/nation_world/nation/usda-a-captive-agency/article_da1abcd7-fdd3-5dec-86ca-8b87944ee8b0.html.

23. Rosenberg, Martha. "Corruption, Mismanagement at USDA's Food Safety and Inspection Service Puts Consumers at Risk, Whistleblower Says." Organic Consumers Association. April 11, 2019. https://www.organicconsumers.org/blog/corruption-mismanagement-usdas-food-safety-and-inspection-services-put-consumers-risk?fbclid=IwAR3oXpJaUbGtITNGnZsGgj2lNoZ3AZ8gkn5IpEIGqa8GepF9hww-TlgiaDM.

24. Azzam, Azzeddine. "Competition in the US Meatpacking Industry: Is It History?" *Agricultural Economics* 18(2), 1998. pp. 107–126. https://www.sciencedirect.com/science/article/abs/pii/S0169515098800091.

25. Organization for Competitive Markets. "Packers and Stockyard Act." https://competitivemarkets.com/gipsa/. 2023.

26. Khan, Lina. "Obama's Game of Chicken." *Washington Monthly.* November 9, 2012.

27. Fassler, Joe. "A New Lawsuit Accuses the 'Big Four' Beef Packers of Conspiring to Fix Cattle Prices." *The Counter.* April 23, 2019. https://newfoodeconomy.org/meatpacker-price-fixing-class-action-lawsuit-cattlemen-tyson-jbs-cargill-

national-beef/?fbclid=IwAR0NRgT-_j0orLDJoLfNFliwiLl6GJEQ3_
hduuiW0Mt6ohUuMweBlfP_Bbc.

28. Garber, Adam, and Viveth Karthikeyan. "New Report: Hazardous Meat & Poultry Recalls Nearly Double." *U.S. Public Interest Research Group*. January 17, 2019. https://uspirg.org/news/usf/new-report-hazardous-meat-poultry-recalls-nearly-double.

29. Khimm, Suzy. "Another Obama Decision Reversed? Now It's About Food Safety." *NBC News*. October 16, 2017. https://www.nbcnews.com/politics/white-house/another-obama-decision-reversed-now-it-s-about-food-safety-n810296.

30. Leonard, Christopher. *The Meat Racket: The Secret Takeover of America's Food Business*. Simon & Schuster. 2014.

31. Taylor, Robert, and David Domina. "Restoring Economic Health to Contract Poultry Production." *Organization for Competitive Markets*. May 13, 2010. http://www.competitivemarkets.com/wp-content/uploads/2012/02/dominareportversion2.pdf

32. Khan, Lina. "Obama's Game of Chicken." *Washington Monthly*. November 9, 2012.

33. Ringgenberg, W., C. Peek-Asa, K. Donham, and M. Ramirez. "Trends and Characteristics of Occupational Suicide and Homicide in Farmers and Agriculture Workers, 1992–2010." *Journal of Rural Health*, 34(3), 2018. pp. 246–253.

34. O'Neil, Colin. "Trump's Agriculture Nominee Brings the Swamp to Washington." *Environmental Working Group*. March 8, 2017. https://www.ewg.org/planet-trump/2017/02/ewg-investigates-trump-s-agriculture-nominee-brings-swamp-washington.

35. State of Georgia. "Governor Perdue Named BIO Governor of the Year." April 23, 2009. https://sonnyperdue.georgia.gov/00/press/detail/0,2668,7800
6749_136688711_139078727,00.html.

36. Kullgren, Ian. "How Perdue's Power Benefits His Friends." *Politico*. March 13, 2017.

37. Schouten, Fredreka. "Many Ex-Governors Work as Lobbyists, Consultants." *USA Today*. August 11, 2013; Perdue Partners. "Governor Sonny Perdue Launches Perdue Partners, LLC. *Business Wire*. April 18, 2011. https://www.businesswire.com/news/home/20110418006352/en/Governor-Sonny-Perdue-Launches-Perdue-Partners-LLC.

38. Kullgren, Ian. "How Perdue's Power Benefits His Friends." *Politico*. March 13, 2017.

39. O'Neil, Colin. "Sonny Perdue's Revolving Door Policy Already in Action." *Environmental Working Group*. March 13, 2017. https://www.ewg.org/planet-trump/2017/03/sonny-perdue-s-revolving-door-policy-already-action.

40. Union of Concerned Scientists. *Betrayal at the USDA: How the Trump Administration Is Sidelining Science and Favoring Industry Over Farmers and the Public.* March 30, 2018. https://www.ucsusa.org/resources/betrayal-usda.

41. Kelloway, Claire. "Trump Administration Guts Office Designed to Protect Farmers from Ag Monopolies." *Food and Power.* December 6, 2018. http://www.foodandpower.net/2018/12/06/trump-administration-guts-office-designed-to-protect-farmers-from-ag-monopolies/.

42. Sommerfeldt, Chris. "Trump Administration Showers Brazilian Crooks with $62M Bailout Money Meant for Struggling U.S. Farmers." *New York Daily News.* May 16, 2019. https://www.nydailynews.com/news/politics/ny-trump-administration-bailout-farmers-brazilian-criminals-20190516-6rdb3ithvfec7fttem7qrny54y-story.html.

43. Runyon, Luke. "JBS, World's Largest Meat Company, Mired in Multiple Corruption Scandals in Brazil." *Harvest Public Media.* August 3, 2017. https://www.harvestpublicmedia.org/post/jbs-worlds-largest-meat-company-mired-multiple-corruption-scandals-brazil.

44. Tomson, Bill. "First US Beef Shipment Arrives in Brazil After 13-Year Ban." *Agri-Pulse.* May 4, 2017. https://www.agri-pulse.com/articles/9217-first-us-beef-shipment-arrives-in-brazil-after-13-year-ban.

45. Kieler, Ashlee. "U.S. Halts Import of Brazilian Beef Following Tainted Meat Scandal." *Consumer Reports.* June 23, 2017. https://www.consumerreports.org/consumerist/u-s-halts-import-of-brazilian-beef-following-tainted-meat-scandal/.

46. Food Safety News. "JBS Taps Almanza to Lead Its Food Safety Program Worldwide." August 4, 2017. https://www.foodsafetynews.com/2017/08/jbs-taps-almanza-to-lead-its-food-safety-program-worldwide/.

47. USDA. "Perdue: USDA Halting Import of Fresh Brazilian Beef." Release No. 0063.17. June 22, 2017. https://www.usda.gov/media/press-releases/2017/06/22/perdue-usda-halting-import-fresh-brazilian-beef.

48. Evich, Helena Bottemiller. "Almanza Hails 'Modernization' in Exit Interview." *Politico.* August 2, 2017.

49. Meating Place. "Bio for Craig Morris." 2022. https://www.meatingplace.com/Industry/Blogs/Bio?forumId=808.

50. Meat and Poultry. "USDA Official to Join National Pork Board." October 18, 2017. https://www.meatpoultry.com/articles/17292-usda-official-to-join-national-pork-board.

51. Note: Morris left the National Pork Board in January of 2019 to take a job in the seafood industry as the CEO of Genuine Alaska Pollock Producers.

52. Vinik, Danny. "A $60 Million Pork Kickback?" *Politico.* August 30, 2015.

53. LinkedIn. "Barry Carpenter." https://www.linkedin.com/in/barry-carpenter-2961478.

54. Table Foods. "Episode 38: Crisis in the Dairy Industry with Sarah Lloyd." September 4, 2019. https://knowbetter.bytablefoods.com/2019/09/04/ep-38-crisis-in-the-dairy-industry-with-sarah-lloyd/.

55. Ho, Justin. "The Trade War's Only the Latest Problem Facing America's Dairy Industry." National Public Radio. August 8, 2019. https://www.marketplace.org/2019/08/08/dairy-farms-more-problems-than-trade-war/.

56. Riviera, Gloria, Marjorie McAfee, Zoe Lake, and Allie Yang. "Wisconsin's Failing Dairy Industry Means Farmers May Play Vital Role in Midterms." ABC News. November 1, 2018. https://abcnews.go.com/Politics/wisconsins-failing-dairy-industry-means-farmers-play-vital/story?id=58886981.

57. Dynes, Erica. "Farmer Solutions Complex: Beef One Idea." *Agri-View*. January 4, 2020. https://www.agupdate.com/agriview/news/business/farmer-solutions-complex----beef-one-idea/article_f8d1a8ed-27e4-5a8c-880b-3ebfbc33bb07.html.

58. Lloyd, Sarah. "Don't Be Distracted by That Burning Pile of Soybeans." *Progressive*. September 4, 2019. https://progressive.org/dispatches/dont-be-distracted-by-that-burning-pile-of-soybeans-lloyd-190904/.

59. Interview with Sarah Lloyd. December 4, 2019.

60. Spivak, Cary. "A Nonprofit That's Supposed to Promote Dairy Pays Its Leaders Millions—While the Farmers Who Fund It Are Going Out of Business." *Milwaukee Journal Sentinel*. September 4, 2019.

61. Spivak, Cary. "Ex-Agriculture Secretary Tom Vilsack Is the Top Paid Executive at Dairy Management." *Milwaukee Journal Sentinel*. December 2, 2019.

62. Lloyd, Sarah. "Milk: Too Much of a Good Thing." *Wisconsin Examiner*. July 29, 2019.

63. Interview with Sarah Lloyd. December 4, 2019.

64. Lloyd, Sarah. "Don't Be Distracted by That Burning Pile of Soybeans." *Progressive*. September 4, 2019. https://progressive.org/dispatches/dont-be-distracted-by-that-burning-pile-of-soybeans-lloyd-190904/.

65. Government Accountability Office. *U.S. Department of Agriculture: Recommendations and Options to Address Management Deficiencies in the Office of the Assistant Secretary for Civil Rights*. Report GAO-09-62. October 22, 2008. https://www.gao.gov/assets/a282840.html.

66. McGinnis, Mike. "Q&A: John Boyd, Founder and President of National Black Farmers Association." *Successful Farming*. September 7, 2018. https://www.agriculture.com/news/business/q-a-john-boyd-founder-and-president-of-national-black-farmers-association.

67. NewsOne. "Black Farmer Wrests Billion-Dollar Settlement from U.S." February 1, 2012. https://newsone.com/1833215/john-boyd-black-farmer-settlement/.

68. Parker, Robin Rose. "John Boyd Jr., 46, President, National Black Farmers Association, Baskerville, Va." *Washington Post.* June 20, 2012.

69. National Black Farmers Association. "The John Boyd Story." http://www.nationalblackfarmersassociation.org/single-post/2018/02/08/The-John-Boyd-Story.

70. NewsOne. "Black Farmer Wrests Billion-Dollar Settlement from U.S." February 1, 2012. https://newsone.com/1833215/john-boyd-black-farmer-settlement/.

71. Parker, Robin Rose. "John Boyd Jr., 46, President, National Black Farmers Association, Baskerville, Va." *Washington Post.* June 20, 2012.

72. DeShong, Travis. "With His New Chicken Documentary, Is Morgan Spurlock Part of the Solution and the Problem?" *Washington Post.* September 12, 2019.

73. Office of the Inspector General. *Evaluation of SBA 7(A) Loans Made to Poultry Farmers.* Small Business Administration. Report No. 18-13. March 6, 2018. https://www.sba.gov/sites/default/files/oig/SBA-OIG-Report-18-13.pdf.

74. Lowery, Annie. "The Rise of the Zombie Small Businesses." *The Atlantic.* September 4, 2018.

75. McLamb, Stephen. "Marshall County Chicken Farmer Plaintiff in Federal Lawsuit Against USDA." NBC-WAFF. December 21, 2017. https://www.waff.com/story/37122257/marshall-county-chicken-farmer-plaintiff-in-federal-lawsuit-against-usda/.

76. Brown, Claire. "Arkansas Lawmakers Oppose a Rule That Would Hurt Big Poultry. They All Receive Campaign Contributions from the Companies Affected." *The Counter.* November 29, 2018. https://newfoodeconomy.org/arkansas-big-poultry-tyson-small-business-administration-political-spending-contract-chicken-growers/.

77. DeCiccio, Emily. "Tainted Beef: How the Meat You Buy Could Be Supporting Venezuela's Socialist Regime." *New York Post.* October 31, 2019.

78. Lowery, Annie. "The Rise of the Zombie Small Businesses." *The Atlantic.* September 4, 2018.

79. Felperin, Leslie. "*Super Size Me 2: Holy Chicken!* Film Review." *Hollywood Reporter.* September 9, 2017. https://www.hollywoodreporter.com/review/super-size-me-2-holy-chicken-review-1037096.

80. Maxwell, Joe. "The Death of the American Dream for Family Farmers." *The Hill.* November 8, 2017. https://thehill.com/opinion/energy-environment/359388-the-death-of-the-american-dream-for-family-farmers.

81. Food Integrity Campaign. "Nationwide Group of Family Farmers to Expose Abuse in Meat Industry, Demand Action from USDA." July 15, 2019. https://www.foodwhistleblower.org/media-alert-nationwide-group-of-family-farmers-to-expose-abuse-in-meat-industry-demand-action-from-usda/.

82. Evich, Helena Bottemiller, Doug Paler, Pradnya Joshi, and Catherine Boudreau. "Suing USDA but Fearing Reprisals." *Politico.* December 15, 2017.

83. McLamb, Stephen. "Marshall County Chicken Farmer Plaintiff in Federal Lawsuit Against USDA." NBC-WAFF. December 21, 2017. https://www.waff.com/story/37122257/marshall-county-chicken-farmer-plaintiff-in-federal-lawsuit-against-usda/.

Chapter 3: Vegans Making Laws: From California to Capitol Hill

1. Rifkin, Rebecca. "In U.S., More Say Animals Should Have Same Rights as People." Gallup. May 18, 2015. https://news.gallup.com/poll/183275/say-animals-rights-people.aspx.

2. Stallwood, Kim. *Growl: Life Lessons, Hard Truths, and Bold Strategies from an Animal Advocate.* Lantern. 2014. p. 216.

3. Tauber, Steven. *Navigating the Jungle: Law, Politics, and the Animal Advocacy Movement.* Routledge. 2016. p. 7.

4. Robert Rutland, Charles Hobson, William Rachal, and Frederika J. Teute (eds.). *The Papers of James Madison*, vol. 10, 27 May 1787–3 March 1788. University of Chicago Press, 1977. pp. 76–78.

5. Delon, Nicolas. "Social Norms and Farm Animal Protection." *Palgrave Communications* 4(139), 2018, pp. 1-6.

6. Wolfson, David, and Mariann Sullivan. "Foxes in the Hen House: Animals, Agribusiness, and the Law." In Cass Sunstein and Martha Nussbaum (eds.). *Animal Rights: Current Debates and New Directions.* Oxford University Press. 2004. pp. 205–233.

7. 49 U.S. Code § 80502.

8. Animal Welfare Institute. *A Review: The Twenty-Eight Hour Law and Its Enforcement.* April 2020. https://awionline.org/sites/default/files/uploads/documents/20TwentyEightHourLawReport.pdf.

9. USDA defines "livestock" as "cattle, sheep, goats, pigs, horses, mules and other equines," but not birds, rabbits, or "'exotic' animals, such as reindeer, elk, deer, antelope, bison and water buffalo." *See also* Animal Welfare Institute. "Humane Slaughter Update: Federal and State Oversight of the Welfare of Farm Animals at Slaughter. April 2020. https://awionline.org/sites/default/files/uploads/documents/20HumaneSlaughterUpdate.pdf. p. 4.

10. Eisnitz, Gail. *Slaughterhouse: The Shocking Story of Greed, Neglect, and Inhumane Treatment Inside the U.S. Meat Industry.* Prometheus Books. 2006; Warrick, Jo. "They Die Piece by Piece." *Washington Post.* April 10, 2001.

11 Mortlock, Samantha. "Standing on New Ground: Underenforcement of Animal Protection Laws Causes Competitive Injury to Complying Entities." *Vermont Law Review* 32, 2007.

12. Animal Welfare Institute. "Humane Slaughter Update: Federal and State Oversight of the Welfare of Farm Animals at Slaughter." April 2020. https://awionline.org/sites/default/files/uploads/documents/20HumaneSlaughterUpdate.pdf.

13. National Agricultural Library. "Humane Methods of Slaughter Act." USDA. https://www.nal.usda.gov/awic/humane-methods-slaughter-act.

14. Jones, Dena. "Custom-Exempt Slaughter Should Not Be Expanded." *Food Safety News*. January 15, 2016. https://www.foodsafetynews.com/2016/01/custom-exempt-slaughter-should-not-be-expanded/.

15. Abbott, Chuck. "USDA Withdraws Proposals on Poultry Plant Line Speeds and SNAP." *Successful Farming*. January 26, 2021. https://www.agriculture.com/news/livestock/usda-withdraws-proposals-on-poultry-plant-line-speeds-and-snap.

16. Kindy, Kimberly. "USDA Plan to Speed Up Poultry-Processing Lines Could Increase Risk of Bird Abuse." *Washington Post*. October 29, 2013.

17. Federal Register Docket 05-19378, "Treatment of Live Poultry Before Slaughter." September 28, 2005.

18. Friedrich, Bruce. "Still in the Jungle: Poultry Slaughter and the USDA." *New York University Environmental Law Journal*, 23, 2015. pp. 247–298.

19. Food Safety and Inspection Service. "Modernization of Swine Slaughter Inspection." *Federal Register*, October 1, 2019, p. 52300. https://www.federalregister.gov/documents/2019/10/01/2019-20245/modernization-of-swine-slaughter-inspection.

20. Monke, Jim. "Agriculture and Related Agencies: FY2020 Appropriations." Congressional Research Service. Report R45974. March 26, 2020. https://crsreports.congress.gov/product/pdf/R/R45974.

21. House Appropriations Committee. "Appropriations Committee Approves Fiscal Year 2020 Agriculture-Rural Development-FDA Funding Bill." June 4, 2019. https://appropriations.house.gov/news/press-releases/appropriations-committee-approves-fiscal-year-2020-agriculture-rural-development.

22. H.B. 3164. "Agriculture, Rural Development, Food and Drug Administration, and Related Agencies Appropriations Act, 2020." 116th Congress. https://www.congress.gov/bill/116th-congress/house-bill/3164/text.

23. House Appropriations Committee. "Appropriations Committee Approves Fiscal Year 2020 Agriculture-Rural Development-FDA Funding Bill." June 4, 2019. https://appropriations.house.gov/news/press-releases/appropriations-committee-approves-fiscal-year-2020-agriculture-rural-development.

24. S.B. 2522. "Agriculture, Rural Development, Food and Drug Administration, and Related Agencies Appropriations Act, 2020." 116th Congress. https://www.congress.gov/bill/116th-congress/senate-bill/2522/text.

25. H.B. 3164. "Agriculture, Rural Development, Food and Drug Administration, and Related Agencies Appropriations Act, 2020." 116th Congress. https://www.congress.gov/bill/116th-congress/house-bill/3164/text.

26. White House Statement on H.R. 3055, June 2019. https://www.whitehouse.gov/wp-content/uploads/2019/06/SAP_HR-3055.pdf. p. 5.

27. Monke, Jim. "Agriculture and Related Agencies: FY2020 Appropriations." Congressional Research Service. Report R45974. March 26, 2020. https://crsreports.congress.gov/product/pdf/R/R45974. p. 2.

28. National Conference of State Legislatures. "Initiative and Referendum States." https://www.ncsl.org/research/elections-and-campaigns/chart-of-the-initiative-states.aspx.

29. There are many legal nuances among the states. Some states require more than a majority vote, and some have different thresholds for statutes versus constitutional amendments.

30. Welch, Tyler. "Can Citizens Better Use the Ballot Initiative to Protect Wildlife?: The Case of the Mountain Lion in the West." *Colorado Natural Resources, Energy & Environmental Law Review*, 25(2), 2014. pp. 419–448.

31. Tischler, Joyce. "A Brief History of Animal Law, Part II (1985–2011)." *Stanford Journal of Animal Law & Policy*, 5, 2012. pp. 72–73.

32. Ibid.

33. Shields, Sara, Paul Shapiro, and Andrew Rowan. "A Decade of Progress Toward Ending the Intensive Confinement of Farm Animals in the United States." *Animals*, 7(40), 2017.

34. Lovvorn, Jonathan, and Nancy Perry. "California Proposition 2: A Watershed Moment for Animal Law." *Animal Law*, 15, 2009. pp. 149–169.

35. Shields, Sara, Paul Shapiro, and Andrew Rowan. "A Decade of Progress Toward Ending the Intensive Confinement of Farm Animals in the United States." *Animals*, 7(40), 2017.

36. Winter, Michael. "Calif. Meat Packer to Pay $317M over Abuse, Recall." *USA Today*. November 16, 2012.

37. Perry, Nancy, and Peter Brandt. "A Case Study on Cruelty to Farm Animals: Lessons Learned from the Hallmark Meat Packing Case." *Michigan Law Review First Impressions*, 106, 2008. pp. 117–122.

38. Ballotpedia. "California Proposition 2, Standards for Confining Farm Animals (2008)." https://ballotpedia.org/California_Proposition_2,_Standards_for_Confining_Farm_Animals_(2008).

39. Runkle, Nathan Milo. *Mercy For Animals: One Man's Quest to Inspire Compassion and Improve the Lives of Farm Animals*. Avery, Penguin Random House. 2017. pp. 135–136.

40. Lovvorn, Jonathan, and Nancy Perry. "California Proposition 2: A Watershed Moment for Animal Law." *Animal Law*, 15, 2009. pp. 163–164.

41. California A.B. 1437. 2009. https://leginfo.legislature.ca.gov/faces/billStatusClient.xhtml?bill_id=200920100AB1437.

42. *State of Missouri, et al. v. Harris, et al.* (E.D. Cal. 2014; 9th Cir. 2016).

43. *Cramer v. Harris*, (9th Cir. 2015).

44. California Secretary of State. "Campaign Finance: Yes on Prop 12: Prevent Cruelty California, a Humane Society Committee." https://cal-access.sos.ca.gov/Campaign/Committees/Detail.aspx?id=1399103&session=2017&view=expenditures.

45. H.R. 272. "Protect Interstate Commerce Act of 2019." 116th Congress. https://www.congress.gov/bill/116th-congress/house-bill/272/text.

46. Linder, Ann. "Legislative Analysis of H.R. 4879: The 'Protect Interstate Commerce Act' of 2018." Harvard Law School Animal Law & Policy Program. April 2018. https://animal.law.harvard.edu/wp-content/uploads/Harvard-ALPP-PICA-Report-1.pdf.

47. Gabriel, Trip. "Before Trump, Steve King Set the Agenda for the Wall and Anti-Immigrant Politics." January 10, 2019. https://www.nytimes.com/2019/01/10/us/politics/steve-king-trump-immigration-wall.html.

48. Topel, Avery. "Ag-Gag in the Aftermath of Free Speech Claims: How Iowa Rewrote Its Unconstitutional Agricultural Protection Law." *Arizona State Law Journal Online*, 2, 2021. pp. 270–297.

49. American Society for the Prevention of Cruelty to Animals. "What Is Ag-Gag Legislation?" http://www.aspca.org/animal-protection/public-policy/ag-gag-legislation-state.

50. Wilson, Larissa. "Ag-Gag Laws: A Shift in the Wrong Direction for Animal Welfare on Farms." *Golden Gate University Law Review*, 44, 2014. p. 311; Potter, Will. "Sentinel Species: The Criminalization of Animal Rights Activists as Terrorists, and What It Means for the Civil Liberties in Trump's America." *Denver Law Review*, 95, 2018. p. 877; Bollard, Lewis. "Ag-Gag: The Unconstitutionality of Laws Restricting Undercover Investigations on Farms." Yale Law School. https://law.yale.edu/sites/default/files/documents/pdf/news/BollardLewis2012Hogan-SmogerEssayContestWinner.pdf.

51. Topel, Avery. "Ag-Gag in the Aftermath of Free Speech Claims: How Iowa Rewrote Its Unconstitutional Agricultural Protection Law." *Arizona State Law Journal Online*, 2, 2021. pp. 270–297.

52. Internal Revenue Service. "Measuring Lobbying Activity: Expenditure Test." https://www.irs.gov/charities-non-profits/measuring-lobbying-activity-expenditure-test.

53. Westen, Drew. *The Political Brain: The Role of Emotion in Deciding the Fate of the Nation.* PublicAffairs. 2008.

54. For a review, *see,* Tauber, Steven. *Navigating the Jungle: Law, Politics, and the Animal Advocacy Movement.* Routledge. 2016. p. 8.

Chapter 4: Building a Movement:
Mercy For Animals and Emotional Intelligence

1. Runkle, Nathan Milo. *Mercy For Animals: One Man's Quest to Inspire Compassion and Improve the Lives of Farm Animals.* Avery, Penguin Random House. 2017.

2. Shields, Sara, Paul Shapiro, and Andrew Rowan. "A Decade of Progress Toward Ending the Intensive Confinement of Farm Animals in the United States." *Animals*, 7(40), 2017.

3. Mercy For Animals. 2005 IRS Form 990. https://projects.propublica. org/nonprofits/display_990/542076145/2006_06_EO%2F54-2076145_990_200512.

4. Mercy For Animals. 2006 IRS Form 990. https://projects.propublica. org/nonprofits/display_990/542076145/2007_04_EO%2F54-2076145_990_200612.

5. Hall, Carla. "L.A.'s Deep Pockets Give Creatures Comfort." *Los Angeles Times.* December 19, 2007.

6. Mercy For Animals. 2010 IRS Form 990. https://projects.propublica. org/nonprofits/display_990/542076145/2011_06_EO%2F54-2076145_990_201012.

7. Animal Charity Evaluators. Charity Review: Mercy For Animals. https:// animalcharityevaluators.org/charity-review/mercy-for-animals/2017-nov/.

8. Goleman, Daniel. "What Makes a Leader?" *Harvard Business Review.* June 1996.

9. McNulty, Timothy. "Jail Time Still Doesn't Deter Philip Berrigan." *Chicago Tribune.* June 20, 1994.

10. Purdy, Chase. "How the Vegan Movement Broke out of Its Echo Chamber and Finally Started Disrupting Things." *Quartz.* November 13, 2016. https:// qz.com/829956/how-the-vegan-movement-broke-out-of-its-echo-chamber-and-finally-started-disrupting-things/.

11. Montgomery, David. "Animal Pragmatism." *Washington Post.* September 8, 2003.

12. Purdy, Chase. "How the Vegan Movement Broke out of Its Echo Chamber and Finally Started Disrupting Things." *Quartz.* November 13, 2016. https:// qz.com/829956/how-the-vegan-movement-broke-out-of-its-echo-chamber-and-finally-started-disrupting-things/.

13. Feder, Barnaby. "Pressuring Perdue." *New York Times Magazine.* November 26, 1989. Peter Singer's *Ethics into Action: Henry Spira and the Animal Rights Movement* (Rowman & Littlefield, 1999) is one of the movement's best biographies.

14. MarketScreener. "Whole Foods Market Receives Award for Commitment to Cage-Free Supply Chain." June 28, 2017. https://www.marketscreener. com/quote/stock/WHOLE-FOODS-MARKET-INC-4930/news/Whole-Foods-Market-nbsp-June-28-2017-Whole-Foods-Market-receives-award-for-commitment-to-cage-f-24668485/.

15. Walmart. "Walmart U.S. Announces Transition to Cage-Free Egg Supply Chain by 2025." Walmart. April 5, 2016. https://news.walmart.com/news-archive/2016/04/05/walmart-us-announces-transition-to-cage-free-egg-supply-chain-by-2025; Bollard, Lewis. "Why Are U.S. Corporate Cage-Free Campaigns Succeeding?" Open Philanthropy Project. April 11, 2017. https://www.openphilanthropy.org/blog/why-are-us-corporate-cage-free-campaigns-succeeding.

16. Open Philanthropy Project. Interview with Leah Garcés and Dawn Rotheram. November 8, 2016. https://www.openphilanthropy.org/sites/default/files/Leah_Garces_Dawn_Rotheram_11-08-16_%28public%29.pdf.

17. Starostinetskaya, Anna. "Leah Garcés Becomes First Female President of Mercy For Animals." *VegNews*. October 11, 2018. https://vegnews.com/2018/10/leah-garces-becomes-first-female-president-of-mercy-for-animals.

18. Scully, Matthew. "The #MeTooing of Wayne Pacelle." *American Spectator*. February 23, 2018. https://spectator.org/the-metooing-of-wayne-pacelle/.

19. Garcés, Leah. *Grilled: Turning Adversaries to Allies to Change the Chicken Industry.* Bloomsbury Sigma. 2019.

20. Ibid.

21. Ibid.

22. Ibid.

23. Kristof, Nicholas. "Abusing the Chickens We Eat." *New York Times*. December 3, 2014.

24. Williams, Wyatt. "Why a North Carolina Chicken Farmer Exposed the Depressing Conditions on His Own Farm." *Vice*. February 23, 2015. https://www.vice.com/en/article/qbeq7p/the-whistle-blower-crows-at-dawn-0000570-v22n2.

25. Garcés, Leah. *Grilled: Turning Adversaries to Allies to Change the Chicken Industry.* Bloomsbury Sigma. 2019.

26. Perdue. "Perdue Response to Mercy For Animals Press Conference." December 10, 2015. https://corporate.perduefarms.com/news/press-releases/perdue-response-to-mercy-for-animals-press-conference/; Bhumitra, Jaya. "Perdue Announces Groundbreaking Policy to Improve Lines of 680 Million Birds After MFA Investigation." Mercy For Animals. June 26, 2016. https://mercyforanimals.org/blog/perdue-announces-groundbreaking-animal-welfare/.

27. McKay, Mark, and Leah Garcés. "How Perdue and Mercy For Animals Found Common Ground." Food Dive. May 24, 2021. https://www.fooddive.com/news/how-perdue-and-mercy-for-animals-found-common-ground/600309/.

28. Shanker, Deena, and Lydia Mulvany. "Perdue Unveils a More Humane Chicken Slaughter Process." *Bloomberg BusinessWeek*. February 26, 2019.

29. Grandin, Temple. "Animal Welfare Evaluation of Gas Stunning (Controlled Atmosphere Stunning) of Chickens and Other Poultry." Colorado State University. January 2013. https://www.grandin.com/gas.stunning.poultry.eval.html.

30. Meyer, Zlati. "Tyson's Chicken Cams Will Be Monitored for Animal Cruelty." *USA Today.* June 21, 2017. Tyson Foods. Animal Welfare Monitoring. https://www.tysonsustainability.com/animal-well-being/animal-welfare-monitoring.php.

31. Honig, Esther. "Cargill Tests Robotic Cattle Driver as a Way to Improve Worker Safety." *National Public Radio.* November 27, 2018. https://www.npr.org/sections/thesalt/2018/11/27/666991079/cargill-tests-robotic-cattle-driver-as-a-way-to-improve-worker-safety.

32. Amelinckx, Andrew. "New Technology Could Keep Billions of Male Chicks from Being Ground Alive." *Modern Farmer.* November 8, 2016. https://modernfarmer.com/2016/11/new-technology-keep-billions-male-chicks-ground-alive/; United Egg Producers. Statement on Eliminating Male Chick Culling. https://uepcertified.com/united-egg-producers-statement-eliminating-male-chick-culling/.

33. Kowitt, Beth. "Inside McDonald's Bold Decision to Go Cage-Free." *Fortune.* August 18, 2016.

34. Bollard, Lewis. "Why This Could Be the Year of the Broiler Chicken." Open Philanthropy Project. January 2019. https://us14.campaign-archive.com/?u=66df320da8400b581cbc1b539&id=2ea3d9ffc0.

Chapter 5: Betrayal of Trust:
Inside the Humane Society's #MeToo Scandal

1. Anonymous. "#TimesUpAR: Guest Blog." *Carol J. Adams Blog.* January 29, 2018. https://caroljadams.com/carol-adams-blog/timesupar.

2. Ibid.

3. Clifton, Merritt. "David Wills, Ex-Humane Society of the U.S. Vice President, Gets Life in Prison." *Animals 24-7.* October 15, 2020. https://www.animals24-7.org/2020/10/15/david-wills-ex-humane-society-of-the-u-s-vice-president-gets-life-in-prison/.

4. Kullgren, Ian. "Female Employees Allege Culture of Sexual Harassment at Humane Society." *Politico.* January 30, 2018. https://www.politico.com/magazine/story/2018/01/30/humane-society-sexual-harassment-allegations-investigation-216553.

5. Heath, Thomas. "Ringling Circus Prevails in 14-Year Legal Case; Collects $16M from Humane Society, Others." *Washington Post.* May 16, 2014.

6. HSUS 2013 IRS Form 990. https://www.humanesociety.org/sites/default/files/archive/assets/pdfs/financials/2013-hsus-form-990.pdf; Fund for Animals 2013 IRS Form 990. https://www.fundforanimals.org/about/financial-reports/ffa-2013-public-disclosure.pdf.

7. Gunther, Marc. "Humane Society CEO Under Investigation for Sexual Relationship with Employee." *Chronicle of Philanthropy.* January 25, 2018.

https://www.philanthropy.com/article/humane-society-ceo-under-investigation-for-sexual-relationship-with-employee/.

8. Paquette, Danielle. "Humane Society CEO Is Subject of Sexual Harassment Complaints from Three Women, According to Internal Investigation." *Washington Post.* January 29, 2018.

9. Ibid.

10. Ibid.

11. Kullgren, Ian. "Humane Society CEO Resigns amid Sexual Harassment Allegations." *Politico.* February 2, 2018. https://www.politico.com/story/2018/02/02/humane-society-sexual-harassment-allegations-323455. The board chair's statement was removed from the HSUS website but is available using the Wayback Machine. https://www.humanesociety.org/news/press_releases/2018/02/statement-from-bernthal.html.

12. Scully, Matthew. "The #MeTooing of Wayne Pacelle." *American Spectator.* February 23, 2018. https://spectator.org/the-metooing-of-wayne-pacelle/.

13. Bosman, Julie, Matt Stevens, and Jonah Engel Bromwich. "Humane Society C.E.O. Resigns amid Sexual Harassment Allegations." *New York Times.* February 2, 2018.

14. Ibid.

15. Coalition Against Nonprofit Harassment and Discrimination. https://www.canhad.org/read-testimonials/.

16. Glassdoor review of Humane Society of the United States. September 27, 2020. https://www.glassdoor.com/Reviews/The-Humane-Society-of-the-United-States-Reviews-E7799_P2.htm.

17. Glassdoor review of Humane Society of the United States. January 3, 2021. https://www.glassdoor.com/Reviews/The-Humane-Society-of-the-United-States-Reviews-E7799.htm.

18. Glassdoor review of Humane Society of the United States. June 24, 2021. https://www.glassdoor.com/Reviews/Employee-Review-The-Humane-Society-of-the-United-States-RVW48812420.htm.

19. Pacelle, Wayne. *The Humane Economy: How Innovators and Enlightened Consumers Are Transforming the Lives of Animals.* HarperCollins. 2016. p. 289.

20. Heath, Thomas. "Ringling Circus Prevails in 14-Year Legal Case; Collects $16M from Humane Society, Others." *Washington Post.* May 16, 2014.

21. *Feld Entertainment Inc. v. ASPCA, HSUS, et al.,* 873 F. Supp. 2d 288 (2012).

22. Paquette, Danielle. "The Humane Society's Sexual Harassment Scandal Just Won't End." *Washington Post.* March 23, 2018.

23. Clifton, Merritt. "Wayne Pacelle & Jurassic World: Fallen Kingdom Celebrate Returns from Extinction." *Animals 24-7.* July 24, 2018. https://www.animals24-7.org/2018/07/24/wayne-pacelle-jurassic-world-fallen-kingdom-celebrate-returns-from-extinction/.

24. HSUS 2018 IRS Form 990. https://www.humanesociety.org/sites/default/files/docs/HSUS%202018%20990.pdf.

25. Pacelle, Wayne. *The Humane Economy: How Innovators and Enlightened Consumers Are Transforming the Lives of Animals.* HarperCollins. 2016. p. 289.

26. Atherton, Susan, and Tom Sabatino. "Update from HSUS Board Co-Chairson Reconciliation Process." HSUS. March 12, 2019. https://www.humanesociety.org/news/update-hsus-board-co-chairs-reconciliation-process.

27. Hungerford, Amanda. "Gender Equity in the Farmed Animal Movement." February 2019. https://mailchi.mp/abd757b6b4b9/research-note-where-are-we-on-gender-equity-and-how-can-we-do-better?e=2822872639.

28. Ibid.

29. Baran, Stephanie. "Visual Patriarchy: PETA Advertising and the Commodification of Sexualized Bodies." In Vakoch, Douglas, and Sam Mickey (eds.). *Woman and Nature? Beyond Dualism in Gender, Body, and Environment.* Routledge. 2019. pp. 43–56.

30. Dowsett, Elisha, Carolyn Semmler, Heather Bray, Rachel Ankeny, and Anna Chur-Hansen. "Neutralizing the Meat Paradox: Cognitive Dissonance, Gender, and Eating Animals." *Appetite*, 123, April 1, 2018. pp. 280–288.

31. Dullaghan, Neil. "EA Survey 2019 Series: Community Demographics & Characteristics." *Rethink Charity.* December 5, 2019. https://forum.effectivealtruism.org/posts/wtQ3XCL35uxjXpwjE/ea-survey-2019-series-community-demographics-and.

32. Dullaghan, Neil. "EA Survey 2019 Series: Cause Prioritization." *Rethink Charity.* January 2, 2020. https://forum.effectivealtruism.org/posts/8hExrLibTEgyzaDxW/ea-survey-2019-series-cause-prioritization.

33. Animal Advocacy Careers. "Effective Animal Advocacy Bottlenecks Surveys." January 5, 2021. https://www.animaladvocacycareers.org/post/effective-animal-advocacy-bottlenecks-surveys.

34. Broad, Garrett. "Effective Altruism, Meet Animal Protection." *HistPhil.* February 18, 2019. https://histphil.org/2019/02/18/effective-altruism-meet-animal-protection/.

35. Graça, João, Maria Calheiros, Abílio Oliveira, and Taciano Milfont. "Why Are Women Less Likely to Support Animal Exploitation than Men? The Mediating Roles of Social Dominance Orientation and Empathy." *Personality and Individual Differences*, 129, 2018. pp. 66–69.

36. Freedman, Paul. "How Steak Became Manly and Salads Became Feminine." *The Conversation.* October 24, 2019. https://theconversation.com/how-steak-became-manly-and-salads-became-feminine-124147.

37. HSUS 2018 IRS Form 990. https://www.humanesociety.org/sites/default/files/docs/HSUS%202018%20990.pdf.

38. Bollard, Lewis. "Humane Society Legislative Fund—Opposing the King Amendment." Open Philanthropy Project. January 2020. https://www.openphilanthropy.org/focus/us-policy/farm-animal-welfare/Humane-Society-Legislative-Fund-Opposing-King-Amendment.

39. Marceau, Justin. "Palliative Animal Law: The War on Animal Cruelty." *Harvard Law Review*, 134(5), 2021. pp. 250–262.

40. Culpepper, Jessica, and Adele Kimmel. "In Fighting Sexual Harassment, Donors Hold Power." *Chronicle of Philanthropy*. February 15, 2018. https://www.philanthropy.com/article/in-fighting-sexual-harassment-donors-hold-power/.

41. Paquette, Danielle. "Humane Society Dismisses Sexual Harassment Complaints Against CEO Citing Lack of Credible Evidence." *Washington Post*. February 1, 2018.

42. Bosman, Julie, Matt Stevens, and Jonah Engel Bromwich. "Humane Society C.E.O. Resigns amid Sexual Harassment Allegations." *New York Times*. February 2, 2018.

43. Gunther, Marc. "The Return of Wayne Pacelle." *Nonprofit Chronicles*. July 19, 2018. https://nonprofitchronicles.com/2018/07/19/the-return-of-wayne-pacelle/.

44. Kullgren, Ian. "Humane Society CEO Resigns amid Sexual Harassment Allegations." *Politico*. February 2, 2018. https://www.politico.com/story/2018/02/02/humane-society-sexual-harassment-allegations-323455.

45. HSUS. "Humane Society of the United States Makes New Leadership Appointments and Important Governance Changes." *HSUS*. January 25, 2019. https://www.humanesociety.org/news/humane-society-united-states-makes-new-leadership-appointments-and-important-governance. *See also*, Kullgren, ibid.

46. Gunther, Marc. "The Humane Society of the US: Still Reckoning with #MeToo." *Nonprofit Chronicles*. February 25, 2019. https://medium.com/nonprofit-chronicles/the-humane-society-of-the-us-still-reckoning-with-metoo-3db0fc8ba336.

47. Block, Kitty. "Update by President and CEO Kitty Block on Reconciliation Process." *HSUS*. March 12, 2019. https://www.humanesociety.org/news/update-president-and-ceo-kitty-block-reconciliation-process; Gunther, Marc. "The Humane Society of the US: Still Reckoning with #MeToo." *Nonprofit Chronicles*. February 25, 2019. https://medium.com/nonprofit-chronicles/the-humane-society-of-the-us-still-reckoning-with-metoo-3db0fc8ba336.

48. Gunther, Marc. "The Humane Society of the US: Still Reckoning with #MeToo." *Nonprofit Chronicles*. February 25, 2019. https://medium.com/nonprofit-chronicles/the-humane-society-of-the-us-still-reckoning-with-metoo-3db0fc8ba336.

49. Babiak, Paul, and Robert Hare. *Snakes in Suits: When Psychopaths Go to Work*. Harper Business. 2007.

50. Clifton, Merritt. "Is Wayne Pacelle on His Way out at the Humane Society of the U.S.?" *Animals 24-7.* January 28, 2018. https://www.animals24-7.org/2018/01/28/is-wayne-pacelle-on-his-way-out-at-the-humane-society-of-the-u-s/.

Chapter 6: "We Are Hurting So Much": Racism and "Color-Blindness"

1. Wrenn, Corey. "Abolition Then and Now: Tactical Comparisons Between the Human Rights Movement and the Modern Nonhuman Animal Rights Movement in the United States." *Journal of Agricultural and Environmental Ethics*, 27(1), 2014. pp. 177–200.

2. Hunter, Gwenna. "Copy-and-Paste Activism Does Not Work: Perspectives from a POC." In Michelson, Brittany. (ed.). *Voices for Animal Liberation: Inspirational Accounts by Animal Rights Activists.* Skyhorse. 2020. pp. 43–50.

3. Rodrigues, Luis. "White Normativity, Animal Advocacy and PETA's Campaigns." *Ethnicities*, 20(1), 2020. pp. 71–92.

4. Adey, Anna. "Racism and Mixed Messages: What's Wrong with Australia's Animal Rights Movement?" *The Liberationist.* January 26, 2015.

5. Kulbaga, Theresa. *"Dangerous Crossings: Race, Species, and Nature in a Multicultural Age* by Claire Jean Kim (review)." *Journal of Asian American Studies*, 19(1), 2016. pp 127–130.

6. Munro, Lyle. "The Animal Rights Movement in Theory and Practice: A Review of the Sociological Literature." *Sociology Compass*, 6(2), 2012. pp. 166–181.

7. Cairney, Paul. *Understanding Public Policy: Theories and Issues.* 2nd ed. Springer. 2020.

8. Philpott, Tom. "Black Farmers Have Been Robbed of Land." *Mother Jones.* November 19, 2020.

9. Olorunnipa, Toluse, and Griff Witte. "Born with Two Strikes: How Systemic Racism Shaped George Floyd's Life and Hobbled His Ambition." *Washington Post.* October 8, 2020.

10. American Society for the Prevention of Cruelty to Animals. "With Compassion and Solidarity, We Stand with You." June 4, 2020. https://www.facebook.com/aspca/photos/with-compassion-and-solidarity-we-stand-with-you/10157432782521139/; Toliver, Z. "Why Animal Rights Activists Must Stand Up for Black Lives." *PETA blog.* June 2, 2020. https://www.peta.org/blog/black-lives-matter/.

11. For this chapter, in autumn 2022, I searched Virginia Commonwealth University's library website (https://www.library.vcu.edu/) for "animal rights" and "racism," receiving 4,692 hits. I reviewed the titles of the first 150; the latter half contained no relevant hits, at which point I stopped reviewing. I also searched the animal rights academic library maintained by the nonprofit Animal Charity Evaluators (https://animalcharityevaluators.

org/researchlibrary/#/) for "racism." I identified a total of fifteen relevant journal articles, one book chapter, and one dissertation. In addition, a new organization, Encompass, was founded in 2020 to help employees of American animal rights charities address racism. Its first *State of the Movement Report* was scheduled to be published in 2021; they instead produced a very good book, also by Lantern (Singer, Jasmin. [ed.]. *Antiracism in Animal Advocacy: Igniting Cultural Transformation.* Lantern. 2021), which was reviewed.

12. Caviola, Lucius, Jim Everett, and Nadira Faber. "The Moral Standing of Animals: Towards a Psychology of Speciesism." *Journal of Personality and Social Psychology*, 116(6), 2019. pp. 1011–1029.

13. Jones, Robert. "Animal Rights Is a Social Justice Issue." *Contemporary Justice Review*, 18(4), 2015. pp. 467–482.

14. Monteiro, Bronwyn, Tamara Preiler, Marcus Patterson, and Michael Milburn. "The Carnism Inventory: Measuring the Ideology of Eating Animals." *Appetite*, 113, 2017. pp. 51–62.

15. Rodrigues, Luis. "White Normativity, Animal Advocacy and PETA's Campaigns." *Ethnicities*, 20(1), 2020. pp. 71–92.

16. Specter, Michael. "The Extremist: Ingrid Newkirk." *The New Yorker.* April 14, 2003.

17. Rodrigues, Luis. "White Normativity, Animal Advocacy and PETA's Campaigns." *Ethnicities*, 20(1), 2020. pp. 71–92.

18. Wrenn, Corey. "Abolition Then and Now: Tactical Comparisons Between the Human Rights Movement and the Modern Nonhuman Animal Rights Movement in the United States." *Journal of Agricultural and Environmental Ethics*, 27(1), 2014. pp. 177–200.

19. Harper, A. Breeze "Connections: Speciesism, Racism, and Whiteness as the Norm." In Kemmerer, Lisa (ed.). *Sister Species: Women, Animals and Social Justice.* Chicago: University of Illinois. 2011. pp. 72–78.

20. Hunter, Gwenna. "Copy-and-Paste Activism Does Not Work: Perspectives from a POC." In Michelson, Brittany. (ed.) *Voices for Animal Liberation: Inspirational Accounts by Animal Rights Activists.* Skyhorse. 2020. pp. 43–50.

21. Ibid.

22. Wrenn, Corey. "An Analysis of Diversity in Nonhuman Animal Rights Media." *Journal of Agricultural and Environmental Ethics*, 29(2), 2015. pp. 143–165.

23. United States Census. "2010 Census Shows America's Diversity." *U.S. Census Bureau.* March 24, 2011. https://www.census.gov/newsroom/releases/archives/2010_census/cb11-cn125.html.

24. Animal Advocacy Careers. "Effective Animal Advocacy Bottlenecks Surveys." January 5, 2021. https://www.animaladvocacycareers.org/post/effective-animal-advocacy-bottlenecks-surveys.

25. Ng, Abigail. "The Plant-Based Meat Industry Is on the Rise, but Challenges Remain." December 25, 2021. CNBC. https://www.cnbc.com/2020/12/25/the-plant-based-meat-industry-is-on-the-rise-but-challenges-remain.html.

26. Meghan Lowery's presentation and email on file with author.

27. Cairney, Paul. *Understanding Public Policy: Theories and Issues.* 2nd ed. Springer. 2020.

28. Lindblom, Charles. "The Science of 'Muddling Through.'" *Public Administration Review*, 19(2), 1959. pp. 79–88.

29. Cairney, Paul. *Understanding Public Policy: Theories and Issues.* 2nd ed. Springer. 2020.

30. Ibid.

31. Foucault, Michel. *Discipline and Punish: The Birth of the Prison.* Vintage. 1975/1995.

32. Yanow, Dvora. *Conducting Interpretive Policy Analysis.* Sage. 2000.

33. Cairney, Paul. *Understanding Public Policy: Theories and Issues.* 2nd ed. Springer. 2020.

34. MacInnis, Cara, and Gordon Hodson. "It Ain't Easy Eating Greens: Evidence of Bias Toward Vegetarians and Vegans from Both Source and Target." *Group Processes & Intergroup Relations*, 20(6), 2017. pp. 721–744.

35. Peters, Guy. "Institutionalism and Public Policy." In Peters, Guy and Philippe Zittoun (eds.). *Contemporary Approaches to Public Policy: Theories, Controversies, and Perspectives.* Palgrave. 2016. pp. 57–72.

Chapter 7: Animal Law and Legal Education: Pathbreakers and Millennials

1. Tischler, Joyce. "The History of Animal Law, Part I (1972–1987)." *Stanford Journal of Animal Law & Policy*, 1, 2008.

2. Blumm, Michael. "Origins of *Animal Law*: Three Perspectives—Part II." *Animal Law*, 10, 2004.

3. Hessler, Kathy. "The Role of the Animal Law Clinic." *Journal of Legal Education* 60(2), 2010. pp. 263–284. "The only animal law clinic that existed before Lewis & Clark's was the one at Rutgers School of Law, Newark. That clinic was an in-house externship model and was long closed when I began my work." p. 271.

4. Glaberson, William. "Legal Pioneers Seek to Raise Lowly Status of Animals." *New York Times.* August 18, 1999.

5. Favre, David. "Twenty Years and Change." *Animal Law Review*, 20(7). p. 19.

6. Pamela Frasch, Sonia Waisman, Bruce Wagman, and Scott Beckstead. *Animal Law* (1st ed.). Carolina Academic Press. 2000.

7. Tischler, Joyce. "A Brief History of Animal Law, Part II (1985–2011)." *Stanford Journal of Animal Law & Policy*, 5, 2012.

8. State Bar of Michigan. Animal Law Section Newsletter. Winter 2005. p. 12.

9. Bryant, Taimie. "The Bob Barker Gifts to Support Animal Rights Law." *Journal of Legal Education*, 60(2), 2010. p. 253.

10. Ibid.

11. Savage, Jenny. "University of Denver Sturm College of Law Launches New Professorship in Animal Rights Law." *Animal Legal Defense Fund*. June 18, 2015. https://aldf.org/article/university-of-denver-sturm-college-of-law-launches-new-professorship-in-animal-rights-law/.

12. Gibbons, Holly Anne. "Origins of *Animal Law*: Three Perspectives—Part III." *Animal Law*, 10, 2004.

13. Tischler, Joyce. "A Brief History of Animal Law, Part II (1985–2011)." *Stanford Journal of Animal Law & Policy*, 5, 2012.

14. Bryant, Taimie. "The Bob Barker Gifts to Support Animal Rights Law." *Journal of Legal Education*, 60(2), 2010. p. 253.

15. Walsh, Colleen. "Putting His Money Where His Mouth Is." *Harvard Gazette*. November 2, 2016.

16. Harvard Law School Faculty Directory. "Kristen A. Stilt." https://hls.harvard.edu/faculty/directory/10852/Stilt. 2023.

17. Walsh, Colleen. "Putting His Money Where His Mouth Is." *Harvard Gazette*. November 2, 2016.

18. Animal Law & Policy Program. "The History of the Animal Law & Policy Program at Harvard Law School." Harvard Law School. https://animal.law.harvard.edu/history/. 2023.

19. Animal Grantmakers. "Plight of Farm Animals Planted Seeds of Animal Welfare Trust Founder's Destiny." September 15, 2020. https://givingcompass.org/partners/animal-philanthropy/plight-of-farm-animals-planted-seeds-of-animal-welfare-trust-founders-destiny.

20. Harvard Law School. "Generous Gift from Bradley L. Goldberg Will Support Animal Advocacy Program at Harvard Law School." *Harvard Law Today*. October 29, 2014. https://today.law.harvard.edu/bradley-l-goldberg-gift-will-support-animal-advocacy-program-at-harvard-law-school/.

21. Vermont Law School Directory. "Delcianna Winders." https://www.vermontlaw.edu/directory/person/winders-delcianna. 2023.

22. Alonso, Erika. "ACE Interviews: Brad Goldberg." Animal Charity Evaluators. October 22, 2016. https://animalcharityevaluators.org/blog/ace-interviews-brad-goldberg/.

23. Walsh, Colleen. "Putting His Money Where His Mouth Is." *Harvard Gazette*. November 2, 2016.

24. Harvard Law School. "Jonathan Lovvorn Appointed Policy Director of the HLS Animal Law and Policy Program." *Harvard Law Today*. September 15, 2017. https://today.law.harvard.edu/jonathan-lovvorn-appointed-policy-director-hls-animal-law-policy-program/.

25. New York University Directory. "Matthew Hayek." https://as.nyu.edu/content/nyu-as/as/faculty/matthew-hayek.html; New York University.

"Elan Abrell Curriculum Vitae." https://as.nyu.edu/content/dam/nyu-as/anthropology/documents/AbrellCV8.19.pdf.

26. Animal Law & Policy Program. "The History of the Animal Law & Policy Program at Harvard Law School." Harvard Law School. https://animal.law.harvard.edu/history/. 2023.

27. Hessler, Kathy. "The Role of the Animal Law Clinic." *Journal of Legal Education*, 60(2), 2010. pp. 267–268, 278–279.

28. The Brooks Institute. "About." https://thebrooksinstitute.org/about. 2023.

29. Brooks McCormick Jr. Trust for Animal Rights Law and Policy 2018 IRS Form 990. https://www.causeiq.com/organizations/view_990/477124844/1410a405779672e593734a205c0a236d.

30. Harvard Law School. "Animal Law and Policy Clinic Launches at Harvard Law School." *Harvard Law Today*. August 5, 2019. https://today.law.harvard.edu/animal-law-and-policy-clinic-launches-at-harvard-law-school/.

31. Animal Law & Policy Program. "Year in Review 2019–2020." Harvard Law School. http://animal.law.harvard.edu/wp-content/uploads/ALPP-Year-in-Review-2019-2020.pdf.

32. Harvard Law School. "$10 Million Endowment Established for the Harvard Law School Animal Law & Policy Program." *Harvard Law Today*. November 10, 2021. https://today.law.harvard.edu/10-million-endowment-established-for-the-harvard-law-school-animal-law-policy-program/.

33. Animal Law & Policy Program. "Year in Review 2019–2020." Harvard Law School. http://animal.law.harvard.edu/wp-content/uploads/ALPP-Year-in-Review-2019-2020.pdf. p. 44.

34. Email on file with author.

35. Amnesty International. "Climate Change Ranks Highest as Vital Issue of Our Times—Generation Z Survey." December 10, 2019. https://www.amnesty.org/en/latest/news/2019/12/climate-change-ranks-highest-as-vital-issue-of-our-time/.

36. Schapiro, Fred. "The Most-Cited Legal Scholars Revisited." *University of Chicago Law Review* 88(1), 2021. pp. 1595–1618.

37. Kysar, Douglas. *Regulating from Nowhere: Environmental Law and the Search for Objectivity*. Yale University Press. 2010. pp. 203–204.

38. Law, Ethics & Animals Program. "People." Yale Law School. https://law.yale.edu/animals/people. 2023.

39. Nylen, Leah. "Biden Launches Assault on Monopolies." *Politico*. July 8, 2021.

40. Law, Ethics & Animals Program. "Big Ag & Antitrust Conference." Yale Law School. https://law.yale.edu/animals/events/big-ag-antitrust-conference. 2021.

41. Law, Ethics & Animals Program. "Big Ag & Antitrust Conference Guide." Yale Law School. https://law.yale.edu/sites/default/files/area/center/leap/document/yale-big-ag-and-antitrust-conference-guide.pdf. 2021.

42. Nylen, Leah. "Biden Launches Assault on Monopolies." *Politico*. July 8, 2021.

43. Yale Law School. "Law, Ethics & Animals Program to Launch." *YLS Today*. https://law.yale.edu/yls-today/news/law-ethics-animals-program-launch. September 3, 2019.

44. Animal Grantmakers. "Plight of Farm Animals Planted Seeds of Animal Welfare Trust Founder's Destiny." September 15, 2020. https://givingcompass. org/partners/animal-philanthropy/plight-of-farm-animals-planted-seeds-of-animal-welfare-trust-founders-destiny.

Chapter 8: Dreamers: The Good Food Institute and Clean Meat

1. Tauber, Steven. *Navigating the Jungle: Law, Politics, and the Animal Advocacy Movement*. Routledge. 2016. p. 53.

2. "Death of Henry Bergh." *New York Times*. March 13, 1888.

3. Johnson, Victoria. "The Man Who Made Us Feel for the Animals." *New York Times*. September 16, 2020.

4. Ibid.

5. Mercy For Animals 2016 IRS 990.

6. Popper, Nathaniel. "This Animal Activist Used to Get in Your Face. Now He's Going After Your Palate." *New York Times Magazine*. March 12, 2019.

7. Ibid.

8. MacInnis, Cara, and Gordon Hodson. "It Ain't Easy Eating Greens: Evidence of Bias Toward Vegetarians and Vegans from Both Source and Target." *Group Processes & Intergroup Relations*, 20(6), 2017. pp. 721–744. doi:10.1177/1368430215618253.

9. Popper, Nathaniel. "This Animal Activist Used to Get in Your Face. Now He's Going After Your Palate." *New York Times Magazine*. March 12, 2019.

10. Good Food Institute IRS Form 990, available at https://projects.propublica. org/nonprofits/organizations/810840578.

11. Shapiro, Paul. *Clean Meat: How Growing Meat Without Animals Will Revolutionize Dinner and Save the World*. Gallery Books. 2018. pp. 48–50.

12. Friedrich, Bruce. "Creating a New Agricultural Revolution." Effective Altruism Global Conference 2019. Transcript at https://forum.effectivealtruism.org/posts/ qFEcGbwzogFSuX4wv/bruce-friedrich-creating-a-new-agricultural-revolution. The Good Food Institute. Research Grants. https://gfi.org/researchgrants/.

13. Shapiro, Paul. *Clean Meat: How Growing Meat Without Animals Will Revolutionize Dinner and Save the World*. Gallery Books. 2018. p. 85.

14. Sample, Ian. "Fish Filets Grow in Tank." *New Scientist*. March 20, 2002. https://www.newscientist.com/article/dn2066-fish-fillets-grow-in-tank/.

15. Stephens, Neil, Alexandra Sexton, and Clemens Driessen. "Making Sense of Making Meat: Key Moments in the First 20 Years of Tissue Engineering

Muscle to Make Food." *Frontiers in Sustainable Food Systems*. July 10, 2019. https://doi.org/10.3389/fsufs.2019.00045.

16. Ibid.

17. Specter, Michael. "Test-Tube Burgers." *New Yorker*. May 16, 2011.

18. Zaraska, Marta. "Lab-Grown Beef Taste Test: 'Almost' Like a Burger." *Washington Post*. August 5, 2013.

19. Stephens, Neil, Alexandra Sexton, and Clemens Driessen. "Making Sense of Making Meat: Key Moments in the First 20 Years of Tissue Engineering Muscle to Make Food." *Frontiers in Sustainable Food Systems*. July 10, 2019. https://doi.org/10.3389/fsufs.2019.00045.

20. Lucas, Amelia. "Beyond Meat Surges 163% in the Best IPO So Far in 2019." *CNBC*. May 2, 2019. https://www.cnbc.com/2019/05/02/beyond-meat-ipo.html.

21. Lipschultz, Bailey, and Drew Singer. "Beyond Meat Makes History with Biggest IPO Pop Since 2008 Crisis." *Bloomberg BusinessWeek*. May 2, 2019. https://www.bloomberg.com/news/articles/2019-05-02/beyond-meat-makes-history-with-biggest-ipo-pop-since-08-crisis.

22. Stoffel, Brian. "If You Invested $10,000 in Beyond Meat's IPO, This Is How Much Money You'd Have Now." *The Motley Fool*. December 11, 2019. https://www.fool.com/investing/2019/12/11/if-you-invested-in-beyond-meats-ipo-how-much-now.aspx.

23. Theurer, Benjamin, and Antonio Hernandez. "Carving Up the Alternative Meat Market." *Barclays Investment Bank*. August 19, 2019. https://www.investmentbank.barclays.com/our-insights/carving-up-the-alternative-meat-market.html.

24. Flavell, Shawna. "They Call Him 'Bruce Poppins.'" *People for the Ethical Treatment of Animals*. May 1, 2009. https://www.peta.org/blog/call-bruce-poppins/.

25. Woods, Bob. "Bill Gates Bets on Growing Demand for Sustainable Foods." *CNBC*. May 14, 2015. https://www.cnbc.com/2015/05/14/hampton-creek-and-impossible-foods-technology.html.

26   Temple, James. "Bill Gates: Rich Nations Should Shift Entirely to Synthetic Beef." *MIT Technology Review*. February 14, 2021. https://www.technologyreview.com/2021/02/14/1018296/bill-gates-climate-change-beef-trees-microsoft/.

27. Firth, Niall. "The Race to Make a Lab-Grown Steak." *MIT Technology Review*. February 27, 2019. https://www.technologyreview.com/2019/02/27/136968/the-race-to-grow-a-more-planet-friendly-burger/.

28. Samuel, Sigal. "It's Not Just Big Oil. Big Meat Also Spends Millions to Crush Good Climate Policy." *Vox*. April 13, 2021. https://www.vox.com/future-perfect/22379909/big-meat-companies-spend-millions-lobbying-climate.

29. Harguess, Jamie, Noe Crespo, and Mee Yong Hong. "Strategies to Reduce Meat Consumption: A Systematic Literature Review of Experimental Studies." *Appetite*, 144, 2020. p. 104478.

30. Popper, Nathaniel. "This Animal Activist Used to Get in Your Face. Now He's Going After Your Palate." *New York Times Magazine*. March 12, 2019.

31. For good reviews, *see* Firth, Niall. "The Race to Make a Lab-Grown Steak." *MIT Technology Review*. February 27, 2019. https://www.technologyreview.com/2019/02/27/136968/the-race-to-grow-a-more-planet-friendly-burger/; Chriki, Sghaier, and Jean-François Hocquette. "The Myth of Cultured Meat: A Review." *Frontiers in Nutrition*. February 7, 2020. https://doi.org/10.3389/fnut.2020.00007.

32. Purdy, Chase. *Billion Dollar Burger: Inside Big Tech's Race for the Future of Food*. Penguin. 2020. p. 11.

33. *Washington Post* Live. "Meet Hampton Creek Founder Josh Tetrick." *Washington Post*. October 23, 2015.

34. de León, Riley. "Plant-Based Food Start-Up Eat Just Receives $200 Million Investment Led by Qatar." *CNBC*. https://www.cnbc.com/2021/03/25/plant-based-food-company-eat-just-nabs-200-million-investment.html.

35. Purdy, Chase. *Billion Dollar Burger: Inside Big Tech's Race for the Future of Food*. Penguin. 2020. pp. 69–70.

36. Jacobsen, Rowan. "The Biography of a Plant-Based Burger." *Pacific Standard Magazine*. July 28, 2017. https://psmag.com/news/the-biography-of-a-plant-based-burger#.1dzfvzx4b.

37. Goetz, Thomas. "Impossible Foods' Founder Didn't Want to Be an Entrepreneur, but His $2 Billion Idea Was Hard to Resist." *Inc. Magazine*. September 2019. https://www.inc.com/magazine/201909/thomas-goetz/impossible-foods-pat-brown-imposter-syndrome-unlikely-entrepreneur.html.

38. Rusli, Evelyn. "The Secret of These New Veggie Burgers: Plant Blood." *Wall Street Journal*. October 7, 2014.

39. Woods, Bob. "Bill Gates Bets on Growing Demand for Sustainable Foods." *CNBC*. May 14, 2015. https://www.cnbc.com/2015/05/14/hampton-creek-and-impossible-foods-technology.html.

40. Robinson, Melia. "Google Wanted to Buy This Startup That Makes Fake Meat—Here's Why the CEO Will Never Sell." *Business Insider*. March 27, 2017. https://www.businessinsider.com/impossible-foods-google-acquisition-rumors-2017-3.

41. Sen, Anirban, and Joshua Franklin. "Exclusive: Impossible Foods in Talks to List on the Stock Market - Sources." *Reuters*. April 8, 2021. https://www.reuters.com/article/us-impossible-foods-m-a-exclusive-idUSKBN2BV2SF.

42. Jacobsen, Rowan. "The Biography of a Plant-Based Burger." *Pacific Standard Magazine*. July 28, 2017. https://psmag.com/news/the-biography-of-a-plant-based-burger#.1dzfvzx4b.

43. Fassler, Joe. "Lab-Grown Meat Is Supposed to Be Inevitable. The Science Tells a Different Story." *The Counter*. September 22, 2021. https://thecounter.org/lab-grown-cultivated-meat-cost-at-scale/.

44. Ibid.

45. Reiley, Laura. "Why the CEO of Impossible Foods Thinks He Can Eliminate All Animal-Based Meat in 15 Years." *Washington Post*. July 16, 2021.

46. Reese, Jacy. *The End of Animal Farming: How Scientists, Entrepreneurs, and Activists Are Building an Animal-Free Food System*. Beacon Press. 2018. pp. 70–71.

47. Corbyn, Zoë. "Out of the Lab and into Your Frying Pan: The Advance of Cultured Meat." *The Guardian* (U.K.). January 19, 2020.

48. Musk, Elon. "The Secret Tesla Motors Master Plan (Just Between You and Me)." Tesla. August 2, 2006. https://www.tesla.com/blog/secret-tesla-motors-master-plan-just-between-you-and-me.

49. "The Chicken." The Chicken Restaurant. https://thechicken.kitchen/. 2023.

50. Mandel, Jonah. "Lab-Grown Chicken 'Food Revolution' Gathers Pace at Ness Ziona Eatery." *The Times of Israel*. June 23, 2021. https://www.timesofisrael.com/lab-grown-chicken-food-revolution-gathers-pace-at-ness-ziona-eatery/.

51. Holmes, Oliver. "I Tried the World's First No-Kill, Lab-Grown Chicken Burger." *The Guardian* (U.K.). December 4, 2020.

52. Pomranz, Mike. "Lab-Grown Chicken Meat Will Make Its Restaurant Debut This Saturday." *Food & Wine*. December 16, 2020. https://www.foodandwine.com/news/lab-grown-meat-first-restaurant.

53. Noyes, Andrew. "Eat Just Makes History (Again) with Restaurant Debut of Cultured Meat." *Business Wire*. December 21, 2020. https://www.businesswire.com/news/home/20201220005063/en/.

54. Scipioni, Jade. "This Restaurant Will Be the First Ever to Serve Lab-Grown Chicken (for $23)." *CNBC*. December 18, 2020. https://www.cnbc.com/2020/12/18/singapore-restaurant-first-ever-to-serve-eat-just-lab-grown-chicken.html.

55. Hanson, Dana. "The 10 Most Expensive Types of Sharks to Eat in the World." *Money, Inc.* https://moneyinc.com/most-expensive-types-of-sharks-to-eat-in-the-world/; Houston, Jack, and Irene Anna Kim. "The Rarest Steak in the World Can Cost over $300. Here's Why Wagyu Beef Is So Expensive." *Business Insider*. January 7, 2021. https://www.businessinsider.com/wagyu-beef-steak-cows-from-japan-so-expensive-2019-8.

56. Palmer, Joshua. "How Much Does Bluefin Tuna Cost?" *Luxury Viewer.* July 1, 2021. https://luxuryviewer.com/how-much-does-bluefin-tuna-cost/.
57. Email on file with author.
58. Purdy, Chase. *Billion Dollar Burger: Inside Big Tech's Race for the Future of Food.* Penguin. 2020. p. 59.
59. Gross, Jenny. "Investors Bet on Foie Gras Grown from Cells in a Lab." *New York Times.* July 17, 2021.
60. Bromwich, Jonah, and Sanam Yar. "The Fake Meat War." *New York Times.* July 25, 2019.
61. Plant-Based Foods Association. "Retail Sales Data: 2020." https://www.plantbasedfoods.org/retail-sales-data/.
62. National Cattlemen's Beef Association. "Issues: Fake Meat." https://policy.ncba.org/home/issues/fake-meat; National Cattlemen's Beef Association. "2018 Scorecard." https://www.ncba.org/CMDocs/BeefUSA/2018%20Priority%20Issue%20Scorecard_FINAL.pdf.
63. Selyukh, Alina. "What Gets to Be a 'Burger'? States Restrict Labels on Plant-Based Meat." National Public Radio. July 23, 2019. https://www.npr.org/sections/thesalt/2019/07/23/744083270/what-gets-to-be-a-burger-states-restrict-labels-on-plant-based-meat.
64. National Agricultural Law Center. "Truth in Labeling Lawsuits Update." University of Arkansas Division of Agriculture Research & Extension. https://nationalaglawcenter.org/truth-in-labeling-lawsuits-update/.
65. Pitz, Lexi. "What's the Beef? Controversy Surrounding the Labeling of Plant-Based and Cell-Based Meat." *Minnesota Law Review*, 104, February 23, 2020.
66. See framework agreement on USDA's Food Safety and Inspection Service's website: https://www.fsis.usda.gov/wps/wcm/connect/0d2d644a-9a65-43c6-944f-ea598aacdec1/Formal-Agreement-FSIS-FDA.pdf.
67. S.B. 3053—Food Safety Modernization for Innovative Technologies Act. 116th Congress.
68. Shapiro, Paul. *Clean Meat: How Growing Meat Without Animals Will Revolutionize Dinner and Save the World.* Gallery Books. 2018. p. 79.
69. University of California–Davis Clean Meat Consortium. https://biotech.ucdavis.edu/cultivated-meat-consortium-cmc.
70. Fell, Andy. "UC Davis Establishes Research, Training in Cultivated Meat." University of California–Davis. September 23, 2020. https://www.ucdavis.edu/news/uc-davis-establishes-research-training-cultivated-meat.
71. North Carolina State University Prestage Department of Poultry Science. "Cellular Agriculture." https://cals.ncsu.edu/prestage-department-of-poultry-science/research/cellular-agriculture/.

72. DeLauro, Rosa. "Chair DeLauro Statement at the U.S. Department of Agriculture—the Year Ahead Hearing." U.S. House Appropriations Committee. https://appropriations.house.gov/news/statements/chair-delauro-statement-at-the-us-department-of-agriculture-the-year-ahead-hearing.

73. Nicholas, Isaac, and Mike Silver. "Tufts Receives $10 Million Grant to Help Develop Cultivated Meat." *Tufts Now.* October 15, 2021. https://now.tufts.edu/articles/tufts-receives-10-million-grant-help-develop-cultivated-meat.

74. Jacobsen, Rowan. "The Biography of a Plant-Based Burger." *Pacific Standard Magazine.* July 28, 2017. https://psmag.com/news/the-biography-of-a-plant-based-burger#.1dzfvzx4b.

75. Goetz, Thomas. "Impossible Foods' Founder Didn't Want to Be an Entrepreneur, but His $2 Billion Idea Was Hard to Resist." *Inc. Magazine.* September 2019. https://www.inc.com/magazine/201909/thomas-goetz/impossible-foods-pat-brown-imposter-syndrome-unlikely-entrepreneur.html.

76. Purdy, Chase. *Billion Dollar Burger: Inside Big Tech's Race for the Future of Food.* Penguin. 2020. pp. 78–79.

77. Wiblin, Robert, and Keiran Harris. "Bruce Friedrich Makes the Case that Inventing Outstanding Meat Replacements Is the Most Effective Way to Help Animals." *80,000 Hours.* February 19, 2018. https://80000hours.org/podcast/episodes/bruce-friedrich-good-food-institute/#transcript.

78. Anderson, Jerry. "Protection for the Powerless: Political Economy History Lessons for the Animal Welfare Movement." *Stanford Journal of Animal Law and Policy*, 4, 2011. pp. 1–63.

79. Fuller, Buckminster. *Critical Path.* Macmillan. 1981. p. xxxviii.

INDEX

About the Author

JEFF THOMAS has longtime professional experience in the farm animal movement and political campaigns. He is also the author of two classic books on modern Virginia politics. He is currently a doctoral candidate at the Virginia Commonwealth University School of Public Policy in his hometown of Richmond. Mr. Thomas received his master's degree from the Tulane University School of Public Health and his undergraduate degree from the Duke University School of Engineering. In his free time, he enjoys filing Freedom of Information Act requests and petting sweet little pups. He welcomes all communications with readers at jeffthomasrva@gmail.com.

ABOUT THE PUBLISHER

LANTERN PUBLISHING & MEDIA was founded in 2020 to follow and expand on the legacy of Lantern Books—a publishing company started in 1999 on the principles of living with a greater depth and commitment to the preservation of the natural world. Like its predecessor, Lantern Publishing & Media produces books on animal advocacy, veganism, religion, social justice, humane education, psychology, family therapy, and recovery. Lantern is dedicated to printing in the United States on recycled paper and saving resources in our day-to-day operations. Our titles are also available as ebooks and audiobooks.

To catch up on Lantern's publishing program, visit us at www.lanternpm.org.

facebook.com/lanternpm
twitter.com/lanternpm
instagram.com/lanternpm